The French Chef
in America

The French Chef in America

★ ★ ★ ★ ★ ★

Julia Child's Second Act

ALEX PRUD'HOMME

ALFRED A. KNOPF
New York
2016

THIS IS A BORZOI BOOK
PUBLISHED BY ALFRED A. KNOPF

www.aaknopf.com

Knopf, Borzoi Books, and the colophon are registered trademarks
of Penguin Random House LLC.

Library of Congress Cataloging-in-Publication Data
Names: Prud'homme, Alex, author.
Title: The French chef in America : Julia Child's second act /
Alex Prud'homme.
Description: First edition. | New York : Alfred A. Knopf, 2016. |
Includes bibliographical references and index.
Identifiers: LCCN 2015043441 (print) | LCCN 2015051459 (ebook) |
ISBN 9780385351751 (hardcover : alk. paper) | ISBN 9780385351768 (ebook)
Subjects: LCSH: Child, Julia. | Cooks—United States—Biography.
Classification: LCC TX649.C47 P78 2016 (print) | LCC TX649.C47 (ebook) |
DDC 641.5092—dc23
LC record available at http://lccn.loc.gov/2015043441

Jacket photograph of Julia Child by Arnold Newman/Getty Images
Colorization by Dana Keller
Jacket design by Carol Devine Carson

Manufactured in the United States of America
First Edition

To Judith B. Jones

CONTENTS

The French Chef
in America

INTRODUCTION

Julia's Second Act

In mid-July 1976, Julia Child attended President Gerald R. Ford's bicentennial celebration in Washington, D.C., where she provided commentary for public television, interviewed the White House chef, and met Queen Elizabeth II. Then, as the somewhat raucous party was still winding down, Julia slipped away to rejoin her husband, Paul, in the quiet anonymity of rural France.

Julia was near the height of her celebrity at the time. Performing as "The French Chef," she had won an Emmy, a Peabody Award, and the French Ordre du Mérite Agricole; appeared on the cover of *Time* magazine; made documentary films; and co-authored two volumes of *Mastering the Art of French Cooking*, which had helped launch a food revolution in America. Flinging baguettes, slapping eggplants, flapping chicken wings, she had proven to be a natural on TV: a knowledgeable, unaffected culinary guide whose comic timing and idiosyncratic vocalizations were lauded and satirized across the country. In France, however, the French Chef was virtually unknown, which was just how the Childs liked it.

Every year, Paul and Julia would retreat to their small, simple house outside of Cannes for a few weeks at a time. They had named the house La Pitchoune—La Peetch, for short—which means "the little thing" in the Provençal dialect. It was the place they went to exhale and rejuvenate. Paul would write, paint, photograph, and tend the garden. Julia would sleep, visit restaurants, and cook with her "French sister," Simone "Simca" Beck. It was a familiar pattern, only this time the Childs invited my family to join them.

Julia and Paul on the terrace at La Pitchoune

We flew from New York to Nice, rented a small olive-green car, and drove along winding roads to the Childs' house overlooking the hill town of Plascassier. That evening the Childs welcomed us with a succulent dinner of roasted lamb and ratatouille. Julia was ebullient. In the coming days, she toured us around the outdoor market in Cannes, where she spoke to nearly every vendor and bought heaps of fish for what she would deem "a great bouillabaisse." Then she was off—visiting with M. F. K. Fisher, negotiating with the plumber, having her hair done, attending to desk work, and always tinkering with something delicious in her compact *cuisine*.

At La Peetch—as in their much larger home kitchen in Cambridge, Massachusetts—Paul had erected Peg-Board on the wall, from which he hung Julia's *batterie de cuisine*. He outlined her copper pots and steel pans with black Magic Marker, so one would know exactly where each should be hung. Julia worked at a small gas stove vented by a window, a tall worktable, and with a row of knives arranged by size on a magnetic strip. It was an efficient space not much bigger than a ship's galley, and it seemed to emit mouthwatering smells at all hours.

Though Julia and Paul never had children (they had tried but it "didn't take," Julia said), they welcomed my sisters and me as surrogate grandchildren. Paul was the twin brother of my maternal grandfather, Charles Child. We had been lucky to spend time with Julia and Paul in Cambridge, New York, and Maine, but this was our first visit to La Pitchoune. I was almost fifteen years old in the summer of 1976, with bushy blond hair down to my shoulders; my sisters were thirteen and nine. While my parents were lodged in a guest room, my sisters slept in an outbuilding, and I was relegated to a couch in the open living-dining room. We children had been warned to be on our best behavior, and made sure to walk slowly and keep our voices down around Paul, who was seventy-four and still recovering from a heart-bypass operation two years earlier.

Paul was an erudite man who was a decade older, and several inches shorter, than Julia. He was pleasant, if reserved, that July. He would appear at meals, but spent much of his time sequestered in the little *cabanon* (cabin) across the driveway, painting, writing, and organizing the

Lunch at La Colombe d'Or in Saint-Paul-de-Vence, July 1976

bottles in his wine *cave*. He had grown thin, his face was often slack, and he seemed mentally present one minute but distant the next. He could be stern and liked to talk about Serious Things, like Politics, Economics, and Culture, which made him an intimidating presence. I would later learn that he was suffering from nightmares and insomnia at the time. Because Julia was a snorer and a thrasher, they slept apart; but when Paul awoke at 4 o'clock one morning, he slipped into her bed for comfort, and, he noted in his date book, they " 'sleep' late."

Our two weeks at La Pitchoune were an idyll. We bought flowers in Grasse, shopped for handblown glass in Biot, picnicked in sunny fields, wandered through Old Nice, lunched at the house of the expat American chef Richard Olney, and swam in the azure Mediterranean. Inspired by the Formula 1 cars that race in nearby Monaco, I ground the gears and spun the tires of our rental car in the bumpy field below La Peetch, teaching myself how to drive a stick shift. After terrorizing a herd of goats, putting a dent in the fender (stone wall), and feeling the adrenaline surge as I bounced through mud patches at warp speed, I declared myself fit for a driver's license, not to mention hot laps around Monte Carlo.

As always, talk at the Childs' house centered on the gastronomic and painterly arts, and these subjects came together for me in a new way on the afternoon that we drove up to Saint-Paul-de-Vence for lunch. It is a secluded medieval town nestled in the steep hills between Nice and the Alpes-Maritimes mountains. There, we ate at La Colombe d'Or, a seemingly modest auberge where a sign reads: *"Ici on loge à cheval, à pied ou en peinture"* ("Here we lodge those on horseback, on foot, or with paintings"). The inn was established in 1920 by Paul Roux, a local farmer, and is decorated with a remarkable collection of artwork by the once-struggling painters and sculptors who traded their work for lodging: Picasso, Braque, Léger, Chagall, Calder, and others.

Perhaps it was the familial warmth, the food and wine, the proximity to such a collection of masterworks, or some other mysterious trigger, but Paul suddenly grew animated. His one good eye came into focus (the other had been blinded in childhood), he smiled for the first time in days, he regaled us with stories about the local *villages-perchés*—the fortified hill towns built to defend against raiding Saracen pirates—and encouraged me to try a glass of rosé. My grumpy granduncle was suddenly entertaining and interesting; it was as if Paul had reverted to his charming, pre-bypass self.

A couple of evenings later we gathered on the terrace at La Pitchoune for dinner. It was hot, the air was still, and we were tired. The sun faded behind the hills, and Julia hummed to herself as she cut up a whole chicken and steeped it in a fantastic marinade, then grilled it one sizzling piece at a time on a tiny hibachi in the corner. Paul ran a long extension cord from the house to a small black-and-white TV placed on a wobbly chair. He turned the TV on to the Summer Olympics, then under way in Montreal. As the graceful Cuban heavyweight boxer Teófilo Stevenson battled Romania's Mircea Şimon, Paul jabbed the air with his fist and translated the French announcer's play-by-play into English with growing excitement. When Stevenson knocked out Şimon to win the gold, we stood to hoot and holler at the little screen. (It was Stevenson's second gold medal, after triumphing in Munich. Winning again in 1980, he was the first boxer to win three Olympic gold medals in one weight class.) Paul was so animated, and Julia's chicken was so delicious, that the evening lingers as memorable.

In ensuing years, Paul would fade into a state he ruefully called "the mental scrambles." Never fully recovering from his operation, he suffered a series of strokes and other ailments that left him weary, confused, and irascible. In retrospect, those days at La Pitchoune in 1976 were the last glimpse I had of the intelligent, warm, and enthusiastic man he had been: the genuine Paul Child.

Julia, on the other hand, was in the midst of a dynamic new phase of her career, when she left behind classical French cuisine and the French Chef, to reinvent—and re-Americanize—herself as "Julia Child."

PAUL AND JULIA HAD MET in Ceylon (Sri Lanka) during the Second World War, married in the United States in 1946, and were posted to Paris by the U.S. Information Service in 1948. In the early fifties, Paul mounted cultural exhibitions for the U.S. Embassy, while Julia graduated from the Cordon Bleu and discovered her raison d'être in cooking *la cuisine bourgeoise*—excellent, middle-class food prepared according to a well-established set of rules. She and her French friends Simone Beck and Louisette Bertholle opened their own cooking school, L'École des

Trois Gourmandes (which Julia translated as "the School of the Three Hearty Eaters"), and toiled for years on the cookbook that would be published in 1961 as *Mastering the Art of French Cooking*. During this time Julia experienced a "flowering of the soul," when she morphed from a too-tall, too-loud, rather unsophisticated social butterfly, as she described herself, into a worldly diplomatic wife and expert on what she liked to call "cookery." This was her gestational period, when she was in her thirties, forties, and early fifties. I think of it as Act One of Julia's adult life, and I helped her write about it in her memoir, *My Life in France*.

The book in your hands is a different kind of project. While Julia's memoir was written in the first person, in her voice, *The French Chef in America* is mostly written in the third person, in my voice, and strives for a more journalistic survey of Julia in the 1970s. It was a period of global upheaval, when she was in her sixties and transformed herself a second time.

The Childs retired from the diplomatic service in 1961, and settled in Cambridge, Massachusetts, outside of Boston. Their large clapboard house stood just behind Harvard Yard, where they were surrounded by "eggheads," the professors, artists, and European refugees who formed Paul and Julia's social circle. In those revolutionary days, protests erupted nearby on a regular basis, sometimes violently, while young restaurateurs, chefs, and farmers helped create a new American cooking.

In the early seventies, Julia began to experiment with recipes from around the world, wrote in the first person, and began to tell personal stories. These tentative steps in a new direction led to a remarkably productive decade, when she produced a stream of books and TV shows, wrote for a slew of newspapers and magazines, was satirized by *Saturday Night Live*, grew more outspoken than ever—she clashed with promoters of health food and nouvelle cuisine, extoled the virtues of butter and cream, championed Planned Parenthood, questioned feminism, left public television for *Good Morning America*—and had other adventures that brought her to the apex of her celebrity. Yet even as Julia achieved wide renown in public, she and Paul suffered some of their darkest moments in private.

I have come to regard this period—roughly the late sixties through the early eighties—as Julia's Second Act: when she retooled her career, embraced her American roots, and finally discovered her true voice.

Part I

The French Chef Faces Life

I

Dinner and Diplomacy

> I never forget that I live in a house owned by all the
> American people.
>
> —FRANKLIN DELANO ROOSEVELT

1. WHITE HOUSE RED CARPET

The sun shone brightly as three flags—the American, Japanese, and District of Columbia—riffled in a breeze. As the camera panned across the Washington, D.C., cityscape, four howitzers boomed a nineteen-gun salute on the South Lawn. It was Tuesday, November 14, 1967, and Julia Child was taking her audience somewhere they had never been before.

"Welcome to Washington. *I'm* Julia Child, out here in front of the East Gate of the White House, where every day *thousands* of visitors go through this historic mansion. And today, something very *special* is going on," she said in her distinctly breathy, high-low warble. Hundreds of tourists streamed through the White House, also known as the People's House, clogging the halls and gawking at the formal dining rooms just hours before an important state dinner.

"These visits are *terribly* important. And also terribly complicated to handle. It's really *fascinating* to see how the White House manages one of them," Julia narrated. "And that's exactly what we're going to see. Not only what goes on in front, but what goes on backstage, and backstairs.

We're going to see *everything*, inside and out, from the start—the official greeting right on through to the White House dinner."

Thus began a public television special called *White House Red Carpet*. Produced by WGBH, Julia's home public television station in Boston, it was the first time that a TV crew had been allowed to document a state dinner. It also marked the first time in more than two years that Julia had appeared on the tube with fresh material. Season One of her cooking show, *The French Chef*, aired from February 1963 through July 1966, when Julia took a break and the show went into reruns. By then she had firmly established herself as "the kitchen magician," as *The Boston Globe* called her. With more than a million viewers a week, Julia encouraged her audience to cook boldly and take risks without fear of failure. "Eat heartily!" she declared, and, "Never apologize!" Her fans referred to her simply as "Julia," as if they knew her personally.

Julia had taken a sabbatical for two reasons: she had been hard at work with her French colleague Simone "Simca" Beck, on a follow-up to their cookbook, *Mastering the Art of French Cooking*; and she was waiting for color television to become a reality. By November 1967, the book was coming together and WGBH had received its first color cameras. With *White House Red Carpet*, Julia was making a dramatic return to the national spotlight.

A robust fifty-five years old, Julia stood more than six feet two inches tall, had a long face with a rounded jaw, frizzy brown hair, lively blue eyes, strong hands, and usually dressed in pearls, a blue apron, and size-twelve sneakers. At the White House she wore a stylish black-and-white checked coat, a shoulder-length brown wig with a flip curl (for convenience: constant hairdos during a multiday TV shoot were a burden), and an impish grin.

The idea for a White House TV special was sparked in 1966—"the year that everyone seems to be cooking in the kitchen with Julia," noted *Time* magazine—when the Public Broadcasting Laboratory (PBL) asked if she would like to do a thirty-minute special about "What's Happening Now." Avid news watchers, Julia and Paul drew up a list of potential ideas.

Paul's voice was important. He was an equal partner in their joint venture: Julia's mentor, editor, manager, confidant, bodyguard, staff photographer, sommelier, and culinary "guinea pig." He avoided the limelight and described himself as "a part of the iceberg that doesn't show." While she was a blast of sound and a ray of sunlight, he was more internalized, with a quieter, moodier demeanor and a sometimes prickly intellect. Julia and Paul were "a team," they said, "two sides of a coin," and they often signed their joint letters "JP" or "Pulia."

In answering PBL's request, the Childs proposed a documentary film about President Charles de Gaulle's decision to relocate the Les Halles food market—dubbed "the belly of Paris" by Émile Zola—from the city center to a suburb near Orly airport to make room for a modern, American-style shopping complex. The move was controversial, and loaded with the symbolism of France leaving behind the darkness of two World Wars, the Suez Crisis, and Vietnam in favor of a shiny, bright, space-age future. The Childs were horrified by the decision. While living in Paris, they had spent countless hours shopping at Les Halles, and loved its teeming Old World alleys, wrought-iron arcades, hollering shopkeeps, bins of varicolored flowers, stacks of raw vegetables, piles of copper pots, racks of knives, bottles of olive oil, barrels of wine, and the like. They wanted to document the lively, odiferous, chaotic marketplace before it was replaced by a smooth concrete, smoked glass, and blandly efficient shopping mall.

PBL accepted their plan to document Les Halles, then rejected it as too expensive. The Childs were disappointed, if not entirely surprised: the lack of funding and clear editorial vision were familiar hurdles in public television. They cast about for a new subject, a food story with "visual drama" located closer to their home in Cambridge, Massachusetts.

It is likely that Paul—a former diplomat, who understood the symbolic and practical aspects of state dinners—suggested a documentary about the White House. And Julia knew that President Johnson employed Henry Haller, a highly regarded Swiss-born, French-trained chef. They both understood that the president could use a positive boost in the media. The year 1967 had been tumultuous: the Vietnam War was grinding painfully on, and race relations were tense at home; Johnson was under attack from both the left and right and had shrunk from public appearances. This dark state of affairs presented public television with an opportunity, Paul thought: "Why not show a side of the People's House that most of the People have never seen?"

The old Les Halles market in Paris before its demolition . . .

. . . and after

The Childs pitched PBL a documentary about what happens behind the scenes at a state dinner. It was a long shot, they knew. But under the circumstances, Julia Child was one of the few people who could have convinced the presidential staff to allow television cameras to poke around 1600 Pennsylvania Avenue—from its elegant public hallways to the first family's private quarters and down into the cramped, quirky kitchen in the basement—during a high-profile event. As Paul explained in a letter to the columnist Herb Caen, a state dinner "isn't about spending the tax payers' money on striped pants and pink champagne. It's a function of diplomacy, and only the culminating, externally visible part of a complex series of discussions, decisions, studies, meetings and agreements involving many parts of government."

PBL withdrew from the Childs' project in order to pursue a civil rights program. But National Educational Television (NET)—the main broadcaster of educational TV at the time—picked up the White House special. It took four months of intensive work behind the scenes to turn the seemingly straightforward idea into an actual telecast.

Julia and her staff at WGBH issued reams of letters, telegrams, and phone messages to convince the White House of the value of such a show (an outspoken Democrat, Julia promised to remain strictly apolitical); stacks of memos to public television brass explaining exactly what they would be getting, and at what cost; and binders of research about the historical, diplomatic, and culinary significance of a state dinner. In a letter to Lady Bird Johnson, the producer Ruth Lockwood explained:

> Everyone is fascinated by the White House and our first family. Millions of us have visited the public rooms, and more millions have toured parts of The White House on television. So far we have seen it only as a shrine with empty rooms. Now we would like to go behind the splendid façade and show how you and your staff make it run so well as an official residence with a home-like atmosphere . . . The American public-at-large has little conception of diplomatic life . . . [and] the tremendous importance that the reception plays in our international affairs.

The Johnsons hesitated. Rock 'n' roll, feminism, environmentalism, racial conflicts, and antiwar protests were roiling America. Moreover, the guest of honor at the diplomatic dinner that November was to be

Japanese prime minister Eisaku Satō. Japan was an especially important and sensitive ally: despite lingering resentments from the Second World War, Japan was America's leading partner in Asia, and the United States was Japan's biggest customer. Johnson was attempting to manage the optics of his presidency carefully, if not particularly successfully, and was doubtless concerned that Julia and her cameras would get in the way of important negotiations. Yet the first family eventually agreed to invite the Childs and a small TV crew to observe the diplomatic dinner.

Over four days WGBH filmed scenic shots of Julia in Washington, interviewing key presidential staff members (though not the first couple, per White House etiquette), and exploring the grand dining rooms and narrow stairwells of the People's House. Then it was time for the main event.

IT HAD BEEN 167 years since John Adams hosted the first diplomatic party at the White House. After touring the building, which was built in the 1790s by George Washington, Paul wrote that it remained "essentially an 18th-century gentleman's mansion in its original conception." In fact, President Harry S. Truman had completely renovated the rickety building in 1952, after he took a bath, felt the floor tremble, and nearly crashed through it onto his wife, Bess, and a group from the Daughters of the American Revolution. Truman insisted on a nearly exact replica of the old rooms, including what seemed to be miles of winding passageways, creaky stairs, and mysterious nooks and crannies.

The state dinner would fill two dining rooms, which were decorated with great crystal chandeliers, tall and heavily draped windows, and round tables graced by flowers, crystal goblets, candles, and gold-and-white plates ornamented with the presidential seal. A floor below, in the basement, the kitchen was tiny, about eighteen feet square, with shiny white walls, gray linoleum floors, roaring ventilation fans, stainless-steel counters, and hanging pots and spoons, all lit by fluorescent lights.

The cramped space, Paul noted, made "the back-of-the-stage operations humanly difficult, so potentially interesting to the American public if the PR people don't insist on a shiny, no-trouble image."

As WGBH's cameras panned down bustling hallways on the afternoon of November 14, the last tourists were being ushered out and the chief housekeeper, Mrs. Mary Kaltman, who oversaw "everything from lightbulbs to lobsters," checked that each of the nineteen tables had a flower bouquet and place cards. Mrs. Carpenter, Lady Bird's press secretary, said of the library: "I love this room, but in the days of Abigail Adams, it's where she kept her milk cows, and so we laughingly say, 'We've moved from moos to news.'"

Until the Eisenhowers hired the first White House chef, food at the People's House was prepared by navy stewards. In 1961, the Kennedys hired René Verdon, a highly regarded French chef from the Carlyle Hotel in New York. Verdon prepared a lamb luncheon for Princess Grace of Monaco, and trout Chablis for the British prime minister Harold Macmillan. After President Kennedy's assassination, Verdon stayed on with the Johnsons. But he resigned in 1965, protesting LBJ's insistence on serving garbanzo bean purée, the use of canned and frozen vegetables (to keep costs down), and other creative differences. "You do not serve barbecued spareribs at a banquet with ladies in white gloves!" huffed Verdon.

The new executive chef, Henry Haller, led a team of four sous-chefs and a staff of many other, mostly African American, assistants. Haller—a confident, robust, hawk-faced man trained in classical French cuisine—had apprenticed in Davos, then immigrated to the United States after the Second Word War. He met his Brooklyn-born wife, Carol, on Martha's Vineyard. When the job offer came from the White House, Haller was executive chef at the Hampshire House hotel in Manhattan, where then Vice President Johnson had enjoyed his cooking.

Haller's workday began at 6:00 a.m. and ended after midnight, but he was paid far less than chefs of his caliber earned in top restaurants. Nevertheless, he declared, "there is no better job" than running the president's kitchen. He was a phlegmatic sort who didn't mind the pressure of the job. When the king of Saudi Arabia arrived with his own food stuffed into five briefcases and with a royal food taster as well, Haller smiled. Though the Johnsons employed Zephyr Wright, an African American woman, to cook Southern-style family meals, there were times when Haller was required to whip up lunch for foreign dignitaries from whatever he could find in the pantry—for which the president was eternally grateful.

"Many Americans who dislike President Johnson half-believe that

Julia with the White House executive chef Henry
Haller, admiring the seafood vol-au-vent, 1967

dinner at the White House is limited to such gustatory curiosities as *Pedernales Chili* and *enchiladas*," Paul wrote in *The Economist*. "Alas for prejudice! The truth is that official food at the White House is delectable."

To prepare for 190 guests, Haller had been cooking for three days by the time that Julia and her camera crew arrived. Dressed in chef's whites and a toque, he barked orders, cracked jokes, and prepared a sumptuous seafood vol-au-vent—lobster, bay scallops, tiny shrimp, and quenelles (fish dumplings) in a pastry crust, topped with a *sauce américaine*.

"*Hmmmm*," Julia murmured, as she craned her tall body over a steaming pot, closed her eyes, and inhaled the seafood aroma. "Can I have a little taste?"

"Czertainly!" Haller replied.

"Oh, it's *awfully* good," she cooed. "That's lovely."

"Ze taste hasz to go wis ze prezentation."

"Everything in the kitchen is timed to the minute from now on," Julia narrated, like a play-by-play announcer. "It's all keyed to what's going on upstairs."

By the front door under the North Portico, string instruments serenaded the guests, who wore black tie and exited limousines to a barrage of flashing bulbs. Vice President and Mrs. Hubert Humphrey made their way through the mob of reporters. Foreign ambassadors and deputy ministers led American governors and local pols, the chairman of the Atomic Energy Commission, the chairman of U.S. Steel, Johnson backers from Waco and Cleveland and Alabama, a poet, a Rockefeller, the president of CBS, and the president of the International Union of Operating Engineers.

Japanese prime minister Satō, a short man dressed in an impeccably tailored suit, and his diminutive wife, wearing glasses and a white kimono, bowed and smiled. Satō was known to be "intensely interested in baseball," and so the commissioner of baseball, General William D.

Julia and Ruth Lockwood working on a script

Eckert, and the St. Louis Cardinals's pitcher Bob Gibson had been invited. Satō was also a jazz lover, and the White House had arranged for a special musical guest to entertain at the end of the evening.

The Johnsons and the Satōs repaired upstairs, to the Yellow Oval Room, the first family's private reception area, to exchange gifts. Johnson offered Satō an elegant Tiffany desk set, while Satō presented Johnson with a bulky portable television camera and videotape recorder.

"The Diplomatic Reception room is filling up with all *kinds* of people," Julia chuckled, as the camera showed her in a flowered dress and Paul in a tuxedo entering the White House. "Business types, politicos, socialites, diplomats," she said. As bejeweled socialites and the actors Kirk Douglas and Ida Lupino smiled, she added, "Plus a scattering of luminaries, to make the evening glitter."

The State Dining Room held fourteen tables that sat ten people apiece; next door, the smaller Blue Dining Room sat five tables of ten. Food was raised from the basement kitchen by two dumbwaiters and an elevator. It arrived in a narrow butler's pantry and was staged on trestle tables. At a signal from the chief butler, a line of nineteen waiters swept into the dining rooms bearing silver platters.

First came the seafood vol-au-vent. "The puff pastry was exceptionally flaky and tender, made only with butter and not the 'other spread,'" Julia said, referring to margarine, which she loathed.

The entrée was a sautéed *noisette* (filet) of lamb, so perfectly cooked that the meat was a pale rose color inside. They were accompanied by artichoke bottoms filled with a *sauce Choron*. Each noisette was topped with a fluted mushroom cap, napped with a brown deglazed sauce, and asparagus. Then came a sprightly salad in a dressing that complemented the wines, an excellent selection of small-batch American wines unknown to the Japanese and most Europeans. With salad came nicely ripened cheeses and bunches of grapes. The dessert, prepared by pastry chef Ferdinand Loubat, was Bavarian cream mousse flavored with fresh strawberries.

"This is an absolutely delicious dinner," Julia declared with feeling. "The tables are elegant, beautiful, softly lighted by candles. The service is impeccable—that's something you rarely see around anymore: perfect service. This is really one of the best dinners I've eaten anywhere.

I'm delighted with it—particularly because it's *here*. If I could do it for six people, I'd be proud indeed. But they're doing it for one hundred ninety."

In a somber toast, President Johnson quoted Abraham Lincoln to explain why he felt he must stand firm in Vietnam: "'I am here; I must do the best I can and bear the responsibility of taking the course which I feel I ought to take.'" Looking owlish, the president peered from the lectern into the shadowy audience (the film crew was not allowed to use extra lights) and intoned with a deep drawl: "It took time and a great deal of patience but Lincoln won peace at home and saved the Union . . . All men must know what it is to be emancipated: to be emancipated from hunger, from sickness, from want, and from fear of aggression . . . We must look beyond the dangers that we all face in Asia now, to the day when our . . . common sense of responsibility to all humankind . . . will finally open the road to peace, to stability, and to prosperity for all humanity."

At the end of the carefully choreographed night, it was time to shift the mood and loosen up. The choice of White House entertainer is determined by the guest of honor: for Haile Selassie's visit, it was grand opera; for the shah of Iran, ballet; for the president of Mexico, Herb Alpert and the Tijuana Brass. To cap this evening, Tony Bennett and his band, including a female harpist, performed in the East Room.

Lean and dapper, Bennett grinned wolfishly from the stage. He loosened his bow tie, flung off his jacket, and let his voice rip: "When I come home to you, Saaaan Fraaaanciscoooo—your golden sun will shiine for meeeeeeeee!"

The audience broke into wide smiles and applauded enthusiastically. "Tony Bennett sang himself right out of his jacket during the final number," Julia quipped. "And is struggling it on again as the presidential party thanks him."

Observing the president and prime minister, she judged, "They really seem relaxed, friendly, and happy together—and that's the point of this whole affair."

Newspaper coverage of the evening played up the diplomatic tension surrounding the president. A story in the Washington, D.C., *Evening Star* was headlined JOHNSON'S SATO TOAST ANSWERS CRITICISM. It noted that "well known New Yorker, Hugh Bullock . . . talked with Rep. Wayne Hays of Ohio about the failure of any New York newspapers to present the administration's point of view. Hays called the campaign of the media against Johnson 'the assassination of Lyndon Johnson.'" The paper added that "Johnson, who has done very little of this [entertaining] of late, retired to his night reading of reports at 11:40. He was a calmly smiling and gracious host, but the words of his dinner toast revealed how deeply the broadscale criticism prevalent today has cut into him."

Paul Child struck a more bemused tone in *The Economist:* "For visitors to the United States who may ask, 'Is there any place out there where one can eat truly excellent food in a beautiful room, with perfect service?' you can answer, 'Yes, there is one. In fact it's quite agreeable, if you can get a table, but it tends to be a bit crowded.'"

The four days' worth of filming were whittled down to a tight, forty-eight-minute-long TV special, and *White House Red Carpet* was scheduled to air nationwide in April 1968. Even before it was televised, in-house reviews of the special were positive, and Julia's golden touch appeared intact.

Buoyed by this, she and Paul began to strategize about ways to change

Tony Bennett rehearses at the White House.

and strengthen *The French Chef,* to keep her audience, and herself, interested when they resumed taping in 1968. Inspired by their failed Les Halles special, the Childs proposed taking Julia out of the studio and into the real world, perhaps to her original inspiration: *la belle France.* It wouldn't be easy. In May 1968, strikes broke out across France, as a million students and factory workers marched in Paris to protest de Gaulle's conservative government and the lack of work. In the United States, President Johnson had asked Americans not to travel, in order to spend their money at home, as a patriotic act. He was particularly annoyed with the French, who had opened relations with the Soviet Union and demanded that all foreign military personnel leave French soil. "With world conditions as they are . . . it is the wrong time to consider doing part of our series in France," the producer Ruthie Lockwood advised Julia.

The Childs were ardent patriots, but they were also stubbornly independent-minded. Julia considered France her "spiritual home," and would not be kept away. So, rather than stay at home to watch the *White House Red Carpet* telecast, the Childs flew to La Pitchoune, their little house in Provence, in the spring of 1968. The plan was to lie low there for several months, resting, reading, cooking, and eating. Julia and her co-author, Simca Beck, had much work to do on *Mastering the Art of French Cooking,* Volume II, which they were behind on. And it all went according to plan, until their idyll was rudely interrupted.

II. How Fortunate We Are

La Pitchoune overlooked a green valley and the town of Plascassier, just north of Cannes, and a few miles from the Mediterranean. It was a simple one-story building, with tan stucco walls and a red tile roof. It had a large living-dining room, a narrow kitchen, modest bedrooms, and a terrace overhung by a trellis coiled with green vines.

The house was built in 1965, in a former potato field on a gently sloping hill. Julia referred to it as "the house the book built," because she had paid for it with proceeds from *Mastering.* She also called it "the house built on friendship," because it was situated on a corner of Bramafam ("the cry of hunger"), the property owned by Simca Beck and her husband, Jean Fischbacher. They had invited the Childs to lease the property and build on it, on the condition that once they were finished using the house it would revert to the Fischbacher family. This was a very un-French and un-American arrangement; but it suited the four friends just fine, and it was sealed with a handshake.

Enveloped by soft warm breezes from the Mediterranean, and perfumed by the scents of wood smoke, manure, mimosa, jasmine, and lavender, La Peetch seemed to exist out of time. The arid gray-brown earth was festooned with low scrub bushes, red and yellow wildflowers, dark green olive trees, and tall, swaying cypresses. The quiet was punctuated by birds chirping, bleating goats, and a chugging tractor. In the distance behind Plascassier, the Alpes-Maritimes rose in a succession of green foothills and blue mountains that appeared to recede into infinity. Southern France is famously laid-back, and the people who lived nearby didn't know, or care, who Julia Child–the-American-TV-star was.

Julia and Paul had flown there right after taping the diplomatic dinner at the Johnson White House, and quickly fell into a contemplative rhythm. Over the course of December and January, Paul painted landscapes, photographed Julia's cookery, and tested bread recipes. Julia corrected proofs for *The Cooking of Provincial France*, a Time Life book on which she was a consultant, and tested recipes with Simca for Volume II of *Mastering*. On a visit to Paris in December, the Childs dove into the chaos of Les Halles one last time, to buy three foie gras and truffles for their holiday celebrations. "God, it was great!" Julia enthused of the market. "Ten thousand smells, sounds, and faces! I kept thinking what a movie we could have made if that plan of ours hadn't fallen through."

Back in Provence, they were invited to watch the slaughter of a three-hundred-pound pig in a traditional ceremony. This was the kind of local, ritualized moment that fascinated Julia. She was inquisitive and not squeamish, and felt it was important to know "all of the hows and whys" of where food comes from.

As Julia kneaded, chopped, and stirred in the kitchen at Christmas, Paul—who affectionately referred to her as "the Mad Woman of La Pitchoune"—found himself "smelling all these breads, chickens, pâtés, dorados, cooking, and hearing my tender little wifelet crashing around in the kitchen, scolding the pussy for meowing, whacking something metallic with something else metallic, like a Peking street vendor. A very jolly house." He wrote his twin, Charlie Child: "How fortunate we are at this moment in our lives! Each doing what he most wants, in a marvelously adapted place, close to each other, superbly fed and housed, with excellent health, and few interruptions."

In early February 1968, Paul and Julia flew home to Cambridge, Massachusetts, for a quick visit. Having rented out their rambling Victorian house, they stayed with Avis DeVoto, the literary scout who had sent *Mastering* to Knopf in 1959, and was the wife of essayist Bernard DeVoto. They planned to catch up with friends and review some paperwork; Julia would record the voice-over for the White House TV special, have a small lump in her left breast examined—"It is a very simple matter," she said—and they would return to France, where work on Volume II of *Mastering* would resume.

Julia was riding high. *White House Red Carpet* had gone extremely well, planning was under way for Season Two of *The French Chef*, and Knopf was about to publish a compilation of recipes called *The French Chef Cookbook*. And so it came as a rude shock when a doctor at New England Sinai Hospital in Boston said that the small lump in her breast was a cancerous tumor, "the size of a lima bean." Julia had been a casual smoker, but was otherwise robust and healthy.

Faced with the unexpected diagnosis, she characteristically instructed the surgeon, "If the tumor is malignant, lop the breast off. I want to get it over with."

Following the standard procedure of the day, the oncologists performed a radical mastectomy, removing the entire breast and the lymph nodes on her left side, to forestall further spread of the disease. (Such invasive surgery would not be used on a small tumor today.)

"Left breast off," Julia wrote in her diary on February 18. She was not given chemotherapy, and at the time breast reconstruction was not widely available. "They just sewed me up and I went home," she recalled. In fact, it wasn't quite that simple. Julia spent ten days recuperating at the hospital. Returning to Avis's house, she sank into a warm bath and allowed herself to cry over her "lost bubby."

With such highs followed by such lows, Julia could have been forgiven for dropping into a funk. But she remained stoic, hardly complained, and dismissed the operation as "a nuisance." In letters to friends, Julia emphasized how fortunate she'd been that the surgery had been on her left side, and not on her dominant right. Friends sympathized, saying,

"That's too bad," but didn't dwell on her condition. "No one took it as a terrible crisis," Julia recalled, not because they were insensitive, but because at the time mastectomy was considered a difficult, extremely personal subject to talk about. Julia did not mention her breast cancer in public for years, and when she finally did, she kept a stiff upper lip: "No radium, no chemotherapy, no caterwauling. I didn't want to be whiny."

Paul suffered on her behalf. Though he was a black belt in judo, he was a worrier bedeviled by existential dread, and was subject to a string of coughs, stomach flus, and eye inflammations in a way that his twin, Charlie, never was. Though Paul put on a brave face, Julia's mastectomy gripped him with fear. "Death and degeneration sat on my chest like twin ghouls, and I had a white night in spite of a double dose of sleeping pills," he wrote. Berating himself for such "damn-fool emotions," Paul imagined the worst: "Planning the funeral, the disposition of La Pitchoune and of our house in Cambridge . . . the problems of whether [Julia's] ashes would better be buried in the Plascassier cemetery, in Pasadena, in Cambridge, or simply scattered somewhere."

Despite his fears, Julia recovered, and willed herself upward and outward into "the world of the living." She began to take short walks around Cambridge, did physical therapy, and, though she wasn't sleeping well, slowly regained her strength. The loss of her breast "didn't really bother me, for I wasn't flapping my breasts around anyway," Julia said. Besides, Paul "made me feel like he loved me."

Years later, in 1975, she appeared on a PBS show called "What You Don't Know Can Hurt You," part of a Dick Cavett series to promote breast cancer awareness. "The leading expert on a woman's body is the woman herself," Julia said. "And the best instruments for the detection of possible breast cancer are a woman's own two hands." When the show aired in New York, the station received more than two thousand calls from viewers wanting to know more. "It's dreadful to lose a breast," Julia told Cavett. "I was in my fifties and married. How would I have felt had I been thirty and hopeful?"

BY MID-MAY 1968, Julia was in the midst of recuperating from her mastectomy when she and Paul plastered smiles on their faces to attend a special screening of *White House Red Carpet* for the WGBH crew in Boston. Driving to the station Julia lit a cigarette, inhaled, and felt nauseated. She flicked the butt out the window and never smoked again.

Everyone has his or her own remedy for trouble. Julia had always turned to work as a salve, and so it was now. The enormous challenge of envisioning *Mastering*, Volume II, testing and retesting recipes, writing them up, and consulting with their editor at Alfred A. Knopf, Judith Jones, gave Julia a goal, structured her time, and nourished her in every way. And, for better and for worse, the process brought her closer to her "French sister" and longtime collaborator, Simca Beck.

When Julia, Simca, and Louisette Bertholle wrote *Mastering the Art of French Cooking* in the fifties, they had to leave aside many recipes that wouldn't fit into the already-crowded 684-page tome. Upon the book's publication in 1961, they vowed that if it sold well they would include the forsaken dishes in a second volume. Judith Jones encouraged this idea.

Jones was an accidental cookbook editor. "The idea had never even occurred to me" before *Mastering* landed on her desk in 1959, she recalled. She had been hired by Knopf as a fiction editor, and to work on translations of Camus and Sartre. But, Jones explained in a series of conversations over many months, she understood the cookbook intuitively. She had lived in Paris at the same time the Childs did, had developed her palate by eating in cafés and brasseries, and had learned to cook with friends and by asking for recipes as she shopped in the outdoor markets. Given the manuscript for *Mastering* in New York, Jones was charmed by the book, and convinced of its potential when she cooked from it at home. "I thought, 'Well, if *I* like it then others will, too!,'" she said.

Mastering was the first cookbook Jones edited, and she would go on to introduce other chefs with distinct voices and culinary expertise to America—including Marion Cunningham (sophisticated home cooking), Lidia Bastianich (Italian food), Claudia Roden (Middle Eastern), Edna Lewis (the American South), Madhur Jaffrey (Indian), and Irene Kuo (Chinese).

When *Mastering* successfully fulfilled its promise and Julia became a TV star in the early sixties, it was logical for the publisher to follow up with a sequel. In 1965, Julia and Simca began to work on *Mastering*, Volume II. (By that point, Louisette Bertholle had dropped out of the collaboration.) Jones set a deadline of December 31, 1967, for the first draft. But that date came and went, with no sign of Volume II.

"It will be ready when it's ready," Julia said. Writing to Simca, she added: "Too bad, but it is a thing we can't hurry, if it is to be the super book we expect."

A year later, she and Simca had produced only three of fourteen planned chapters. Jones was growing concerned—in part because the authors gave the appearance that "they could keep going well into the next century," and in part because she noticed that the Child-Beck collaboration was starting to buckle and crack under pressure.

III. Made for Each Other

The air was chilly and the sky was overcast and portending rain until the late afternoon, when the sun sent shafts of light through the gloom and warmed up their little corner of Provence. It was December 27, 1968. The Childs were at La Pitchoune for Christmas, the Fischbachers were next door at Bramafam, and Julia and Simca were knuckling down to "cookery bookery." They had spent the afternoon in front of a tiny black-and-white TV, watching NASA's *Apollo 8* capsule—the first manned spaceflight to orbit the moon—reenter the atmosphere from space and splash down into the Pacific. They were "dazed and thrilled" by the sight, Paul wrote. "Its courage, its perfection, and its imagination are almost beyond belief. What a triumph for human beings."

That afternoon, the American journalist Mary Roblee Henry drove up the rutted driveway to chronicle the making of Volume II for *Vogue*. "Tonight you are our guinea pigs!" Julia greeted Henry and the French photographer Marc Riboud enthusiastically. "We're going to cook up a storm, testing two tremendously secret recipes from the new book."

Julia heaved a weighty black stone mortar onto the worktable in her La Pitchoune kitchen, and used the pestle to mash crawfish shells together with butter. "It takes strong hands to be a good cook," she said, with a zealous gleam in her eye. "You have to be rough and tough." With hard strokes she squeezed the pink butter through a sieve into a bowl. "This flexes the muscles, and the butter gets far better mixing than in a blender . . . The crawfish go into the sauce, the shells into the butter, and the rest into the soup!"

Simca Beck watched impatiently. She was a tall, pale-skinned, sharp-featured, headstrong blond Frenchwoman who was just as obsessed with *la cuisine bourgeoise* as Julia was. They called each other *ma belle soeur*, which can mean either "my dear sister" or "sister-in-law." Like blood sisters, they loved each other most of the time and clashed spectacularly some of the time.

Simca dipped a finger into the crawfish mousse and scowled. "I find that very buttery."

"*Zut alors*, more shells!" said Julia, who seemed to relish the work. "This is only the sixth time we've done this dish. We tried it out on Sam Chamberlain [the American artist and writer], but so far it hasn't even a name."

As Madame Henry took notes on a yellow legal pad, Riboud snapped pictures. Paul acted as sous-chef and dishwasher, and quietly observed the proceedings.

As far as Henry and Riboud could tell, Julia and Simca were working in perfect harmony. It was an impression the authors encouraged. "Some people don't want others around because they don't know what they're doing," Julia said. "I *know* what I'm doing so I don't mind company. One of the great pleasures is working with Simca."

"We were made for each other." Simca nodded.

As the cooks finished and the sun set, drinks were served in front of the fireplace in the open living-dining room. The floor at La Peetch was lined with red tile, the white stucco walls were decorated with Paul's paintings, and a vase of fresh mimosas graced the round dining table.

Dinner began with a sole mousse accompanied by the hard-won crawfish butter sauce. Paul poured a cool Alsatian Sporen 1964, which they sipped from distinctive amber-colored, handblown wineglasses bought in neighboring Biot. Conversation was light and convivial. As they ate, Riboud focused his cameras on Julia, creating a series of images of her tasting food at the stove and laughing as she poked the fish mousse with a fork. He didn't take many pictures of Simca.

The entrée was a duck that had been poached, boned, molded with foie gras, and chilled in a port wine aspic. It was served on glazed pottery plates that were a house gift from the eminent American chef James Beard. Paul uncorked bottles of Château Lynch-Bages 1959 and cut "thighs" of a peasant loaf that Julia had baked. Simca's husband, Jean Fischbacher, turned the salad leaves in their dressing eighty times. Julia served ripe cheeses bought in Cannes, and Simca brought out her signature dessert, an apple *tarte normande*.

The meal was sublime, "one of the most unforgettable dinners ever cooked by Julia Child," Henry declared in her *Vogue* article, which appeared six months later. Julia had thoroughly enjoyed herself, and understood that a story about the making of their book in a high-profile magazine would provide fantastic publicity. Now she was eager to finish work on Volume II.

Paul wasn't convinced the evening had gone so well. "The concentration of both Mary Henry and Marc was on Julia," he observed, "which may have hurt Simca's feelings."

Out of respect for her colleague, Julia did not discuss her success in the States, or the media apparatus that had helped make it possible. Simca rarely watched television and knew little about *The French Chef;* she did not appreciate why Julia's portrait on the cover of *Time* in 1966 was groundbreaking, or how a feature in *Vogue* would publicize their book. As far as Simca was concerned, nothing had changed since they worked on the original *Mastering* in the fifties: she and Julia were equal partners in teaching and writing, and Simca considered herself the better cook.

But when it dawned on her, as Paul wrote, that "Julia has so sedulously protected her (against my urgings) from knowing how popular, how beloved and well known, what a household word Julia has become," Simca grew quietly resentful. How was it that her old friend had become such a major celebrity in America?

2

The French Chef

I. 103 IRVING STREET

In January 1959, the Childs were living in a small house on Olive Avenue, in Washington, D.C. Paul had been temporarily named the chief of exhibits for the USIA (U.S. Information Agency, formerly USIS, the U.S. Information Service), and Julia was fine-tuning the manuscript for what would become *Mastering the Art of French Cooking*. To all outward appearances, they were happily committed to a career in diplomacy. But behind closed doors, they had made a momentous decision: after one more posting—to Oslo, Norway—Paul would retire from the USIA, and the Childs would return to civilian life in America.

He had just turned fifty-seven and she would soon turn forty-seven. They had enjoyed their time abroad—most of all in France—but it was tiring, and they were ready to settle down. They had a quiet life already planned out. Julia would cook, write, and teach classes. Paul would paint, write, and take photographs. They would find a nice house, surround themselves with good friends and sophisticated culture, and enjoy delicious wine and food.

After much consideration, they chose Cambridge, Massachusetts, over other cities, such as Washington, D.C. (which they liked, but didn't love), Los Angeles (Julia's hometown, though "too far from family and friends"), and New York (too much hustle and bustle). Paul had spent much of his youth in Boston, and had lived in Cambridge with his first great love, Edith Kennedy, in 1930, when he taught at the Shady Hill School. (He and Kennedy, who was a sophisticated divorcée twenty years older than Paul, did not marry; she died of heart troubles and edema in 1942.) Paul had friends in Cambridge and felt comfortable in its leafy, left-leaning, academic milieu. As did Julia: though raised in Pasadena, California, her family was rooted in Massachusetts, and she often mentioned her "New England Yankee" lineage. She graduated from Smith College, in Northampton, Massachusetts, and had grown fond of Cambridge during visits to Avis DeVoto and other friends.

Cambridge was a charming town, intimate enough to provide a genuine community, but just across the Charles River from the city of Boston. Best of all, to Julia's eye, Cambridge was populated by "eggheads"— intellectuals from widely varied backgrounds, some of whom taught at Harvard, MIT, and Boston University, others who were architects, historians, economists, or restaurateurs.

The Childs had taken several scouting trips to Cambridge but had yet to find a house that felt like home. Then, in January 1959, Avis DeVoto called to say, "I've heard about a special house. It's not on the market yet, but it will be soon. It's perfect for you. Drop everything and come up here immediately."

The Childs demurred. They were about to depart for the Norwegian fjords, and, besides, there was an icy rain outside. But Avis advised that house shopping in Cambridge was a competitive sport, and insisted that this might be their only chance for a "special" place. Reluctantly, Paul and Julia boarded the train north.

In Cambridge, they made their way to 103 Irving Street, on a leafy lane behind the Harvard campus. The house was a wide, three-story-tall, gray clapboard Victorian built in 1889 by the philosopher Josiah Royce. It had a short driveway, a modest garden, a full basement, and a long kitchen. As they entered, another couple was exploring the rooms and whispering. Paul inspected the cellar, the fine dining room, two living rooms, a large space on the second floor (suitable for an office/painting studio), the attic, and an adjoining apartment that could be rented out. Julia stood in the kitchen on the first floor and tried to imagine herself cooking there. Eighteen feet wide by twenty-four feet long, it was "ample," she judged.

The big gray house needed refurbishment, but Avis was right: there was something special about it. "It spoke to us," Julia recalled. As a third couple toured 103 Irving Street, the Childs figured they'd never find anything better and made a generous offer—about $48,000—on the spot. Their bid was accepted.

"Hooray!" they cheered. Then they rented the house out and decamped for Norway for exactly two years and two days.

On May 19, 1961, Paul Child quit his job after sixteen years in the Foreign Service. "Ah, freedom at last—no more of this hurly-burly, thank you very much," he and Julia said to each other. Upon returning to the States, the Childs moved into 103 Irving Street and set to making it their own. It was their first permanent home together. While it had good bones, there were many refinements to be made, especially to the kitchen.

The kitchen of their new house was the ninth that Julia and Paul designed together, though they'd never had such a generous canvas to work on before. "We intended to make it both practical and beautiful, a working laboratory as well as a living and dining room," Julia said.

Visitors entered not through the front door facing Irving Street but through a side door that led from the driveway into the kitchen. The first object you encountered there was the "big black monster," your hostess's most essential piece of equipment: a six-burner Garland restaurant range, which the Childs purchased in Washington, D.C., in the late 1940s for $400. It hunkered to the left, by the door, produced "a fierce high heat," was equipped with an oven "large enough for two 25-pound turkeys," and never needed repair. There was usually a pot of tea on the stove and pans filled with foods in various stages of experimentation; occasionally you'd see handmade sausages hanging from the stove hood as they cured, or a homemade baguette cooling nearby.

To the right as you entered, an electric self-cleaning oven with a peekaboo window and a thermostatically regulated warming drawer were recessed into the wall. Julia was always tinkering with something in those ovens, such as the slow-roasted pears in a velvety purple wine sauce I encountered one day, which suffused the house with an ethereal aroma.

The Childs' architect, Robert Woods Kennedy, suggested they move the double sink from a cramped corner to a more central spot against the right wall, beneath a set of windows, making room for a large butcher block, a dishwasher, and a refrigerator they had shipped from Washington.

Julia didn't care about establishing the "golden triangle"—a configuration allowing a cook to take as few steps as possible between stove, refrigerator, and sink—declaring in typical fashion, "the more exercise the better." But she was adamant that she have as much "working and putting-down space as possible." Kennedy installed maple work surfaces, one and a half inches thick, along every available wall. The oven and the gas range required countertops nearby, as places for hot pans to rest and where oven mitts and basting brushes were at the ready. The counters were raised to thirty-nine inches from the floor, to accommodate Julia's height. One lasting regret for Julia was that she did not specify that the counters have a two-inch overhang, which makes it easy to scrape crumbs or chopped vegetables into a bowl held below the work surface.

While she preached the necessity for "moderation," Julia admitted that she suffered from a kitchenware "megalomania." She was rendered helpless by Dehillerin, her favorite shop in Paris, where she would buy armloads of kettles, parfait molds, ice-cream makers, knives, whisks, colanders, and—most of all—copper pots. According to Paul, Julia acquired enough gadgets to outfit at least two medium-size restaurants. "My excuse is that I need this equipment for television and cooking demonstrations and certainly I must try out everything new so that I can have a valid opinion of it," she wrote. "But even I have almost come to the point where any further acquisition must mean the getting rid of an existing object, and that is a terrible wrench because I love almost every piece. I therefore have no helpful advice to give those with limited space except to suggest puritan restraint, strict discipline, and super organization."

Julia was a "hanger-upper" who liked to "see where everything is" in the kitchen. Paul hung her *batterie de cuisine* on simple Peg-Board, painted a blue green: dozens of copper saucepans and skillets, her serving platters, and whimsical molds in the shapes of fish or hearts. He outlined each with black Magic Marker, so you would know exactly where to return it. "Since we rejoice in the shapes of tools, cooking utensils become decorative objects, all carefully orchestrated by Paul from pots and pot lids to skillets, trivets, and flan rings," Julia explained to *Architectural Digest*. "Glass measures and earthenware pitchers are hung just so, while scissors hang in harmony with olive pitters, bottle openers, and nut-crackers . . . in a stunning array of colors and shapes."

Having suffered from the unyielding beauty of red tiles in Provence and large vinyl squares in Cambridge, Julia insisted on an airport-strength vinyl flooring, in a pebble pattern, to ease the strain of hours of standing in her kitchen. The vinyl was comfortable, durable, and required washing only when Julia needed "the psychological release," she said. (She used the same material to floor the kitchen at La Pitchoune.)

The Childs turned one of their two pantries into a mini bakery, with a large, thick piece of white pastry marble on a countertop. Julia liked to *wham* her bread dough, knead her *pâtes feuilletées*, and roll out piecrusts on that cool, smooth surface. Paul used the back pantry for storage and as a cocktail laboratory.

To the left of the alcove where the Childs stashed their little television stood a large black refrigerator. It was decorated with a Valentine designed by Paul, along with his colorful photographs of Julia's *boeuf daube en gelée*, and a *pâté en croûte*. To the right of the fridge stood a bookcase laden with dictionaries, atlases, and references like *Peterson Field Guide to Birds*, *Bartlett's Familiar Quotations*, *Bulfinch's Mythology*, and a full set of *Encyclopaedia Britannica*. The walls were graced by art made by friends and family—a painting of an artichoke, another of white eggs on a blue background, and a rubbing of a bluefish Julia caught in Maine.

Though the Childs occasionally used the spacious dining room—for large dinner parties or Thanksgiving feasts, at which they served a rich pumpkin-and-cream soup in a hollowed-out pumpkin, for instance—that was an exception. More often, they ate at the kitchen table they'd brought from Norway. It sat six comfortably and eight in a squeeze. Julia covered it with a colorful oilcloth, and usually piled it with stacks of newspapers and mail. "I want the dining table in the middle of the room," she said, "because, like a sheepdog, I need to be right there in the midst of everyone."

The Childs had made 103 Irving their own: "a supremely comfortable house to cherish," Julia called it, though that description doesn't do it justice. The second floor held her office (decorated with a large typewriter, a mug of tea, precarious stacks of books, a blizzard of papers on and around her desk, and an exercise machine), Paul's painting/photography studio (impeccably organized easels, paints, camera paraphernalia, negatives, logbooks, and a mug of tea), and their bedrooms; the third floor held a guest room and storage; a small extension held an apartment the Childs often rented to college students. What the foregoing omits is the sensation that upon entering 103 Irving Street you were stepping into Paul's and Julia's conjoined brains. It was the decoration that gave that impression. The front hallway held one of Paul's hand-carved wooden chests, while nearly every wall was decorated by his etchings, photographs, and paintings—wartime charts of Japanese aircraft, Cubistic Parisian rooftops, red tobacco barns, watery reflections of Venice, portraits of Julia, and the like.

When Edith Efron of *TV Guide* visited in 1970, she was stunned by the house, which appeared to be a complex nineteenth-century artwork. "Why has no one written about you?" she asked Paul ("an attractive gentleman who is actually 68, looks to be about 55, and assures us that he feels like 40"). He smiled and quietly replied, "They don't see me. They only see Julia." But, Efron noted, "the joke is on them. If you don't 'see' Paul, you don't 'see' Julia either. This beautiful world that Paul Child has created is the world that Julia lives in. And the 'pale, assistant/husband,' whose paintings are eagerly bought by the Boston University population, is the creative lord of it."

Conversation in the Child house would flow from Robert Frost to Frank Lloyd Wright, Goethe, Ibsen, Mozart, Chopin, and—Julia's favorite—Balzac. The Childs said they wanted to make documentary films about woodworking and silversmithing, to preserve traditional artisanal skills before they disappeared. As Vietnam raged, and race relations worsened, and the Nixon White house plotted, the Childs debated good and evil. "Julia," Paul told Efron, "is an essentially conable woman. She's naïve in the nicest possible way. She just can't believe people have bad motives, when it's a palpable fact . . . The problem is that the baddies have pre-empted the good symbols, like peace . . . You know, Korzybski said that those who control the symbols control society."

Julia listened to this, walloped veal cutlets flat with a mallet, and, with a grin, digressed: "I've never met Mary McCarthy, but I suspect she's an intellectual snob. I have a feeling she'd go after my husband and ignore me. I'd scratch her eyes out!"

Inevitably, guests would end up in the kitchen, which Julia described as "the beating heart and social center" of the house. "It was certainly the most-loved and most-used room." Friends felt free to knock on the door at 103 Irving, and when they did, Julia would usher them into the kitchen to chop cold butter into cubes, baste the goose, or haul wine up from the basement:

> They walk about, then sit at the table, and we have aperitifs and talk while I am finishing the dinner. It is easy and pleasant, and I am one of the party the way I like to be. Food is better, too, infinitely better, because the cook is in the kitchen, the way a chef is in his restaurant. No fresh green beans sit to warm up, losing their texture and color while I am in a dining room; no sauce will boil away nor custard curdle. Furthermore, nobody minds a bit of public stirring, tossing, and tasting . . . [After eating] I pile the plates in my double sink and hide them under big stainless trays, while all finished pots are covered discreetly, and the stove light doused. Everything looks shipshape, in other words . . . Then out we go . . . to have coffee in the clean and well-ordered living room. That is my idea of a proper kitchen.

11. Friends, Neighbors, Cantabrigians

After moving into 103 Irving Street in 1961, Julia met Dorothy Zinberg, a graduate student in sociology at Harvard, at the Legal Sea Foods fish market. Looking over the haddock, lobsters, and clams, chatting with the store's owner, George Berkowitz, the two conversed as any other housewives might. Except that Julia Child happened to be unusually inquisitive and well informed about food.

The postwar culinary revolution was just getting under way in New York. French classics like coq au vin and *boeuf bourguignon* gave way to the "gourmet trend" of Spanish paella, Peruvian seviche, Indonesian pork satay, and Arabian chicken roasted with cloves and honey. But Cambridge was essentially a provincial New England town, Zinberg recalled, "like living in the country." While Boston had some fine establishments, Cambridge restaurants tended to serve meat-and-potatoes basics, or red-sauce Italian food, though there was one first-rate French restaurant, the Henri IV, a favorite of artists such as Joan Miró, William Faulkner, Thornton Wilder, and Alexander Calder. "This was an era when dinner party menus consisted of grilled Spam, pineapple chunks, and gelatin-mold salad stuffed with marshmallows," Zinberg said with a shudder. Yet, as home to Harvard, Radcliffe, and MIT, Cambridge became a magnet for European academics, who brought Old World foods, like borscht, dark bread, and kielbasa with them.

The Childs had a remarkable set of neighbors, most of whom lived within a few blocks of one another. The economist and former ambassador to India, John Kenneth Galbraith, and his wife, Catherine ("Kitty"), lived behind Paul and Julia. Avis and Bernard DeVoto lived close by, as did Dorothy and her husband, Norman Zinberg, who was an influential psychoanalyst at Harvard. Not far away were historian Arthur Schlesinger Sr., Arthur Schlesinger Jr., and his wife, the author Marian Schlesinger.

Some friends became professional collaborators who influenced Paul and Julia as much as the Childs influenced them. Ben and Jane Thompson, for instance, ran the influential home furnishings store Design Research in Cambridge, which would later supply cookware and Marimekko prints for *The French Chef* set. In the early seventies, the Thompsons opened Harvest, a modern American restaurant on Harvard Square that operated in the same spirit as Alice Waters's Chez Panisse in Berkeley, California, and trained many of Boston's leading chefs. (Harvest remains in business today.) And, in 1976, the Thompsons and the developer James Rouse—with the Childs' vocal support—renovated Boston's decrepit Faneuil Hall into a "festival marketplace" inspired by Les Halles.

In Cambridge there was a vast corps of overeducated, underemployed women who "were ready for Julia," said Zinberg. "We didn't know who she was, at first. But then she changed our lives—in every way you can imagine."

Mastering the Art of French Cooking was published in October 1961. It was intended, Julia wrote, for "the servantless American cook who can be unconcerned on occasion with budgets, waistlines, time schedules, children's meals, the parent-chauffeur-den-mother syndrome, or anything else which might interfere with the enjoyment of producing something wonderful to eat."

Those last few words are the key to understanding Julia's ethos. For, she added, in what could be a credo to her career: "All of the techniques employed in French cooking are aimed at one goal: how does it taste?"

With a rave review in *The New York Times*, Craig Claiborne launched *Mastering* into the American mainstream, calling it "probably the most comprehensive, laudable, and monumental work" on French cooking in English, and predicting that it would "remain as the definitive work for nonprofessionals."

Mastering arrived at an auspicious moment. The economy was booming, Americans were traveling abroad and eager to embrace new foods, and the Kennedys had hired René Verdon to cook for them. Years later, Julia recalled, "With the Kennedys in the White House, people were very interested in [French food], so I had the field to myself, which was just damn lucky. It would be very, very much more difficult now."

By early 1962, *Mastering* went into its third printing of ten thousand copies, and Julia received her first royalty check, for $2,610.85. "Yahoo!" she crowed, noting that she, Simca, and Louisette were now within $632.12 of paying off the expenses they'd incurred writing the book.

On February 20, 1962, Paul was transfixed by radio accounts of John Glenn's orbit of Earth aboard the *Friendship* 7 capsule. Julia, meanwhile, appeared on "an egghead TV show" called *I've Been Reading*. It was hosted by Boston University English professor Albert Duhamel and aired on WGBH, Boston's fledgling public television station. Duhamel put Julia at ease, and she proved naturally comfortable in front of a TV camera. Perhaps too comfortable. So intent was she on demonstrating how to "turn" a mushroom and flip an omelet the French way that she forgot to mention the title of her book. But it hardly mattered. Twenty-seven people wrote to the station to say, "Get that tall, loud woman back on television. We want to see more cooking!"

This was an unexpectedly warm response. The WGBH honchos looked at one another and wondered: Is there enough interest in this Julia Child to warrant a cooking show on public television?

III. THEMES AND VARIATIONS

Though she did not own a TV set, Julia had been bitten by the television bug from the moment she set foot on a studio set. In October 1961, she and Simca had appeared on NBC's *Today* show to promote *Mastering*, and afterward Julia wrote: "TV was certainly an impressive new medium." (She would soon buy her first television with the proceeds from book sales.) By then, she had been teaching cooking for nine years, and was on a mission to spread the gospel of *"le goût français"*—the very essence of French taste—which she fervently believed could be reproduced by American cooks in their home kitchens. All that was needed, Julia said, were a set of clear instructions, the right tools and ingredients, and a little encouragement.

In April 1962, shortly after appearing on *I've Been Reading*, Julia typed a memo to WGBH in which she laid out a vision for "an interesting, adult series of half-hour TV programs on French cooking addressed to an intelligent, reasonably sophisticated audience which likes good food and cooking."

Each program, Julia suggested, should focus on just a few recipes, and her cooking demonstration—"informal, easy, conversational, yet timed to the minute"—should lead to a discussion of broader culinary matters, such as "a significant book on cooking or wine, an interesting piece of equipment, or a special product." To keep the audience from getting bored of the same old chef nattering on, Julia suggested that other experts, such as a pastry chef or a wine sommelier, appear as guests, and that well-known chefs—such as James Beard or Joseph Donan (a master French *cuisinier*)—cook side by side with her on the show.

French food was particularly well suited to teaching, Julia thought: not only was it the best tasting, it had a clear set of rules to follow. The master chef Auguste Escoffier, whom Julia referred to as "the great codifier," had established a set of procedures to cook by in his reference book *Le Guide Culinaire*, which is still in use today. Explicit rules appealed to Julia's need for order and respect for "the scientific method."

"Because the French have treated cooking as a serious profession as well as an art, they are far more precise about their methods than any other national group," she wrote. Once a cook learned the basics of French technique, she taught, they could be applied to Spanish, Russian, Italian, Japanese, or any other cuisine.

"As I conceive of cooking . . . the whole business boils down to a series of themes and variations in which one learns the basic techniques, then varies the ingredient," Julia wrote. "Once you have learned the coq au vin, you can make any similar type of stew, whether it be beef, lamb or lobster." This focus on theme and variation, which had been ingrained by Chef Max Bugnard, her mentor at the Cordon Bleu, would prove a hallmark of Julia's teaching throughout her career.

WGBH HAD NEVER PRODUCED a cooking program, had a small audience, was largely run by volunteers, and operated on a shoestring budget. But encouraged by the public's strong response to Julia on *I've Been Reading*, the station arranged for her to shoot three pilot (or trial) episodes of a televised cookery show.

On June 18, 1962, the Childs arrived at a borrowed "studio" in downtown Boston—actually, the demonstration kitchen of the Boston Gas Company—to shoot the first pilot, "The French Omelette." (Julia preferred the French spelling of that word.) Julia brought her own frying pan, spatula, butter, and eggs. The lights flicked on, and the show's pro-

Julia on the set at WGBH, Boston

ducer, twenty-eight-year-old Russell "Russ" Morash, directed two stationary cameras. Because videotape was so dear, the show was essentially shot "live" in one continuous half-hour take. "I careened around the stove for the allotted twenty-eight minutes, flashing whisks and bowls and pans, and panting a bit under the hot lights," she recalled. "The omelette came out just fine. And with that, WGBH-TV had lurched into educational television's first cooking program."

The second and third pilot episodes, "Coq au Vin" and "Soufflés," were both shot on June 25. This time, Julia had rehearsed the shows at home. Paul built a replica of the set in their kitchen, labeled utensils, made sure the ingredients were measured beforehand, and coached Julia with a stopwatch. Though she continued to gasp and misplace things, she grew more self-assured with each performance.

Julia's special sauce—her ability to blend deep knowledge, broad experience, precise technique, self-deprecating humor, and infectious enthusiasm—won the public's heart. There was simply no one quite like her on TV. Julia loved this "high-wire act," but admitted that she was "a complete amateur" and had no idea how she came across on TV. The answer was simple: the camera, and audience, loved her.

In response to the "Coq au Vin" show, a viewer named Irene McHogue wrote:

> Not only did I get a wonderfully refreshing new approach to the preparation and cooking of said poultry, but really and truly one of the most surprisingly entertaining half hours I have ever spent before the TV in many a moon. I love the way she projected over the camera directly to me the watcher. Loved watching her catch the frying pan as it almost went off the counter; loved her looking for the cover of the casserole. It was fascinating to watch her hand motions which were so firm and sure with the food. And her to-do about the brandy-firing was without parallel for that rare tongue-in-cheek sort of humor the viewer longs for in this day of the over-rehearsed ad-lib.

Encouraged, WGBH signed Julia up for a twenty-six-episode series. Ruth Lockwood, the assistant producer, scrounged up a track of bouncy French theme music. Unable to decide on a name for the program, Julia called it *The French Chef*—though she was neither French nor a professional chef (she called herself "a cook")—until she could invent a better title. Taping of the new series would begin in January 1963, and the show would start broadcasting in February.

Julia was fifty years old. And her stated goal was to teach people "how to make cooking make sense."

IV. A NEW WINDOW ON THE WORLD

After years of scrimping through the breadlines of the Depression, and subsisting on canned basics during the war, Americans craved something *more*—to open their senses, luxuriate in taste, and experiment with new ingredients and flavors—after the Second World War. In 1947, Pan Am introduced affordable transatlantic flights, which made travel more achievable than ever. As Americans investigated other cultures, they tasted a wide range of new cuisines and wanted to replicate them at home.

Fueling this curiosity was a burgeoning food media. In 1941, *Gourmet*, the first American magazine to cover food and wine in a serious way, was launched. That same year, Henri Soulé and Pierre Franey—who had cooked at the French pavilion during the 1939 World's Fair, in New York, and stayed after the outbreak of war—opened Le Pavillon. It would become a temple of haute cuisine, and the training ground for many star chefs.

As they traveled abroad, Americans harbored a special, romantic fondness for France above all other destinations. This reverence was perhaps tinged by an unspoken, big brotherly sense of superiority: America had once again saved France from the Germans, after all, and were welcomed as saviors who delighted in the pleasure of the French table. In 1942, Humphrey Bogart told Ingrid Bergman, "We'll always have Paris," in *Casablanca*. In 1943, Samuel Chamberlain published *Clementine in the Kitchen*, about the French chef who charmed his Massachusetts neighbors. In the postwar years, members of the Lost Generation, such as Ernest Hemingway, Gertrude Stein, Josephine Baker, James Baldwin, and Alexander Calder, spent time in France and produced art inspired there.

In the meantime, another type of revolution was under way: between 1948 and 1955, nearly two-thirds of all American families bought a television set. The "boob tube" would have a profound impact on people's daily lives, and on the culture at large. With millions of people watching the same shows at the same time, TV created a virtual community. It brought an exciting blend of travel, art and science, politics, sitcoms, space travel, and the Vietnam War into the nation's living rooms, and provided a new "window on the world."

It was against this backdrop that WGBH launched *The French Chef*. In the first episode, which aired on February 11, 1963, a slightly nervous, fresh-faced Julia Child demonstrated how to make *boeuf bourguignon*, the venerable beef stew that would run as a leitmotif through her career. At the end of the show, she tucked a dish towel into her apron, and spontaneously said: "This is Julia Child. *Bon appétit!*"

v. THE FRENCH CHEF

Many people assume that Julia had the first cooking show on television, but that was not the case. While the broad success of *The French Chef* understandably led to this impression, Julia had benefited from two decades' worth of culinary programming.

The earliest TV cooking shows appeared in the 1940s—such as Florence Hanford's *Television Kitchen*, in which the host dispensed menu-planning tips for dinner parties on Philadelphia's WPTZ. Other shows, like Shirley Marshall's *Ladies Fare*, in the mid-fifties, explained "how to make average food appetizing" on WAVE-TV in Louisville, Kentucky. Mary Wilson interviewed celebrities, dispensed kitchen advice, and sang songs on *Pots, Pans and Personalities* on WPTZ. Trudy McNall gave us *Home Cooking* on WHAM-TV, in Rochester, New York. And Marjorie Hume presented *What's Cookin'* on KFMB in San Diego.

Jessie DeBoth, of Detroit, established herself as what might be called a vaudevillian–home economist in the 1930s. She performed a live show that mixed cooking with song, dance, comic patter, and prize giveaways. In 1951, she appeared on TV, hollering "HiYo!" and wearing fashionable hats while mixing flour. In a raucous show featuring Pino and Fedora Bontempi, on New Haven's WTNH, a dog wandered onto the set while Pino hectored Fedora, she cooked and yelled at him, and he would exit the kitchen singing opera. Perhaps the most unusual cooking show was aired in San Francisco in the 1950s, starring the blind Mexican cookbook author and restaurateur Elena Zelayeta and her son Billy. While she stared straight at the camera and presented a dish as if she were sighted, he would silently chop, stir, and cook around her.

There were a few male presenters, such as Chef George Rector, who ran a culinary segment on *Radio City Matinee*, a 1946 show on WNBT in New York. His segments were aired in daytime for women, and presented cooking as a means of self-improvement and social advancement. Rector was replaced by James Beard, a rising chef from Portland, Oregon, whose show, *I Love to Eat*, ran on NBC from 1946 to 1947. In an audio recording Beard said he was commonly asked: Should fish be cooked with the head on? To which he replied yes, since "the people who cook better than any other people, the Chinese and the French, always serve their fishes like this, and why not follow their example?" (Julia and Paul Child held the same view.) Like Julia, Beard made silly jokes— "Chicken, I've got you under my skin," he'd sing. But also like Julia, he emphasized that joy in one's food trumped expediency.

In 1950, the rubber-faced comedian Ernie Kovacs took over the cooking show *Deadline for Dinner* (which he pronounced "Dead Lion for Dinner") on WPTZ. One of his gags was to invite a local chef onto the show and engage in wacky banter while they cooked together. Kovacs portrayed a kitchen naïf who assaulted a recipe, and it was up to the sober-minded chef to talk him through it. Kovacs used this stooge versus straight man shtick to demonstrate that a delicious meal can be made despite various (self-inflicted) challenges.

By 1962, when Julia's pilot shows ran on WGBH, the food and home economics program was an established genre. Most of the hosts were women of a specific type: the wise older matron or the cheerful wholesome housewife. Some would address the camera as if lecturing naughty children; others mixed showbiz with pedagogy. In both cases, their aim was to teach homemakers how to provide sustenance for the family. Julia Child, on the other hand, was focused on making cooking "fun" and "attractive" for men, women, and children, and produced food that she happily declared was "toothsome" and "delicious."

WHILE JULIA BUILT her show on the scaffolding of earlier programs, there was no exact template for *The French Chef*. Operating on instinct,

Julia invented her own, exuberant-yet-exact style of presentation, trusting herself and her small team to complete each recipe in just under thirty minutes, week after week.

A big part of Julia's allure was her natural ease on TV. Her combination of grace and awkwardness built a sense of trust and intimacy with the audience, which was reinforced by her deep knowledge and sure technique. Like Kovacs, she used humor to keep her viewers engaged, but because she was so technically adept Julia (usually) managed to triumph over adversity in the end, sometimes in the waning seconds of an episode.

She would start making a quiche, misplace her glasses or lose her train of thought, find them again, and carry on. She would rapidly and expertly dice a pile of mushrooms, fillet a trout, and demonstrate how to encase poached eggs in a delicate consommé gelatin (*oeufs en gelée*). But in the next instant, a spoon would go flying offscreen, an apple charlotte would collapse and she'd mash it back together with her fingers ("It will taste even better this way"), or she'd incinerate the croutons atop a French onion soup into charcoal briquettes ("That's beautiful! There you are. I think that possibly that browned a little bit too much. But I don't know. It gives a very good effect.")

Confronted by a mishap, Julia would look momentarily befuddled, cuss under her breath, or just tilt her head back and laugh.

Many established TV chefs, such as Jim Beard or the English chef Dione Lucas, were accomplished cooks but stilted performers who delivered their recipes like sermons from the Mount. Julia took the opposite approach: smiling into the camera, clearly explaining what she was doing, burning her fingers, and waving around a giant rolling pin, she seemed to implicate her viewers in a mischievous caper. She would lift a gargantuan monkfish up by the tail and talk to it ("Hello, you ugly old thing!"), mention that she had brushed the teeth of a roast suckling pig, demonstrate the making of a liver-filled omelet for a mother-in-law ("that'll fix her up!"), or identify cuts of beef by pointing to parts of her own body—neck, shoulder, rack, fillet, loin—with dramatic acrobatics.

Not only was Julia entertaining, she was unapologetically sensual. Sipping a spoonful of *bourride à l'aïoli* (fish soup), she would close her eyes and moan a deep "*yuummmmmmm.*" That lusty enthusiasm was fun to watch. The sight of Julia sipping, nibbling, grunting, adding a dash more salt or garlic to her food inspired people to do the same at home. If tarragon was important to Julia, then it suddenly became important to her viewers, who demanded that their grocers carry fresher, more varied produce. Julia egged them on, and her words bore results almost instantly.

"Through your efforts, our stores are now stocking leeks and fresh mushrooms, something unheard of 3 months ago," a fan from Oklahoma wrote in the mid-1960s.

In this disarming way, Julia became a cultural translator of sorts who mediated between French gourmets and regular Americans. She took the starch out of cookery with her own breezy version of Franglais— pronouncing the word *cuisine* "kweezeen," and reminding viewers that highfalutin coq au vin was just "good-old chicken stew." Having discovered cooking "late," while in her thirties, Julia empathized with her viewers and was unafraid to ask obvious, "dumb" questions, which made cooking comprehensible: What's the best way to boil an egg? How do you make a chocolate cake? What kind of wine should I serve with cheese?

"The idea was to take the bugaboo out of French cooking, to demonstrate that it is not merely good cooking but that it follows definite rules," Julia said. "One of the secrets of cooking is to learn to correct something if you can, and bear with it if you cannot."

The audience responded viscerally. "You are a delight!" wrote housewives, hippies, taxi drivers, MIT scientists, and Wall Streeters. *The French Chef* was "educational TV's answer to underground movie and pop/op cults," Joan Barthel wrote in *The New York Times Magazine*. "The program can be campier than 'Batman,' farther-out than 'Lost in Space,' and more penetrating than 'Meet the Press' as it probes the question: Can a Society be Great if its bread tastes like Kleenex?"

There was something intimate and subverbal, even primal, about the experience of watching Julia cook. Her food was so lovingly portrayed that there are moments, even now, when it transports you. Julia liked to point the TV camera straight down into a pot of softly bubbling *boeuf bourguignon* to show you what it should look like as it cooked. It was instructive, but it also activated your taste buds, and tempted you to dive right through the screen to dig into a heaping bowl of that succulent comfort food.

Julia having fun on the set of *The French Chef.*

"To do *that* is not easy," observed the chef Jacques Pépin. "She had a very rare quality."

An important, if little-remarked-upon aspect of *The French Chef* was the implied narrative of each episode—from Julia's often-humorous opening ("Julia Child presents the chicken sisters!"), through the instruction, to the triumphal digestion of a meal. While TV chefs like Beard and Lucas would end their shows by holding up their handiwork for the camera's clinical inspection, Julia would proudly march a pot of ratatouille from the kitchen to the dining-room set—"bearing the finished dish like rubies on velvet," Barthel noted—place it on a table decorated with actual candles and silverware, pour a glass of "wine," serve herself a plateful of the vegetable mélange, and dig in with palpable hunger. This seemingly logical coda to a cooking show was an innovation. It completed the "journey" of the meal from conception to creation to consumption.

"Julia was revolutionary," said Judith Jones. "The first time I saw her on TV, I just knew, 'She's got it.' People ask: 'How can you be so sure?' Well, you just *know*. When you are passionate about something and it arouses something in you, it's just instinctual. It was like having a teacher right there beside you in the kitchen, and everything really worked."

Though she disliked "tooting my own horn," Julia had a messianic zeal for spreading culinary knowledge. In championing the pleasure of shopping, cooking, eating, and even of cleaning the dishes, she became a role model for people of all genders, races, ages, and creeds. For Julia, kitchen work was not "domestic drudgery," it was "such fun!" With the battle cry *"Bon appétit!,"* she reinvented what it meant to be a television chef, and brought a growing audience along for the ride.

VI. WGBH: A WHOLE NEW APPROACH

On Wednesday, April 21, 1965, a dozen technicians and executives huddled around a television monitor at WGBH, Boston's public television station. On the black-and-white screen Julia Child was making a tart decorated with strawberries and cream. The camera focused on the berries, then zoomed in closer and closer, when the lumpy gray fruit suddenly exploded into bright red orbs and the dull *crème pâtissière* flashed a startling white.

The group at the monitor jumped up from their seats and threw their arms in the air, laughing and cheering. "It was the first time Julia and her food had appeared in living color," recalled Russell Morash, the director and producer of *The French Chef* since the show's inception. "It was a kind of mind-blowing moment."

"It was absolutely beautiful," Paul Child wrote of this *Wizard of Oz*–like colorization. "The Boys in the Back Room believe that within 3 to 5 years most people who own television[s] in this country will have color sets and that most emissions will be in color, *must* be, in fact, if the producers aren't to be swamped by competitors."

While the red-and-white tart wasn't the future, exactly, it was a glimpse of things to come, a hint of the great possibilities just around the corner. It would take another five years before WGBH had the proper equipment to broadcast Season Two of *The French Chef* in color. But the

1965 color test was an exciting development, one that Julia had been waiting for impatiently.

"I'm tired of gray food," she griped.

To WGBH, color TV was both a threat and an opportunity. At the time news programs and documentaries were aired in black and white, a palette that connoted rigorous fact and serious journalism. Color, on the other hand, was a relatively new and expensive technology that was still gaining acceptance. The first nationwide broadcast in color was NBC's airing of the Tournament of Roses Parade on January 1, 1954. A decade later, only 3.1 percent of households with televisions owned color sets.

Yet color was catching on quickly. If black and white denoted serious, stodgy fare, then color TV was seen as hip, fun, modern, and youthful. NBC, ABC, and CBS embarked on a color TV arms race, and by the 1966–67 season the three major networks were airing their full prime-time schedules—including shows such as *Bewitched* and *Star Trek*—in color.

Public television executives watched this rapid shift in technology and consumer tastes warily. In March 1967, Dave Davis, WGBH's station manager, wrote a heartfelt memo to his staff: the old, black-and-white order was under assault from every quarter, he warned, and the station's audience was hungry for vibrant, provocative, risky programming. If WGBH didn't respond, it would be left behind. "The visual electronic world is providing a total assault on our senses," Davis wrote. "The pressure is on for Public Television. It's probably now or never— and we don't intend to sit back and wait. With color, we will create a whole new approach to the presentation of the visual arts."

After reading the memo, Julia wrote to Ruth Lockwood urging WGBH to adapt to the changing times and "get out of its somewhat ladylike rut." That was a typical Julia sentiment. She was a strong, earthy personality who embraced new technology. To her, words such as "lady-like," "housewife," and "home ec" were synonyms for "prim," "amateur," "fearful," or "conventional"—all that she was not. "Home economics [is] a person with a white uniform and a dry look, preaching . . . food as medicine, not food as food, and that's a horrid approach," she'd say. "I talked about food as joy, comfort, and delight—food as fun."

———

BY LUCK more than by design, Julia had launched her television career at one of the nation's leading public stations at a crucial moment in the development of the medium.

WGBH got its start in 1946, when Harvard president James Conant pushed for the spread of public education through new media. Conant and Robert Lowell, a wealthy relation of another Harvard president, helped to build a consortium to fund a new radio station. It was given the call letters WGBH (which allegedly stood for "God Bless Harvard," but actually stood for "Great Blue Hill," named after the land it sat on), and began to transmit in 1951. WGBH-TV followed, and first broadcast in 1955, with a children's folk-music show. The station went on to air the Boston Symphony, science and arts programming, and college extension courses.

In the early sixties, the Federal Communications Commission (FCC) mandated that just over a tenth of the two thousand licenses granted to stations across the country be used for "noncommercial" or "educational" programming. There was no national educational TV system: instead, there was a smattering of local stations, like WGBH, that served their own communities. This proto–public TV was known for well-intentioned but uninspired programming, a televisual cod-liver oil in which talking heads droned on about Worthy Subjects.

When *The French Chef* hit the Boston airwaves in 1963, WGBH shared copies of the tapes with sister stations, allowing viewers in New Hampshire, Maine, Pennsylvania, and parts of New York to watch Julia a week after she aired in Boston. *The French Chef* was distributed nationally in the fall of 1964, and two years later, Julia won educational TV's first Emmy Award. Her success was a significant boon to public television stations across the country.

In 1967, the Carnegie Commission issued a report on the feasibility of building a nationwide educational television network. The commission's report pointed to *The French Chef* as a shining example of the kind of programming public television could provide its audiences. Julia had a home-field advantage: the board of the Carnegie Commission was filled with Boston Brahmins, including James Conant of Harvard, James Killian of MIT, and Ralph Lowell of the Lowell Institute. Indeed, WGBH general manager Hartford Gunn wrote the report, and Lowell delivered it to President Johnson in 1967. In 1970, Gunn founded

Julia and Paul with her Emmy Award in 1966

the not-for-profit Public Broadcasting Service (PBS), which remains the nation's largest distributor of public television programming. He used *The French Chef* to illustrate the potential for public TV to transmit culture and education nationwide.

But making television is not cheap. Public TV was notoriously short of funds and unable to raise money in conventional ways, such as by running paid advertising. WGBH's attorneys interpreted FCC rules to read that as long as specific brands were not mentioned on air, then commercial underwriting support was acceptable. The station earned its income from viewer donations and corporate largesse rather than from direct ad sales.

As WGBH prepared to air *The French Chef* in 1963, S&H Green Stamps agreed to finance the first season, and Safeway stores and Hills Bros. Coffee stepped in for later episodes. The show's audience was a desirable demographic: well-educated, middle-class families with enough income to enjoy cooking at home, eating out, and travel. As Julia's audience increased, bigger companies took notice. In 1965, the Polaroid Corporation—a Cambridge-based success story—became *The French Chef*'s lead underwriter.

Some chefs, notably James Beard, plugged products such as Borden's milk, Omaha Steaks, Green Giant Niblets, Old Crow Bourbon, Shasta soft drinks, and DuPont chemicals somewhat shamelessly for the money. Julia refused to endorse products, restaurants, chefs, or stores. She covered the brand names of goods she used on TV—even on sugar and salt containers—with masking tape. She tried to persuade appliance makers to donate a well-made stove to the show, but was unsuccessful. Yet when Oster sent her an Osterizer blender—presumably in the hope that she'd use it on air—she politely declined. And when companies sold products with names like "Julia Chives," or Ocean Spray used "Julia Chicken" in its advertising, Julia's lawyer sent them a stern letter; they pulled their ads and paid restitutions that ranged from $5,000 to $40,000, which Julia donated to pubic television.

Julia's public TV series were hardly moneymaking ventures, as today's extravagant cooking shows decidedly are. She earned income from book sales, magazine columns, personal performances, and from a modest family inheritance, not to mention Paul's income from the State Department and his artwork. Julia's aversion to corporate sponsorship was an article of faith. "Just last week I was offered a million dollars if I would endorse a new product, but I said no," she observed in 1980. "Once you start endorsing products, you're no longer a free agent. Your value is gone."

VII. The New World of Publishing

In 1968, as the old order was being upended around the world, Julia Child's fortunes were soaring. She and Simca Beck were finishing *Mastering*, Volume II, and Julia was planning new television programs. In the meantime, Judith Jones and Robert Gottlieb, Knopf's canny editor in chief, recognized that a tie-in book based on *The French Chef* had great commercial potential. "We hardly needed to discuss it," Jones recalled, "it was so obvious."

Thus *The French Chef Cookbook* was quickly cobbled together. It was a simple, straightforward paperback made up of little more than an introduction by Julia, followed by 119 recipes taken directly from Season One of *The French Chef.* The recipes ranged from chicken breasts and risotto (from show number 14: the tapes of the first thirteen shows had been reused, a circumstance that delighted Julia, who did not care for her inexpert early work) to turban of sole (labeled show number 134, for some reason). Each recipe featured a brief preamble and a set of cooking instructions. Quite a few of them were slightly altered versions of dishes that had appeared in *Mastering*. The cover featured a photograph of a smiling Julia about to whack a turkey carcass with a mallet. Inside, the book was illustrated with Paul's photographs of Julia smelling, tasting, and presenting her food; here and there were a few of his line drawings of jars, pots, and wineglasses. Julia was paid a handsome $25,000 advance for the book, which made a nice contrast to the $2,500 advance in total she and her two co-authors had received for *Mastering*. Out of a sense of fairness, Julia chose to share her latest advance with Simca, Louisette, Ruth Lockwood, and WGBH.

As Knopf prepared to publish *The French Chef Cookbook*, Judith Jones and Bob Gottlieb met for lunch one day to discuss marketing. "How many copies are you planning to print?" Gottlieb asked.

Jones steeled herself. Because of her successful run as an editor, she had been given latitude on such decisions by the house's founder, Alfred A. Knopf. But now she worried she might have been overly optimistic about the prospects for this new book of familiar recipes.

"Twenty-five thousand copies," she mumbled.

Gottlieb raised his eyebrows. "Are you crazy?!"

"Is that too much?"

"No! Don't you know what you've got here?"

Though the Childs had moderate ambitions for this quickly done book, Gottlieb ordered a first print run of one hundred thousand copies.

Brooklyn-born, educated at Columbia and Cambridge, Gottlieb was bright, ambitious, and quirky (he collected vintage plastic handbags, among other things). As an editor at Simon & Schuster, he had discovered Joseph Heller's *Catch-22*, and was later elevated to editor in chief. Now at Knopf, his mandate was to "bring us into this new world of publishing," Jones said. It was a heady, disorienting time, when stodgy book publishers were suddenly asked to synergize their product with television, journalism, public relations, and Hollywood. Gottlieb understood this new media ecosystem, and the role Julia could play in it.

"Crazy!" Paul scribbled on a note after taking a phone call from Judith Jones. "Gottlieb has made a contract w/Bantam [for the paperback] for a $340,000 guarantee for the *French Chef*! . . . They'll flood every drugstore in America!"

By May 1971, the book had already sold more than two hundred thousand copies. Julia was pleasantly surprised by this success, though she considered *The French Chef Cookbook* a minor sidelight to her primary focus: *Mastering the Art of French Cooking*, Volume II.

3

Volume II

1. LOUP EN CROÛTE

One afternoon in 1969 Julia, Simca, and Paul took Patricia Simon, a writer for *McCall's* magazine, to lunch at L'Oasis, a two-star restaurant in Mandelieu-la-Napoule, just south of Cannes. They wanted to try a special "wonder dish" called *Loup de Mer en Croûte*. Invented by Chef Paul Bocuse, the "Lion of Lyon," it is a sea bass baked in a brioche crust and served with a *sauce suprême*, a white sauce of butter, flour, and cream.

They began lunch with aperitifs under the plane trees on the restaurant's patio, then ate a pâté of fresh duck livers and truffles, big slices of *pain brioche*, a timbale, tomatoes, and a *salade verte*. And then came the star of the meal, the *loup* ("lou"): the bass was baked in a brioche crust made to look like a fish—complete with pastry fins, eyes, and scales—and came out of the oven "enormous, brown, and glistening," Julia enthused. To serve it, the headwaiter cut around the edges of the crust and carefully lifted the top off. There lay the fish, steaming and fragrant. It was, Julia wrote, "a really remarkable sight."

The waiter peeled the skin off the top of the fish and lifted pieces of fillet from the topside of the bone; he plucked out the skeleton and served the *loup*'s bottom side. With each portion, he added a piece of the golden brioche crust, a spoonful of the *sauce suprême*, and another of fresh tomato fondue.

Like an investigative reporter, or a spy, Julia pleasantly quizzed him:

"Is the bottom molded ahead of time? Are those shallots and herbs in the fondue? Which herbs did the chef use on the fish?"

Paul chuckled, and explained to Patricia Simon, "No one knows us here. Julia just bats her eyes at the waiter and asks very dumb questions, 'What kind of knife did you use?'—that sort of thing—and the waiter takes pity on her and tells her everything she wants to know."

Paul called this technique *"la Juliafication des gens"* ("the Juliafication of people"), and she had used it to great effect while working on *Mastering* in the fifties. It placated ornery policemen, buttered up rude waiters, and extracted valuable culinary tips from tight-lipped chefs. "She could charm a polecat," Paul marveled. It also cast a spell on journalists.

Seated on the restaurant's terrace, surrounded by palm trees and geraniums beneath a leafy trellis, Patricia Simon fell into a reverie. "Much had I traveled in the realms of gold in New York restaurants, but sitting there in that lovely French restaurant, I felt that none of them could compare, and never would," she wrote in *McCall's*. "The originality, the buoyancy, the genuine delight of the waiters, the great style and presentation and service—$200 in New York could not buy it. At once quiet and irrepressibly gay, at once light and *sérieux*. And this spirit, I thought, spoke in every line of Julia and Simca's magnificent book."

As soon as they finished lunch, Julia and Simca rushed back to La Pitchoune to reverse engineer the *Loup de Mer en Croûte* and adapt the recipe for Volume II. They stuffed a fresh *loup* with fennel, parsley, and lemon, then seasoned it with salt and pepper. When two cats from a nearby farm appeared, meowing for attention, Simca and Patricia got sidetracked. Julia guided them back to the task: *"Less talking* or the crust will get too soft," she admonished.

As Julia attempted to wrap the *loup* in brioche, she struggled. "Difficult, this tucking under . . . Ha! *Ça va très bien!* That's going to be very nice!"

Paul snapped photographs and sliced a black olive to make the fish's eye. Simca cut brioche fins and scales. Julia wondered out loud how to glaze the crust: paint it with water or egg white? "Subject it to the operational proof, Julie!" Paul commanded. It was his way of saying: *Don't rely on guesswork or conventional wisdom; do it for yourself, and decide which way is best.* Like careful scientists, the cooks painted half the crust with water,

Julia and Simca Beck with their *loup en croûte*

half with egg yolk, to see which worked best. (The egg glaze was the unanimous decision.) After the *loup* had cooked for forty-five minutes, Paul set the fish on the dining table, arranged parsley and sliced lemons around it, and snapped a photo.

The *loup*, Simon reported, looked "perfectly golden and perfectly fishlike." And it tasted, all agreed, "perfectly delicious."

Patricia Simon's presence in that kitchen at that moment was a coup for the chefs, and for Simon. *McCall's* was a popular and influential monthly magazine aimed at married women. Founded by James McCall in 1873, it was one of the "Seven Sisters"—a group of magazines that included *Better Homes and Gardens, Good Housekeeping, Family Circle, Ladies' Home Journal, Redbook,* and *Woman's Day.* With large budgets to hire leading writers and photographers, including Eleanor Roosevelt during the fifties, *McCall's* had built a circulation of 8.4 million readers by the late sixties.

Competition for popular stories and competent writers was fierce, and securing Child's and Beck's cooperation was a good "get" for *McCall's.* The magazine threw significant resources into the story. According to the carefully worked-out arrangement between Julia, Simca, Knopf, and the magazine, Simon's three-part story about the making of Volume II would be published at the end of 1970, to coincide with the book's publication. Her articles would be accompanied by recipes from the book, and illustrated with photographs taken by Paul Child. Done right, the arrangement would provide a publicity bonanza for all involved.

In the meantime, the world of French cuisine was changing in mysterious ways. Patricia Simon had caught a whiff of this change on her way to France. Delayed at Heathrow Airport, in London, at 5:00 a.m., she met a young French couple. They had never heard of Julia Child, and weren't interested in *The French Chef*, or cooking. "Oh, we couldn't care *less* about food," they said. "It's so silly, spending a lot of time and trouble worrying about food and talking about it and eating it," the husband added. "You see," said his wife, "we just don't have the time."

Simon was taken aback: *But these people are* French. *They're supposed to care about food and know all about it.*

It was only later that she'd realize what the couple represented: they were heralds of a new order, the postwar, modernized—Americanized—France. It was a trend that sent a chill down Julia's spine. She worried that quick burgers, frozen foods, and plastic wrap were insinuating themselves into the hallowed precincts of *la cuisine française*, and would tear apart the country's traditional social fabric, built around food.

Patricia Simon stayed with Simca and Jean at Bramafam, which was twice the size of La Pitchoune, for a week. Simca's dining room was an intimate, low-ceilinged space decorated with antiques and flowers; in the kitchen, a potholder hanging on the wall read: "I love Julia Child."

Several days before the field trip to L'Oasis, Simca and Julia communicated in a swirling gust of Franglais as they set out lunch at Bramafam: cold mushrooms with garlic, lemon, and rosemary; sweet new radishes accompanied by a baguette and fresh butter; *rognons de veau et mirepoix; pommes chasseur;* an elaborate *salade verte;* and white wine. The cheese course included Gruyère and Gorgonzola, and, for dessert, cherries picked from the tree outside.

"Simca is *une force de la nature*," Julia said.

"You are rather energetic yourself, my dear," Paul interjected.

While Simca had hints of the refined British actress Margaret Leighton and the cool detachment of the German Marlene Dietrich, Simon discerned, she was "above all French, the most French person I had ever encountered."

II. *"La Super Française"*

Like Julia, Simca had been raised in a wealthy family in a large house with staff, had adventures with her husband during the Second World War, attended the Cordon Bleu cooking school in Paris, was childless, drove like a maniac, and was married to an accommodating gourmet. Unlike Julia, Simca was a devout Catholic (Julia was a committed atheist), had little patience for children, preferred dogs to cats, and was resolutely unconcerned about the nitty-gritty details of recipes.

The Childs referred to Simca as *"La Super Française"* because she embodied a dynamic, self-reliant, bullheaded kind of Frenchwoman whom Julia admired. But the nickname was used half in compliment and half in regret, for Simca could be warm and charming one minute but cold and harshly critical the next. She focused on whatever task was at hand—reading, talking, cooking, driving—with a ferocious, monomaniacal energy. She told Patricia Simon:

> In the morning I do my research. I *read*, I *read*, I *read* all what I am reading. I *make notes*. Books, newspapers. Many times I read old books— bought years and years ago—out of print fifty years. It's so useful to see what people did then. The people who wrote those old books—they had no idea of expensive. Dozens of eggs or pounds of butter meant nothing to them! But in the recipe—ah!, very often, something interesting about how it is done, some special interesting detail, a little trick of making something.
>
> I also of course read modern books, too . . . In the afternoon, if I have a very special appointment, I go out. But usually it is then that I begin to typewrite my notes. And then I begin to try recipes. My maid, Camille, helps me. If something seems not correct or perfect, I wait to do it again, until it's *good*. Then I send it to Julia. Then she sometimes tries it three or four times.
>
> . . . You see, I could be doing something—going to a party or playing bridge—but I am doing something who is so important, so *sérieux*, that I wouldn't want to do that. I have my *work*. You see, what I am trying to do is a kind of cooking who is not *classique*, who is very good and easy. I am doing something who is so exciting, I want to do it fully, so completely.

"SIMCA" WAS a nickname. She had been baptized Simone Suzanne Renée Madeleine Beck, and was raised in an aristocratic household in Normandy. She detested the name Simone, and her brothers Maurice and Bernard nicknamed her "Nonne." The Becks lived in a grand house in Rainfreville, northeastern France, about ten miles from the English Channel. The family took food and wine seriously, and insisted on sit-down meals that highlighted Norman specialties—a diet famously based on butter, cream, pork, beef, apples, and Calvados, the fiery brandy known as "the spirit of Normandy."

As a chatelaine (a woman in charge of a large household), Simca's mother, Madeleine Le Grand, did not cook. But she was a stylish dame with a sophisticated palate, whose family had made a fortune manufacturing Benedictine, a popular liqueur. She taught her children how to manage people efficiently, if not warmly. Simca's father, Maurice Beck, was a tall, charming man who ran a factory that made silicate powder for ceramic tiles. And he was a crack shot who brought home partridge, rabbit, and venison in season.

In the Beck household, children were not allowed in the kitchen. But as a seven-year-old, Simone bonded with the cook, Zulma, a sturdy Norman woman who clandestinely taught her how to work with food. Their first lesson was on *boeuf bourguignon*. A typical Zulma lunch menu included a beetroot salad with apples and potatoes, chicken in tarragon cream sauce, and flan with apples. Simca learned them all by heart. "Zulma had a lifelong influence on me . . . she was gifted with an almost atavistic sense of how to cook, how to use food, how to prepare it in ways that make it both delicious and healthy," Simca recalled. "Under her tutelage, I got a physical grasp of how to deal with food . . . How to make short pastry, good desserts, sauce bases, and much more."

As a girl, Simone was opinionated and impulsive, an energetic tomboy who would rather compete with her brothers at running, swimming, or horseback riding than play with dolls. Her father taught her basic car repair, and Simone drove, she admitted, "like a demon." She had a crush on Charles Lindbergh and dreamed of becoming a pilot, but her parents forbade it and steered her into more feminine pursuits, such as piano, singing, and bookbinding.

At nineteen, Simone married an ineffectual older man and lived what she called "a butterfly life" in Paris. But in 1933, when she was twenty-nine, everything changed: her father died of leukemia, she divorced her husband (a rare occurrence for a Catholic woman), and she dedicated herself to cooking. The latter was considered nearly heretical for members of her class, but Simone Beck was nothing if not willful.

Enrolling at Le Cordon Bleu in Paris, Simone arranged for private lessons with Henri-Paul Pellaprat, co-founder of the school and author of the classic *L'Art Culinaire Moderne* (*Modern Culinary Art*). He helped Simone broaden her repertoire to include Escoffier-worthy haute cuisine dishes, such as *turbot en soufflé*, galantines, iced soufflés, and the like.

Simone Beck stood five feet eight inches tall, which was large for a Frenchwoman at the time, and was rapier-thin. One day in 1936, she was trying to wedge her lanky frame into her small car—a Renault Simca—when a handsome man chuckled, and said, "What a big chassis for such a little car!"

His name was Jean Fischbacher. He was a dermatological chemist from Alsace. His flirtatious opening line would lead to her nickname, "Simca," which Simone far preferred to her given name.

Jean wooed Simca with his good looks, humor, and impeccable manners. His knowledge of wine and skill at deboning a fish "were terribly important to me—the signs of breeding and good manners," Simca wrote. Jean was far more sensuous than her first husband, encouraging this "proper woman" to drink Champagne, lounge on satin cushions, and make love. "I was beginning to discover something I guess I could call happiness, even euphoria, emotions I began to feel I'd been cheated out of [in my first marriage]," she recalled.

Though he was a Protestant and she was a divorced Catholic, they managed to placate their parents and church authorities, and married in 1937. Two years later, the war arrived on their doorstep.

Simca hid her family's valuable collection of wine and Champagne in the basement at Rainfreville, while Jean joined the infantry and fought the Boches on the Maginot Line. He was awarded the Croix de Guerre for valor, but in 1940 was captured and imprisoned for the remainder of the war. Twice, Simca managed to convince the Nazis to allow her to visit Jean (she sewed secret messages into the figs she brought him), but the war was a time of great deprivation and sacrifice.

When he was released in 1945, Jean was awarded the Legion of Honor by Charles de Gaulle. Simca cooked a fabulous meal and hosted a welcome-home party for him, but after the gruel he had subsisted on in the prison camps, he became violently ill on her rich food. Jean and Simca "felt almost like strangers" at first. But as they reacquainted, food became more central to their lives than ever.

Living in Paris, Jean invented a successful face cream made from ground oyster shells. Simca joined an exclusive women's food club, Le Cercle des Gourmettes. By 1951, she was working with a fellow *gourmette*, Louisette Bertholle, on a French cookbook for the American market. Louisette had traveled widely in America, where she'd met plenty of people who loved French food, and had suggested the project. The two cooks created a large, if unfocused, pile of recipes and handed them to a freelance food editor, who was supposed to Americanize them. The freelancer disappeared shortly after that.

It was then, at a Parisian party in the fall of 1951, that George Artamonoff, the former president of Sears International, introduced Simca to a thirty-nine-year-old American named Julia Child. Within days, Simca had introduced Julia to Louisette, and by early 1952 the three friends had started to teach cookery to American women at L'École des Trois Gourmandes (the School of the Three Hearty Eaters) in the Childs' apartment on the Rue de l'Université. Once they had established a good working relationship, Simca and Louisette tentatively asked if Julia might, possibly, be willing to help them finish a French cookbook for the American market that they had been working on for two years. *"Mais oui!"* Julia cried in delight. She loved the idea, but was disappointed to find that her friends had created a "jumble of recipes." So, in her pleasant way, she set about to quietly reinvent the book for readers like herself.

Drawing from their lesson plans, the three co-authored the 684-page *Mastering the Art of French Cooking*, which, after nine years of work, one failed publishing deal, and two rejections, was published by Alfred A. Knopf in the States in the fall of 1961. Their aim, Julia wrote, was to take "French cooking out of cuckoo land and bring it down to where everybody is."

Since then, Louisette had moved on to other things, but Simca continued to give cooking classes in her apartment in Neuilly, on the outskirts of Paris. She was an intuitive, inspired cook, who "had a highly developed palate," said Judith Jones. "You could trust her taste. And she developed many more recipes than Julia. But she wasn't careful about [quantities] and timing."

In contrast to Simca's "artistic" approach, Julia took a more dogged, pragmatic approach to cookery, and wanted to know "everything about everything." Julia—who had lots of questions, and was a veteran diplomatic party giver—put herself in her reader's shoes. She included notes about ingredients, cookware, and how much of a recipe could be done ahead of time—"these were absolute innovations," Jones said. Paul also contributed: he wrote a primer on wine and drew many of the technical illustrations in the book; working together, he and Julia invented a new way to depict the steps of a recipe from the cook's perspective.

The Julia Child–Simca Beck collaboration was remarkable and history making. In 1966, Avis DeVoto visited La Pitchoune and observed of the two at work:

> This is certainly one of the great collaborations in history. They are absolutely necessary to each other and it is a happy miracle that they found each other. It is the *combination* which makes their work so revolutionary, and for my money they are benefactors of the human race.
>
> Simca is a creative genius, as Julia wrote me, "a great fountain of ideas." She is also inaccurate, illogical, hard to pin down, and stubborn as a mule. Julia is also very creative and is becoming more so. But the two women think differently. Julia is deeply logical, orderly, accurate, painstaking, patient, determined to get all this knowledge clearly on paper. And she can be just as stubborn as Simca is, and will plug away trying to convince Simca until suddenly Simca changes her position, and from then on she will talk as if it were her own idea all along . . .
>
> Simca would come in [to Julia's kitchen] at any time, no planning ahead, looking determined. "*Ma chérie . . .*" and off to the races. These sessions might last an hour, or all morning, or all afternoon. And while it was going on, the two ladies were absolutely oblivious to anything else going on in the house, and I understood why Paul absented himself— shut himself in his room, or moved out to the *cabanon*. I would hear Simca's voice going on and on, floods of French, Julia saying *oui, oui,*

oui, at intervals, Simca's voice rising. Simca had an idea and Simca was taking the lead. Julia was following, and trying to get Simca to measure, use measuring cups and spoons, be accurate. Simca thinks this is all a big joke, and sometimes forgets to do it, but if she remembers, or is reminded, she winks and shrugs shoulders, and does it . . . Julia always won in the end, because she keeps her head.

III. The Third Woman

While writing *Mastering the Art of French Cooking* in the 1950s, Simca said, "I feel I was the prime mover, more of an authority on French food, more of a 'boss.'" In the following decade, however, Julia found her stride and began to assert herself. "Julia had gained confidence and authority, especially as she was the one living in America, with instant access to the American food mentality and knowledge of products available there," Simca recalled in her book *Food & Friends*. "I consider Volume II more Julia's book than mine."

Judith Jones concurred. "If I had questions or comments on Volume II, I always addressed them to Julia," she said. "She was a *force* by then. Less humble, more confident than during Volume I." As was Jones herself.

JUDITH JONES IS an elfin figure, standing about five feet five inches tall, with shoulder-length brown-gray hair parted in the middle, high cheekbones, watchful eyes, and a strong will. She admits to having "an instinctive modesty," and can appear flinty; but she is also quick to laugh and has an incisive mind. Paul Child described her as "an Irish faerie." Julia thought of her as a "peerless editor," trusted confidante, and stalwart friend. "Writing does not come easily for me," Julia said. "But Judith makes it easier. Since she is a cook and a writer, she knows instinctively what I am trying to say. She knows how to bring it out of me."

Mrs. Jones was born Judith Bailey in 1924, which made her a dozen years younger than Julia. Her mother was English, her father was from Vermont, and the family divided its time between an apartment in New York City and a farm in East Hardwick, in Vermont's Northeast Kingdom. Fine food was not a priority in the Bailey household. Judith came of age during the Depression and the Second World War, a period that marked a nadir in modern American cookery. Although her mother subscribed to a half dozen women's magazines, she considered cooking a "demeaning" chore, and "European" foods, such as garlic, smelly and uncouth. It was an era of "hideous Puritanism," Jones recalled. "We just didn't talk about food at the table. I related it to sex in a way. There was an appetite, but you didn't talk about it—which made it all the more fun."

The family maid, Mrs. Cooney, did the cooking and kept to a regimented diet: chipped beef on Wednesdays, pork chops on Thursdays, "the dreaded boiled cod and potatoes" on Fridays, and plenty of gray, overboiled vegetables at all times. "Bland, bland, bland," Jones said with a scowl. "I had the feel for cooking, but no one to teach me."

After graduating from Bennington College in 1945, Judith Bailey returned to New York to work in publishing—first at Dutton, then at Doubleday—as an editorial assistant. In 1948, she and a friend embarked on what was supposed to be a three-week European vacation. She enjoyed Rome and Florence, but it was Paris that gripped Judith with a nearly mystical pull. Arriving in the city at dusk, she recalled, "something just happened inside of me in a way that I'd never experienced before. I just fell in love with the beauty of the light." She also fell in love with the food, the excitement of shopping in the markets, and the French themselves. "I loved that the women could take a scarf and tie it so beautifully, and that they loved their men."

Her allotted days there swept by, and her friend returned to New York. On the day that Judith was scheduled to leave, she accidentally on purpose left her wallet and passport in the Tuileries and was "forced" to stay in Paris. "I wanted to live like the French and shop and cook and get into publishing." Wandering past the American Express office, she happened to meet a young American named Paul Chapin. He invited her to stay at his aunt's large apartment on the Rue du Cirque, for free. Down the hall the painter Balthus had a room.

Though she had no cookbook, and couldn't afford cooking school, Judith began to cook for her roommates. Then she and a French boyfriend opened the apartment as a supper club for Americans. On a trip to southern France, she stumbled over Restaurant La Pyramide, the celebrated restaurant in Vienne, near Lyon. The chef was Fernand Point, a three-star chef generally acknowledged as "the father of modern French cooking," whose experiments with lighter fare in the fifties led to the nouvelle cuisine revolution in the seventies. Jones's meal that day was "a *great* experience—a turning point in my life," she said, because it was so delicious and expertly presented. Back in Paris, she asked the butcher's wife for recipes, and was inspired by eating briny cockles and wonderful entrecôte in restaurants, dishes she re-created at home. "I learned to cook by asking questions," she said. "I needed to know *why* the *coquilles Saint Jacques* I ate at the little bistro was so much better than mine."

Doubleday opened an office in Paris and hired Judith Bailey as an editorial assistant. Intrigued by a rejected manuscript that had a photograph of a young girl on the cover, she eventually convinced her editors to publish it. The book was *Anne Frank: The Diary of a Young Girl*.

In December 1948, Judith Bailey knocked on the door of Evan Jones, the American editor and publisher of *Weekend* magazine, looking for a job. Jones was a native of Minneapolis, where his father edited *The St. Paul Dispatch*; was divorced (he had two daughters in the United States); and adored France and its garlicky sausages. She was hired immediately. They courted in Paris's outdoor markets, smoky bistros, and grand cafés, and took occasional forays into the countryside. Judith and Evan Jones married in Vienna in 1951. Her family didn't approve of Evan in much the way that Julia's father, John "Big John" McWilliams (a conservative Republican businessman), didn't approve of Paul Child (a liberal Democratic artist). "I was *supposed* to find a nice husband on Wall Street, join a club, and be in the Social Register," Jones recalled. "It was that kind of insidious snobbery. What *I* wanted to be was *free* . . . I picked up some very bad habits in Paris, and I picked up a very nice husband."

After three and a half years in France, the Joneses returned to New York and settled into a modest but comfortable apartment on East Sixty-sixth Street. Judith went in search of fresh mushrooms and good recipe books, but was quickly frustrated. "I wanted to keep cooking French," she said. But the plastic-wrapped cabbages and lack of baguettes were dispiriting. Cookbooks of the day were crammed with short, uninstructive recipes. "Everything was supposed to be quick and easy," Jones groaned.

Evan worked as a freelance writer, and in 1957, Judith was hired as a translator and editor of French books by Blanche Knopf, the intimidating wife of Alfred A. Knopf. Publishing was a gentleman's profession: Knopf held its sales conferences at the Harvard Club, and Jones was the firm's only female editor. She translated leading French writers such as Albert Camus and Jean-Paul Sartre. Later, she would edit American fiction writers such as John Updike, Anne Tyler, John Hersey, and William Maxwell. But it was in the underappreciated specialty of cookbooks that Jones made her mark.

"By the late 1950s the food industry had pretty much convinced us American women that we should not get our hands dirty and be kitchen slaves, and that they would take care of the cooking for us," she said. The result was food in a can, iceberg lettuce, and Jell-O with spray-on whipped cream. "Cookbooks were so demeaned then," said Jones. " 'In a bowl, combine the first mixture with the second mixture. Set aside.' But what *size* bowl? What's *in* the second mixture? Set aside *where*—throw it out? It's just bad thinking."

In the fall of 1959, a thick, heavy manuscript landed on her desk with a thud. It was a cookbook written by three unknown women—Beck, Bertholle, and Child. It had fared poorly with a small publisher, Ives Washburn, and had been rejected—twice—by a rival publisher, Houghton Mifflin, as too complicated: "Americans don't want an encyclopedia," a manager sniffed. "They want something quick, with a mix."

Undaunted, Jones took the hand-typed pages home and began to cook from them. Following the clear, logical steps, she learned to make *boeuf bourguignon* every bit as good as the one she'd had in Paris, how to flip an omelet the French way, and compose her first successful crème caramel. She was enamored of the authors' innovations, such as listing the ingredients in a column adjacent to the cooking instructions.

Though she had never edited a cookbook before, Jones took on the project. "It was exactly the kind of book I had been looking for. Revolutionary. I was *bouleversée*—'knocked out.' And I thought that if *I* was interested, then others would be, too."

After nine years of work, the last seven of which Julia had collaborated on, the book had arrived as a near fait accompli. "It was so beautifully thought out, a real teaching book, so I didn't make too many suggestions," Jones said. She cut a few recipes and, though she had no way of knowing how well the book would sell, told the authors to save them for a possible follow-up book.

Mastering was a hit and helped ignite the American food revolution of the sixties and seventies. Jones recalled that roller-coaster ride as thrilling: "Once the lid was off and the respect for food and wine had started in America, you were *awakened*, and it was hard to turn back," she said. "Who wanted to turn back? Some did. My cousin hated *Mastering* because the recipes were so long. But generally people saw there was so much to learn. And Julia made it fun."

The success of *Mastering* led Jones to edit books by chefs and writers who would become the vanguard of a new, multicultural culinary movement in America: "Ms. Jones may not be the mother of the revolution in American taste that began in the 1960s and transformed the food Americans cook at home," *The New York Times* reported in 2007. "But she remains its most productive midwife."

For her first cookbook, Jones said, "Julia liked the gerund master*ing* in the title because learning to cook is an ongoing process. You never really *master* all of French cooking." Volume II was a continuation of the first book, but it had to stand on its own merits and provide readers with new and significant information.

For the second volume, Louisette Bertholle was no longer involved. (In what Julia called the "Louisette Purchase," she and Simca purchased Bertholle's 18 percent share of the business for $30,000 in 1968.) The third, unnamed, but crucial, partner on Volume II was Judith B. Jones. Unlike for *Mastering*, Jones played an active role in shaping the new book, undertaking culinary research, testing recipes, asking detailed questions, and pushing Julia and Simca to tackle recipes unprecedented in American cookbooks. The result was a series of master classes on French classics.

IV. THE SECRETS OF VOLUME II

Two of the star chapters, and most closely guarded secrets, of Volume II were detailed instruction on how to make French bread and charcuterie in the home kitchen. "They came out of my own frustration," Jones recalled. In France one could buy expertly made croissants, brioches, petits fours, and pastries at the local *boulangerie*, and pâtés, terrines, and sausages at the neighborhood *charcutier*. But these delicacies were not available in the United States. Americans had two choices: they could pay exorbitantly to import them, or they could book a trip to Paris. Jones was determined to teach Americans how to make these foods at home. "Selfishly, I wanted a good baguette and some delicious pâté, and you couldn't find them in New York," she said. "So we decided to make our own."

In May 1967, Jones wrote Julia a provocative note: "Don't you think Volume II should include a good honest recipe for French bread that would come as close as possible to the real thing? It is so hard to get even a phony Italian loaf in the sticks—and what's a *vrai* [real] French meal without some bread to mop it up?"

Early in her TV career Julia had considered then rejected a show about French bread because almost no one in France bakes bread at home, and she felt it would be "insincere" to pretend they did. Responding to Jones's suggestion, Julia balked: "This is something we have been able to avoid, as no French home types ever make French bread."

But Jones had been impressed by the countercultural bread makers she'd met in Vermont who were churning out delicious multigrain loaves in their home ovens. And Paul was intrigued by the idea. He had been an avid baker as a young man, and volunteered to conduct a few baguette-baking experiments in Cambridge. He soon became obsessed. Happily covered in flour from head to toe, he worked on French bread at all hours. Noticing Paul's glee, Julia couldn't bear to miss out on the fun at "the Irving Street *boulangerie*." The intellectual challenge of adapting traditional French recipes to the modern American kitchen drew her in, and when Paul decided to turn their home appliance into a domestic version of a professional baker's oven, Julia was hooked.

As they experimented, the Childs learned many lessons: that different types of flour and butter produce different loaves; that most American kitchens are kept warm, causing the dough to rise too fast; that dropping a superheated iron into a tub of water produces just the right puff of steam; that "bread should lie directly on a hot oven floor," which the Childs simulated with a piece of asbestos tile. To create a home baker's oven, "We even researched the medieval method of dampening a bundle of straw and throwing it into the oven to keep the air moist," Paul wrote.

Julia and Simca with the bread maestro Professor Raymond Calvel in Paris

"We used wet whisk brooms in our American electric oven . . . but it didn't work."

After baking sixty mediocre loaves, they had yet to crack the code.

Ultimately, Paul and Julia took pounds of American flour and butter to Paris and apprenticed themselves to the master *boulanger* Professor Raymond Calvel. The first breakthrough was in chemistry: American flour is made from hard wheat, while French flour uses soft wheat; Calvel adjusted the recipe to compensate. The second insight was about technique: "It's all in the folding and shaping of the loaf," Julia reported. *Voilà*, with Calvel's tutoring the Childs were able to produce nearly perfect baguettes in their American kitchen.

It took something like two years of experimenting, and two hundred and eighty-four pounds of flour, but they finally got the recipe for French bread right.

From these lessons, Julia composed a ninety-three-page chapter on baking for Volume II. It was a tour de force. The first section—which included a basic recipe for French bread, a tutorial on "Using the Simulated Baker's Oven," and a section titled "Self-Criticism—Or How to Improve the Product," in which the authors diagnose common maladies, such as a tough crust, a heavy loaf with no holes, or unpleasantly yeasty-flavored bread—ran for twenty-one pages.

(Around this time, Judith Jones pitched the idea of a bread book to James Beard. It took some prodding, but *Beard on Bread* was published in 1973, and remains a classic.)

Simca was only peripherally involved in the Childs' bread work. Like most French people, she bought her croissants fresh from the *boulangerie* every morning, and seemed uninterested in learning how to bake them at home. To Paul and Julia's chagrin, Simca never attempted to create a Simulated Baker's Oven to make baguettes at home.

Yet, Simca had developed her own obsessive interest in bread and pastry, a preoccupation that began with a bad hip. In 1958, when she was fifty-four, Simca was diagnosed with arthrosis—a degenerative condition in which the cartilage of joints deteriorates—and osteoporosis, or brittle bones. To help ease the pain, and add bone-strengthening minerals to her body, Simca took to the "infernal hot baths" at Bourbonne-les-Bains, a spa in the Haute-Marne of Northeastern France. Like many of her compatriots, Simca believed that the mineral-rich spa waters were therapeutic, and indeed she never had to undergo a hip operation.

Every morning Simca ate the delicious croissants served at the spa's hotel, and, curious, she joined the chef at 5:30 one morning to cut and roll croissants. "I immediately understood the necessary speed, the ways elastic dough acts and reacts to your hands as you fashion the little triangles," she recalled. Soon, she was allowed to make the *détrempe*, the layered butter-flour croissant dough. Dressed in her bathrobe at dawn, Simca participated in making 350 croissants every morning—"the routine so fixed in my head and hands that it would become automatic"—then breathlessly rushed away to her cure. "By the time I was finished with my first bath of the day I was ravenous. I'd sit there soaking in the hot water and feel I'd truly earned my breakfast!"

In subsequent years, she met a master *boulanger* named Monsieur Boulanger ("Mr. Baker"), who made delicious baguettes in Bourbonne. Again, Simca volunteered. She found cooking to be therapeutic, an activity that made her sometimes painful and monotonous cures bearable. Starting at midnight, she would knead dough by hand until 2:00 a.m. "Knead that dough! Beat it around, let it rise," Boulanger exhorted. "Yeast is a living thing!" It was hard work. "We pulled the dough, twisted it, threw it down on the table time after time, kneaded it. Started again. It smelled delicious," Simca wrote. "By the time we had put the dough into straw baskets for the final rising and I heaved myself into bed, I felt as if I were a candidate for an Olympic weight-lifting contest, or maybe for a rest home, if not an asylum. But learning what goes into making a baguette made it all worthwhile."

In the sixties and seventies, Simca combined the methods of Boulanger, Paul Troisgros (another chef in Bourbonne), and Professor Calvel (the master baker in Paris) to teach baking to her cooking classes. As she "threw the dough around with abandon," she instructed her students: "Don't be afraid. You've got to knock the daylights out of this stuff to make it supple and light-rising."

ANOTHER TYPE OF FOOD that Judith Jones craved for Volume II was the smoked meats, terrines, and savory pies sold at charcuteries, quintessentially French specialty food stores that don't have an exact analogue in the States. "In Paris people are willing to stand in line for hours, with their toes sticking through their slippers, to pay for good charcuterie," said Jones. "It's an essential part of the French flavor. And I thought it would be a wonderful thing to bring to America."

In this case, Child and Beck immediately embraced her suggestion. But working together—and sometimes against each other—on this chapter led to one of their fiercest clashes.

It began with cassoulet, the rich bean-meat combination that is "as much a part of southwestern France as Boston baked beans are of New England," Child and Beck would write. "I just loved the sweet baked beans of cassoulet—it's home cooking, close to the earth," said Jones. As with their research into *bouillabaisse à la Marseillaise* for the original *Mastering*, Child and Beck discovered that every cook had his or her own recipe for cassoulet. Toulousains insisted the dish must include preserved goose; others said the dish came from Castelnaudary and was made only of beans, pork, and sausages; yet others suggested the dish originated from Arabian fava bean and mutton stews. In any event, Julia and Simca went at it with hammer and tongs, eventually producing a sheaf of bean- and pork-stained notes two inches thick. Jones felt overwhelmed, both by the number of pages and by the intensity of her authors. "That was

A charcuterie stand in France

my first exposure to how they worked together," she recalled. "And how Julia got around, and accommodated, Simca. It was interesting."

Julia strove to make the dish—which can take hours or days to prepare—accessible by breaking the steps down into a simplified "order of battle," and suggesting that components of the dish could be made ahead and assembled for the meal. She substituted store-bought Polish kielbasa for homemade sausage cakes, and left out ingredients like *confit d'oie* (preserved goose) not generally available in America.

Simca was an originalist who shook her finger and scolded Julia on this point: "*Non!* We French—we never make cassoulet like this!" she asserted. "There is only *one* way to make this dish properly—avec *confit d'oie!*"

"That was ridiculous, of course," Jones observed drily. "Simca could be didactic."

After arguing in circles, the authors reached a compromise: Julia crafted a five-page "master recipe" (theme) to which Simca added "additions or substitutions" (variations), including the use of canned *confit d'oie*, which was available at certain imported food stores in America.

As for the other delicacies found in French charcuterie, Julia and Simca characterized roasted hams, garlic sausages, and duck terrines as "a marvelous keystone of French civilization . . . there are few things more satisfying to the soul."

In pushing her writers, Jones was not above the occasional nudge or didacticism herself. When, for instance, she could not find garlic sausage—which she considered essential to cassoulet—in New York, she suggested that Julia develop a homemade sausage recipe. This was just the kind of aesthetic/scientific/engineering challenge that Julia relished. The next time Jones visited Cambridge, she was pleased to find Julia elbow deep in sausage meat and spices, with homemade links strung from cabinet handle to window frame to stove hood, curing. Paul had erected a giant piece of white cardboard on a wall in the kitchen, which Julia had covered with notes about her sausage experiments. "She was absolutely delighted with herself," Jones said with satisfaction. In the resulting fifty-three-page chapter on charcuterie, the authors exhorted fellow cooks not to be intimidated by the details of sausage casings and caul fat: "It is so easy to make your own sausage meat and it is so good that you will wonder, once you have made it, why you were ever so foolish as to buy it."

In this spirit, Julia and Simca delved into traditional French dishes that had largely been ignored by American cooks yet were, Julia maintained, "perfectly delicious." These included: cutting up a live lobster for bisque ("The serious cook really must face up to the task personally"); using cockscombs or braised sweetbreads (thymus gland) in a *ris de veau;* roasting a whole suckling pig ("not an everyday item," but "wonderfully dramatic to serve, delicious to eat, and hardly more difficult to cook than a turkey"); beef tongue braised in aromatic vegetables ("makes such a welcome change from the usual fare . . . that you need have no hesitation at all in serving it for company"); tripe (cow stomach: "Like scrapple and head cheese, it is a rather old-fashioned taste—a fragrant, earthy reminder of the past when every edible morsel of the beast was used . . . our forefathers consumed it with relish . . . If you are one of those who has never tried tripe before, yet enjoys new foods and new tastes, we think you will find this a happy introduction"); rabbit ("very much like chicken in taste and texture"); preserved goose ("The taste . . . has a very special quality quite unlike fresh goose"); and gooseneck sausage ("Pluck and singe skin thoroughly, then peel it off the neck in one piece, turning the skin inside out as you go").

Reading these instructions caused some readers to squirm or cry out in protest—"Disgusting!" "Lobster murderer!" "How could you eat a bunny rabbit?!" Others found them inspiring, challenging, or fun. Plenty of people bought Volume II with no intention of cooking cockscombs or gooseneck sausage at home, but simply because they enjoyed the vicarious thrill of reading about it.

Julia took her culinary spelunking very seriously. In asserting herself in Volume II, she was determined to push her audience, and her collaborators, to new extremes. This gung-ho attitude occasionally put her at odds with Judith Jones, whom Julia accused of being fainthearted and capitulating to pallid mainstream tastes: "I am worried by your growing attitude of catering entirely to the timid and squeamish," Julia admonished her editor. "Do not, please, forget that we have chefs, men, and professionals who also read and follow these recipes."

Julia wanted to encourage people to cook and eat boldly: "I shall try and urge people to toughen up, be earthy, etc.," she wrote to Jones. In

Julia was curious about every step of the food chain.

the case of lamb kidneys, for instance, she wanted her readers to take charge: "If they smell bad or strong, they are awful, and if timid people don't dare smell, they'll get rotten meat, fish, and everything else . . . On trimming your own beef tenderloin—if people will get scared off by being advised to watch a good butcher at work, where are we?"

At the end of her diatribe, Julia allowed, "I am not, naturally, discounting at all your suggestions, because I believe (almost) everything you say. I am resisting tendencies I do not like for our book."

With a wry smile, Jones conceded that Julia's knuckle rapping still smarted forty-five years later. At the time, she replied to her author:

> I am distressed that you think I am suddenly defending the frightened persnickety American housewife because my whole thrust is to try to get them to do things they wouldn't ordinarily touch. And that is your great talent. But I've been thinking back to the time I spent a summer in a small town in Minnesota. Where would I have found a butcher to demonstrate preparing a filet of beef for me? The whole point is that you're instructing these ladies so carefully that they can do anything on their own. But if you say maybe you'd better watch a butcher first, you may have made that woman in Minnesota not quite trust your directions. By the same token a cook who has never used kidneys before might become too fussy by that *very* fresh-smelling note. I used some kidneys the other night that probably wouldn't pass that *very* test but I rinsed them off to freshen them and they were absolutely perfect in our stuffing. (The supermarket habit of wrapping them in plastic tends to encourage a bit of odor that seems to be perfectly harmless.) I'm really not trying to argue. Obviously you know best what you're after, but my comments were in the interest of encouraging people to be *less* timid and fussy.

v. It Will Be Done

In December 1969, six months after Julia and Simca reverse engineered the *loup*, the manuscript for Volume II—which Julia called "Son of *Mastering*"—remained unfinished, and Judith Jones put her foot down. She had previously reduced the book from fourteen to eleven chapters, to save time, and then to nine. Now, in order to meet her production schedule, Jones further limited the book's scope to seven subject chapters: soups, baking, meats, chicken, charcuterie, vegetables, and desserts. She set a final, hard-and-fast, absolutely nonnegotiable deadline of March 15, 1970.

This left no margin for error. There was just enough time to finish and copyedit the manuscript, prepare the art, print the book, and ship it by the official publishing date of October 22, 1970, during the all-important run-up to the December holiday shopping season.

The deadline was not just a psychological ploy, Jones explained: "We had to reserve the presses months in advance," she said. "There was real money at stake." Moreover, with *McCall's* scheduled to run Patricia Simon's three articles between October and December, Knopf was contractually obliged to produce Volume II on time. Meanwhile, Season Two of *The French Chef* was scheduled to begin shooting in the late summer of 1970.

To add to the pressure, Julia had endured a biopsy on her right, remaining breast in January. "I am sure there is nothing wrong, but they won't take any chances even with a pimple, it seems, once you've had the works" of a mastectomy, she wrote Jones. "Anyway, I . . . am plowing along as fast as possible, though it is never fast, as you know."

The biopsy was negative. Julia hardly paused before turning back to the stove and typewriter. Her kitchen table and home office were stacked with hundreds of files and dozens of notebooks filled with recipes, scientific papers, notes on meals eaten at restaurants, culinary inventions of her own, Paul's food photographs, and references for temperatures, weights, and measures.

The pace was relentless. "I just can't do writing, indexing, testing, proofreading, and do anything else at all," Julia wailed. "I work seven days a week. Up at seven, breakfast at nine, work, lunch, work again, tea, work, and then stop to hear the news."

THE CRUCIBLE OF Volume II revealed Julia's and Simca's essential natures. Sometimes the two were in complete sync, other times they were in complete opposition; and there were moments when Judith Jones had to referee between them.

Simca tended to be a romantic, who relied on an instinctual, pinch-of-salt, "French" style of cooking. Julia was a pragmatist, who preferred a step-by-step, researched and engineered, "American" style; and in spite of her disaffection from her father, Big John McWilliams, she had absorbed some of his brusque business acumen.

An early point of tension between the writing partners arose in October 1967, when Julia wrote Simca a frank professional letter. In it, she stressed the importance of hiring separate lawyers to negotiate business issues between them, allowing Julia and Simca to preserve their friendship (the lawyers "can be tough for each of us and eventually the right solutions will be worked out"). They should also maintain copyright protection for *Mastering*, she advised, and ensure that "nothing that notre chère colleague's heirs can do will hurt our mutual property." Then Julia remarked: "One thing we have never taken into consideration at all is my role in publicizing the book."

Noting that sales of *Mastering* had started strong in 1961 but steadily weakened into 1962 (when only 103 copies sold in June), Julia observed that business "immediately picked up" after February 1963, when *The French Chef* began to air. Thereafter trade in *Mastering* was brisk—with 1,129 copies sold in March, 2,283 in May, and an average of 3,000 a month after that. When *Time* anointed Julia "Our Lady of the Ladle" and put her on its cover in November 1966, sales skyrocketed: between November and February 1967, 47,770 copies of *Mastering* sold, representing a third of total previous sales—figures that Julia called "tremendous" and "history for us." This success was "due entirely to the television," she wrote. But, she reminded Simca, "this has been a tremendous amount of work for me, for Paul, and for Ruth Lockwood . . . in fact, this has been a 7-day week since we began . . . almost without stopping."

Educational television was akin to "charity," Julia wrote, and barely covered her expenses. Her only compensation for the elaborate preparation and work was through book sales. Julia considered *The French Chef* "a vehicle to promote our book," and she often mentioned that the recipes and techniques she used on air were "based on *Mastering*." This claim was somewhat disingenuous, she explained to Simca, as 70 percent of the recipes she used on television "had nothing to do with the book at all." In light of this, Julia wrote, "Some serious consideration must be taken of my contribution . . . you would have to pay a minimum of 30 or 40% of your profits for this kind of publicity. I have never made a point of this, but I do think it must enter into our mutual thoughts."

This would be the only time that Julia raised the issue of proportionality and used the power of her television celebrity as a bargaining chip with her colleague. After some back-and-forth between their lawyers, Simca acquiesced, and they came up with an agreeable solution: They agreed to a revised share of revenue from Volume II; Julia would be responsible for expenses.

When the two were not together in France, Julia and Simca corresponded daily, in great flowing letters that went on for thousands of words. They analyzed, tested, and evaluated dishes, and discussed them in minute detail. The letters were usually typewritten, single spaced, and often filled two, three, four, five, or even nine pages. Simca typed in pale blue ink and signed her name with a big, swooping *S* in red pen. Julia liked to use capital letters and exclamation points for emphasis, XX-ed out mistakes, jotted additional thoughts in the margins, and usually signed off with a drawing of a heart pierced by an arrow.

But the pressure was wearying. Often, Julia would work late into the night. "I don't even have time to pee!" she wailed. "I need five more years to finish this book!"

While Julia strove to make her recipes "idiot-proof" for the reader, Simca would modify measurements as she went, eschewing the teaspoon-by-teaspoon method. "Julia and I work very well together," *La Super Française* told *The New York Times*. "She is more scientific. I never measure; I am perhaps more intuitive. I like to create out of my head. I consider myself an old-fashioned cook . . . Sometimes I go further with ideas than Julia. I test and retest before I share the results. My husband is my best taster . . . Julia thinks in American and I think in French. We speak in *Franglaise*."

But when Julia pushed Simca to be accurate and consistent, she would lash out, saying, "*Non!* We French would never do it that way. *Ce n'est pas français!*" ("This is not French!")

When it came to perfecting a formula for *pâte feuilletée*, Julia toiled on draft after draft while Simca wrote one version of the recipe and moved on. *Pâte feuilletée* is a light, flaky pastry that puffs up when cooked, and is made from hundreds of layers of dough separated by hundreds of layers of butter—"seven hundred and twenty-nine layers, to be exact," Julia said. "Tremendously useful," it ennobles everything from cocktail party tarts to turnovers, vol-au-vent (a pastry shell filled with, say, a seafood mélange, as Chef Haller did at the White House), or *gigot en croûte* (lamb wrapped in puff pastry), and desserts like Napoleons and pies. "It most definitely takes practice to perfect," Julia wrote, "but when you have mastered puff pastry you will find it such a satisfying and splendid accomplishment you will bless yourself for every moment you spent learning its technique."

Judith Jones attempted to make a *pâte feuilletée* from a draft of the recipe, but her pastry was hard and lumpy. She was embarrassed, thinking she had done something wrong. But one of her roles as editor was to ask obvious questions. "Julia would give me assignments—investigate shallots, or mushrooms, or kitchen superstitions. I liked that," she said. One day in Julia's Cambridge kitchen, she summoned the courage to say: "Julia, I can't visualize the *pâte feuilletée*. I can't follow what you're saying."

"Go into the pantry, dearie, and I'll watch while you make it," Julia instructed.

As Judith struggled to knead layers of pastry and butter on the white marble slab, Julia took notes and gently coached from the sidelines. They spent two days reworking the recipe, trying different proportions of flour and butter, and, Jones recalled, "It suddenly made sense!" In a difficult recipe like this one, she said, "what you really want to know is *what to expect:* Why do all these layers? What are you gaining from all that butter and air? Julia was able to step back and give the overall picture, explain why it was worth the effort. Very few writers can do that."

In writing to Simca about a similar recipe, for *pâté en croûte* (pastry dough filled with pâté and baked in a hinged mold, used for charcuterie), Julia stated the method behind her madness: "I shall make several more, or as many as necessary. I want to be sure that we have the best possible *croûte*, and that all problems and pitfalls are solved. I shall also take notes on every method of *pâté-en-croûte* making that I run into—I am sure this drives you crazy, but it is the only way I can work—I want to know everything, and why, and what's no good and why, so that when our master recipe is done there are no unsolved questions."

Julia's perfectionism was rooted in a desire to encourage home cooks. She cooked each recipe ten or twelve times to ensure that she had anticipated every mistake her readers might make, and she included advice on how to avoid pitfalls or recover from missteps. Clarity and accuracy were mandatory for Julia, who chided herself for not catching errors before they went into print. But perfection is elusive. Despite her attention to detail, a few of Julia's recipes included errors. And she was vexed to discover that Simca had barely checked the recipes she contributed.

In the years since *Mastering* was first published in 1961, Knopf had received a steady stream of letters from confused readers who found that this or that dish did not work, even when they had followed a recipe to the ounce or teaspoon. Simca blithely dismissed such concerns as unimportant details. But, said Jones, "Julia was appalled by the mistakes" and insisted on making corrections to almost every edition of the book. "Julia took it personally."

"You're only as good as your worst recipe," Julia averred. "I assume all the responsibility for the contents, even down to the commas. I test and retest my recipes until they come out perfect. The book is not Judith's responsibility. It's mine."

THE CLOCK SPUN, the calendar pages fluttered off the wall, and the deadline for Volume II loomed. *Clickety-clack* went their typewriters. "I have no desire to get into another big book like Vol. II for a long time to come, if ever. Too much work," Julia wrote Simca. "I am anxious to get back into TV teaching, and out of this little room with the typewriter. Screw it."

Simca, meanwhile, continued to produce reams and reams of recipes. Julia tried many of them, and if she found them unclear or incomplete, she would query her friend. Frequently, Simca would rear back and claim that "this—*this*—is *la véritable cuisine à la française!*" ("real French cooking"). As their deadline approached, Simca began to lash out at Julia, the United States, and even her own work.

In January 1970, Simca wrote a memo to Julia titled *"Petites Remarques et Modifications, si possible"* ("Small Remarks and Modifications, if Possible"), in which she made a suggestion about egg whites that Julia agreed with. But then Simca added, "I regret that you have omitted in the introduction on broccoli that this vegetable is also a delicious accompaniment to roasted pork and veal." In the margin, Julia scribbled in irritation: "Why did she not suggest this before? When she had the carbons? Not the place."

In February, Julia fact-checked a Simca missive entitled *"Lettre avec Commentaires Indispensables"* ("Letter with Indispensable Comments"), in which *La Super Française* criticized a recipe that she had submitted. Julia wrote:

Ma Chérie: You did this commentary when at Bramafam, without the rest of your files, and have done *ta mauvaise habitude* [bad habit] of wanting to change everything in the recipes as soon as you have seen it again. You have been reading Pierre Lacam . . . His Crème a succès has a crème anglaise with 16 yolks . . . but that is neither our Volume I anglaise . . . Nor have you remembered your own recipe, ma Chérie—but that is the way life is. You had this same recipe for Les Succès, Feb 1969, and you reported that everything was just fine. I am therefore not going to pay too much attention to this "letter with commentaires 'indispensables' " because I am sure when you see the recipe again (were it changed as you have directed), you would say *NON NON NON—ce n'est pas correct, ce n'est pas français*—and as often happens (as it does in this case) that it is your very own recipe (that you have forgotten about) that you are now attacking.

And when Simca insisted "I know officially that this cake we brought from the Bordeaux region," Julia typed in a self-therapeutic note that she did not send to France: "Why not give the source of Lacam? [meaning the pastry chef Pierre Lacam, who wrote *Le Mémorial Historique et Géographique de la Pâtisserie* in 1890] . . . This is entirely M*A*D—like dealing with a madwoman!"

At a certain point Julia stopped reading Simca's letters.

"I'm feeling terribly the pressure of time as I know you are," Jones wrote from New York. "How are we doing?"

With just days left before the nonnegotiable cutoff, Julia lamented that "it is like a sweat shop around here," and warned Jones: "Under no circumstances shall we send any galleys or page proofs to Simca—that is hopeless, and would really ruin us."

With a final push, Julia managed to hand the finished manuscript in on time. She was exhausted, but she had finished. Consoling her partner over the recipes sacrificed to deadline triage, she had written: "It may not be the book of your dreams, *ma chérie*, but it will be done."

4

The French Chef in France

1. To Press a Duck

As Julia's chipper voice narrated, bouncy theme music swelled and the camera zoomed in on a heavy, silver-plated machine about the size of a mailbox standing on end. It was a shiny round canister, with a small spout, elegant metal feet, surmounted by a metal wheel that would have looked at home aboard a dreadnought.

"This elaborate, expensive, silver-plated instrument is a duck press. Its only purpose is to *squeeze* the juices out of a duck," Julia narrated. "We will do two flaming duck recipes today—one in France, the other here—not in a press, *en salmis*. Today, on *The French Chef*!"

The camera pulled back, and viewers found themselves transported to the dining room of La Couronne (The Crown), the oldest restaurant in France. It was in Rouen, the capital of Normandy. A large fire crackled in the fireplace, with a row of glistening ducks roasting before it. For an American TV audience in 1970, this was an exotic, appealing, mysterious scene. And it was just the kind of presentation Julia enjoyed most: a sumptuous, traditional meal made with great care and presented with elegance and drama.

Julia called this scene "The Battle of the Duck." It was part of a series of short documentary films that she and a crew shot in France in a concentrated, three-week burst in the spring of 1970, between finishing *Mastering*, Volume II, and the book's publication. The short films were later spliced into sixteen of the thirty-nine episodes of *The French Chef*,

Season Two, and Julia rounded out the package with voice-overs and cooking demonstrations in the WGBH studio.

The documentaries were a risky escapade. They were shot guerrilla-style, with a tight deadline, minimal budget, skeleton crew, on 16-millimeter color film, to record traditional French foodways before they disappeared forever. The Childs referred to their adventure as "The French Chef in France," or "FCiF." As in *White House Red Carpet*, Julia was taking her audience somewhere they had never been before: this time to the France that most tourists never see, the *arrière-pays* ("back-country") of rustic charcuteries, olive oileries, cheese shops, screaming fishwives, skilled butchers, medieval bakeries, Parisian chocolatiers, and subterranean wine *caves*—the people and places that had originally inspired Julia in the 1950s.

There had never been anything like the "FCiF" films on American television before. In many ways these episodic inserts anticipated today's globe-traveling cooking shows, with a focus on local specialties, unfamiliar ingredients, classical techniques, and surprising locations brought to you by a compelling host.

As the camera panned around the La Couronne dining room, Julia stepped into the frame to interview the maître d'hôtel about his famous dish *Canard à la Rouennaise* (duck from Rouen). Julia wore a dashing silver-white dress with an orange scarf around her neck—a chic ensemble that was a far cry from the sensible blue work shirt, green apron, and purple dish towel she usually favored. Her sartorial choices telegraphed a message about Season Two: Julia was taking her mission, and herself, seriously.

Monsieur Dorin, the master of the duck press, was a lean, bearded man dressed in a dark suit and tie, with thick plastic-framed glasses. He looked more like an accountant or a cousin of Sigmund Freud than the manager of a famed restaurant. In accented English, he explained how he roasted a duck on a spit, then carved off the legs and wings, peeled the skin from the pink breast, and sprinkled it with minced shallots, coarse salt, and exactly forty grinds of pepper.

He worked with the practiced, economical movements of a surgeon, and Julia said, "It looks as though you've done this before, several times."

Dorin knit his brow and nodded solemnly.

As the bird's wings and legs, coated in mustard and bread crumbs, were whisked off to the kitchen for roasting, Dorin placed the bird's carcass into the duck press and added a gurgle of deep red Burgundy. He spun the handle down and gave it a good tug. With the sound of cracking bones, the silver machine crushed the carcass and issued a stream of red wine and duck essence from the spout. Dorin collected the juices in a small copper saucepan and mixed in a splash of cognac. Then he set the blood-brandy pool alight and gently warmed sliced duck breast in the mixture.

"Very careful," he intoned.

Julia stood with her hands behind her back, watching raptly. "Why do you have to be so careful?"

"The blood will become hard, scrambled," if you allow it to overcook, he replied.

"Yours is the most pure recipe I've seen for *canard*." Julia nodded.

Rouen is known for its duck, and those roasted at La Couronne were a beautiful half-wild, half-domestic hybrid. Though Dorin enacted the ritual with priestly seriousness, much of it, Julia noted, was theatrics. "If you *do* happen to have a duck press of your own, you can do it like Monsieur Dorin," she trilled. "But you don't have to rush out and rent a duck press because you can do almost the same at home."

At that point, the screen switched, and the viewer was transported back to the *French Chef* set in Boston, where Julia demonstrated how to cook a perfectly delicious duck in your own kitchen.

The "FCiF" team shot similar documentary segments in three culinary regions of France: Provence, in the south (where Julia and Simca shared a property); Paris, in the central north (where Julia had learned to cook, and Simca lived); and Normandy, in the northwest (where Simca was raised and Julia had vacationed).

The choice to highlight La Couronne was no accident. The restaurant was the site of Julia's very first meal in France, a revelatory lunch of *sole meunière* that took place on November 3, 1948. Much had changed in the intervening years. At the time, Paul was the "senior" member of the marriage, a worldly forty-six-year-old diplomat to Julia's "rather loud and unserious" thirty-six-year-old ingenue. By June 1970, however, Julia had grown into a best-selling author and zesty television celebrity. Like the Sorcerer's Apprentice—or Eliza Doolittle in *My Fair Lady*—Julia had virtually reversed roles with Paul. While she became a superstar,

Paul stepped out of the limelight to support her career, which he was glad to do. "I feel Nature is restoring an upset balance," he wrote to Charlie.

The filming at La Couronne marked the rounding of a circle. It was a homecoming to the site of Julia's culinary awakening, and, though no one knew it at the time, it would prove to be the beginning of the end of Phase One of her career.

11. A Cook's Tour

The final push to complete Volume II had been such a strain that Julia swore off books and, like a horse from the barn, bolted the confines of her study: "Never again am I going to get into anything like this book—never able to go anywhere, do anything, learn something new. NON," she vented to Simca in April 1970. "All of this takes hours and hours of work . . . but at last—it shall be done. H*O*O*R*A*Y." Eagerly returning to the WGBH studio, Julia began to prepare for Season Two of *The French Chef*, which would air in October. "It is such fun to be back there again, and so jolly, and to finally be out of this house and away from this typewriter." It was then that she proposed "The French Chef in France" documentaries.

"I have felt that we needed something new . . . when we came on again in color, and this is it!" Julia said of taking a small crew across the Atlantic to record traditional foodways. "I keep talking so much about France . . . and I am itching to show the actual country, life, people and food. And I envisage our doing it in a very intimate and personal manner."

WGBH welcomed her documentary plan, and outlined it in a handsome brochure for potential underwriters. Julia proposed a luxe "Cook's tour" that would take her from a private home in Champagne to a three-star restaurant in Paris, a picnic on the Eiffel Tower, a truffle hunt in Périgord, and a winepress in Beaune. It was an ambitious idea, but not an easy sell. While *The French Chef* boasted more than a million viewers a week, Season Two would feature more episodes than ever, and would be shot in color for the first time, which made it expensive. Production costs for the Cook's tour alone were estimated at more than $500,000.

This was a large sum for public television, and the station's executives struggled to find a corporate underwriter. It was a sobering moment.

Julia had no choice but to scale back and propose a more modest slate of documentaries: they would be shot on a tight schedule in places where the Childs knew people, which would help cut time and costs, and would focus on simpler foods. This scheme was more appealing, and at the eleventh hour two familiar patrons—Polaroid (which funded *The French Chef*) and Hills Bros. Coffee (which had sponsored *White House Red Carpet*)—agreed to fund Julia's documentary experiment.

Despite this apparent setback an innovative and subversive spirit lingered deep inside the project. Julia had sold the "FCiF" documentaries as a useful teaching tool, and as a way to show her television audience the kinds of food and people that had originally inspired her to cook. But this pitch was something of a Trojan horse. As she revealed years later in *My Life in France*, Julia's true agenda with the "FCiF" documentaries was to "save" classical *cuisine* from being crushed by American-style supermarkets and fast-food joints that were popping up around France like poisonous mushrooms. The French, it turned out, liked convenience as much as everyone else did. Julia feared this was a grave threat to the traditional handmade foods that defined the nation's heritage. In essence, she believed that her documentaries would help preserve the soul of France:

> Although I never mentioned this blatantly, I was convinced that our footage would prove to be an important historical document. Mechanization was taking over the food business, even in France, and it seemed clear to me that many of the artisanal skills we were going to record—the making of *glacéed* fruits, the hand-cutting of meat, the decorative skills of traditional *pâtissiers*—would disappear within a generation or two. Of course, film itself can fade or break. But if our little documentaries survived, they might be one of the few records showing how food was once made almost entirely by human hands rather than by machines.

She had not voiced this motivation at the time for fear of scaring away her audience, her bosses, and her sponsors.

Yet there was a mild irony at work in Julia's attitude. In France she was a stalwart defender of tradition, while in America she was an enthusiastic agent of change. But Julia did not like to analyze her own complex and sometimes contradictory impulses. Though she was measured and pragmatic as a cook, she lived her life instinctually and moved ever forward.

With a green light to proceed on "The French Chef in France," Paul and Julia created detailed schedules, lists of equipment, and questions to be answered on the ground to ensure that everything went smoothly. Naturally, it didn't.

III. The Experience of Age and the Enthusiasm of Youth

Olive trees twisted against a blue sky. Red roses nodded in the warm breeze. There was bright sun, wispy clouds, and the smell of honey in the air at La Pitchoune. Down the road, the Mediterranean glittered and the Cannes Film Festival was in full carnivalesque swing under the palm trees. Paul and Julia sipped tea on the veranda and plotted out the next few weeks. It was mid-May 1970: a moment of calm before the storm.

At 9:00 that night the phone rang. It was Shana Alexander, the editor of *McCall's*, calling from New York. She made pleasant conversation, then got to the point. For $40,000, *McCall's* had procured the exclusive right from Knopf to use a host of recipes—from broiled eggplant slices to a mold of parslied aspic and apricot sherbet—excerpted from Volume II. The recipes would accompany the three-part series of articles that Patricia Simon had written about the making of Volume II after her visit to La Pitchoune the year before. But there was a catch: reneging on its promise to use the hundreds of photos Paul had taken of Julia and Simca at work, *McCall's* had decided to use the celebrity photographer Arnold Newman instead. The real purpose of Alexander's call was to convince Julia and Simca to participate in a photo shoot with Newman, and to allow him to produce a series of mouthwatering images of the duo's completed recipes. To sweeten the deal, the magazine would cover the costs of food and laundry, and would throw in a $200 per diem. All Julia and Simca had to do, Alexander purred, was to pose for Arnold Newman.

McCall's was pulling out all the stops for their series on Volume II, and the publicity value of such attention in a major magazine, timed to the publication of the book, was incalculable.

La Pitchoune

Julia wasn't interested. For one thing, Paul was deeply insulted that the magazine had unceremoniously dropped him. For another, every minute of Julia's time for the next few months had already been scheduled. "Cooking with us is <u>NOT</u> a hot-dog-stand operation," Paul harrumphed to his brother. "Our standards are perfection, visually as well as gastronomically. For us, the cooking and serving of food (and instructing others to do it as we do) is not something we can toss together at the last minute." Once the "FCiF" shoot wrapped at the end of June, the Childs would return to Cambridge to tape Season Two in the studio at WGBH. "We have no staff of writers, idea-men, gag-men, or anyone but ourselves," Paul thundered. "A group of 24 people is involved in the final shooting. They depend on us."

Well, then, Alexander countered, what if Simca Beck were to pose for the great lensman, alone? *"Oui!"* Simca replied; she would be delighted to pose for Mr. Arnold Newman.

The Pan Am jet carrying the WGBH film crew touched down in Nice on May 20. An hour later, Julia, Paul, and five groggy Americans huddled beneath a blue awning at a restaurant in Cannes, eating lunch. Ruth Lockwood was Julia's trusted producer and all-around fix-it

Morning on the Côte d'Azur

woman. She was solidly built, with short brown-gray hair, an oval face, big glasses, and a foghorn voice. It was Ruthie who often came up with the silly props Julia used on air, like the blowtorch and fireman's hat she used for a show on crème brûlée. But Ruth could also be a relentless perfectionist, insisting that reams of research about the White House or French provincial cooking be prepared before a shoot. As trying as she could be, Paul noted, Ruthie was very useful.

The director was David Atwood, a tall Mainer with straight brown hair. He had directed WGBH's coverage of the race riots in Boston in 1969, and the night that James Brown had persuaded an angry crowd not to rampage in the streets. But the "FCiF" was Atwood's first overseas assignment, and the responsibility weighed on him. The cameraman was Peter Hoving, a wry Dutch Canadian with a red beard and a sure sense of himself. He had shot film in Moscow and Western Europe, and spoke a smattering of French. Sound recording was the province of Willie Morton, who hid beneath tables and around corners to pick up sound on his long microphone while out of sight. The crew's production assistant was Nancy Troland, a bespectacled Massachusetts native who had traveled through France with her aunt and spoke a bit of French.

Five of the seven—Paul and Julia, Lockwood, Hoving, and Morton—had worked together on Julia's pilot episodes for WGBH in 1962. Hoving and Morton had worked on *White House Red Carpet* in 1967. As they ate *salade niçoise*, they reminisced about their naïve efforts to produce those shows in rudimentary conditions, and agreed the experience had forged a strong working relationship.

After lunch, David Atwood strolled through an outdoor market and used a Polaroid camera to take instant portraits of the vegetable sellers. The wizened market women were astonished to see the camera spit out a fully developed color picture moments after it was taken. It was as if the young American had "made an apple grow from its seed in 60 seconds," Paul wrote in his diary.

As a former schoolteacher and diplomat, Paul seemed intent on educating the young WGBHers about the importance of building trust and adapting themselves to local customs; he worried that the Yanks' obses-

Julia at a marketplace in France

sion with speed and technology would not mesh well with the slower-paced, tradition-bound French.

"Remember, France is halfway to the Orient," he advised the crew. The message was: *You are no longer in America, kids. For our documentary project to succeed, you must adjust to the French way of doing things. Don't rush through a marketplace too quickly, push people too hard, or take their goodwill for granted.* Unlike most people, the Childs had lived for extended periods in three cultures—American, Chinese, and French—each of which had distinct shopping traditions and relationships to time. Raised in the States, Julia and Paul understood the efficient, but essentially nonsocial, way of buying goods in an American supermarket. They had also lived in the ancient city of Kunming, China, at the end of the Second World War, where even simple transactions required lengthy negotiations. And after the war they lived in Paris and Marseille, where shoppers were expected to interact with vendors as part of doing business. So, while purchasing frozen chicken breasts in Boston took minutes, deliberating the price of a live chicken in a Chinese market could stretch for a day, and buying premium chicken thighs in France would take at least an hour.

Sensitive to cultural differences, Julia believed in the importance of what she called "les human relations." Paul emphasized building "linguistic bridges" with butchers, cheese ladies, or fruit purveyors. If the young WGBHers followed suit, he explained, they would be rewarded with the finest pork loin, ripest triangle of Camembert, and freshest strawberries in the market—and perhaps a few well-guarded family recipes. If not, they would be shut out and the "FCiF" project would fail.

The final member of the team was Daniel Berger, an affable, twenty-eight-year-old French "fixer." He had a mop of curly brown hair, bright eyes, a creamy complexion, a tentative mustache, and an affinity for colorful shirts. Appropriately enough, "berger" means "shepherd" in English: his job was to make things happen when, how, and where they were supposed to. In a 2009 blog post, Berger looked back at his three weeks with the Childs as an adventure that altered the course of his life: "Nixon and Pompidou were presidents, Ungaretti had died, the Renault 12 was popular, Miles [Davis] was playing at the festival of the Isle of Wight, and Michel Le Bris was sentenced to eight months in prison for subversion. Julia Child, the U.S. star unknown in France, was inhabited by a sense of delight, genuinely interested in others, and was to me a female equivalent of the 'perfect gentleman.' "

Summing up the "FCiF" team, Paul quoted Fernand Point, the famed chef at La Pyramide: *"Lorsqu'on dirige un personnel, il est nécessaire d'amalgamer l'expérience des anciens à l'enthousiasme des jeunes"* ("When one heads up a group of people one must combine the experience of age with the enthusiasm of youth").

IV. THE OLD-FASHIONED AND THE NEW

Grasse is a romantic vision of a French town, known for its flowers, fountains, arcaded streets, dank alleyways, long staircases, and sublime courtyards. It was an ideal setting for the opening shots of Julia's documentary. Early on the morning of Thursday, May 21, Julia wandered through the Place aux Aires marketplace, admiring the tulips and fresh vegetables for sale, and bought just-made crème fraîche from a stern woman at a *crémerie*. The film crew trailed behind, capturing the sights and sounds of the moment.

David Atwood silently gestured his directions while Peter Hoving focused his camera on the vendors' rugged hands. Willie Morton crouched to pick up sound with his mike. Nancy Troland clacked the "slate," which identified each shot. Then she scribbled notes about what happened in each scene and where, kept track of film footage, and planned the shooting schedule. Paul Child still snapped photos with his Rolleiflex.

On Friday, the team walked along Rue Meynadier, a winding street in Cannes lined with shops selling wineglasses, butcher's knives, and dining-room furniture. There was cheese at the *fromageries*, terrines and cured meats at charcuteries, voices speaking in dozens of tongues, the clatter of cutlery, and snatches of music emanating from cafés. At Maiffret, where glacéed (candied) fruit had been made since 1885, wicker baskets filled with preserved fruits and boxes of candies were on display. In the back room, peaches and strawberries bubbled in vats of sugar syrup. Women peeled oranges and pitted cherries, and punctured holes into pineapples and lemons, to allow the sugar syrup to penetrate the fruit.

Once cooked, the fruits were marinated in shallow terra-cotta bowls for months, to deepen the flavors.

As Peter's camera rolled, Julia entered the store and spoke with the owner and the director, over and over again. She was happy to do multiple takes, but Paul was increasingly frustrated. He had developed an executive instinct in his diplomatic career, and it was difficult for him to stand by.

"A psychological difficulty for me is to remind myself that I am *not* the leader of this group," he wrote in his diary. "I find that I am constantly planning, trying to think ahead about such things as whether the budget will allow certain expenditures, whether or not the baker who helped us was thanked, if the team had found a place to park," and so on. "I am only the photographer, I make no decisions for the team, I salve no hurt feelings . . . and I keep my mouth shut when the 40-year-younger David decides to shoot a sequence which I feel certain we shall never use."

David Atwood had spent most of the morning filming bowls of fruit and salesclerks tying packages, while Julia stood by mutely. Though she was in full makeup, she was filmed only entering the shop and admiring its sweets, not interacting with anyone. "Julia was not sent to France at considerable expense to Polaroid Corporation and WGBH merely to interpret . . . what might as well be stock footage," Paul muttered. The sequence "won't be quite personal enough." This message was transmitted to David, who vowed to adjust.

On Monday, May 25, the crew arrived at Le Festival, a two-star restaurant in Cannes, where the chef was preparing a spectacular dish: *un loup grillé et flambé au fenouil* (sea bass that is grilled and flambéed over fennel). The bass was cleaned, oiled, and grilled; then the *loup* was placed in a fish-shape wire basket and smoked with flaming fennel stalks; the fish was then filleted and served with melted butter. It was a dramatic but fairly easy dish to make, and, Paul said, "nothing could be more mouthwatering."

As Paul dabbed the sweat from Julia's forehead, she leaned in toward him, and, in hushed voices, they discussed how to re-create the *loup* at the Child family house in Maine, where fennel was not available. Paul wondered if they could use fir tree fronds instead, but Julia concluded the flavor would not be quite right. They were completely absorbed with each other and the task of adapting a classical French dish to an American context. It was a small but telling moment, when the two kindred spirits were content, alert, and working in sync.

Stove doors slammed, pans banged on grills, lids clattered, knives chopped. *"Silence, s'il vous plaît!"* Daniel Berger said, and the noise dropped. Waiters and cooks stood still as the camera whirred and a scene was shot.

"Cut!" said David, and the cacophony resumed.

As the dining room filled with visitors, a woman from Michigan interrupted: "My goodness, it's Julier Chiles! It sure is wonderful to see you in action. My daughter and I watch your program every Thursday night. My friends won't *believe* it when I tell them I actually *saw* you in person!"

The clock ticked and the crew waited while Julia graciously chatted with the fan. The Michigander left, and they picked up where they had left off.

On Tuesday morning, the "FCiF" company headed into the crowded Nice marketplace to procure ingredients for a *salade niçoise*. Down the line of food stalls stood tables groaning with pizzas, *soccas*, and *pissaladières*, traditional Mediterranean finger foods. Periodically, a boy on a red bike appeared from the backstreets, hauling a wagon holding freshly baked pizzas under a conical iron cover. In the market, the boy retrieved empty trays and replaced them with the fresh, bubbling-hot pizzas. Julia and her crew followed the boy back up a cobblestoned hill into the winding maze of the Old City. In a small courtyard surrounded by ocher-colored walls, an open doorway led to a large wood-burning oven. A sweaty, sooty, demonic-looking baker poured beige *socca* (chickpea) batter onto a large, well-oiled, circular black pan and slid it toward the flames. As the fresh *socca* was loaded onto the boy's trailer, Hoving lifted the heavy camera and tracked him as he pedaled around a sharp corner, flew down the hill, and disappeared into the hubbub of the market.

Back at La Pitchoune, Julia encouraged Simca to participate in the "FCiF" documentaries. Though she was an inventive cook and a popular teacher, Simca was not a natural performer, nor did she understand the power of television. She agreed to participate in a couple of quick scenes, then abruptly departed for Paris. This irked Julia and Paul. They knew that *The French Chef* had been crucial to the popularity of *Mastering*—the book would not have had the sales or cultural impact it did without Julia's exposure on television—and hoped for a similar success with Volume II.

On Thursday, May 28, Julia and Simca shot "The Spinach Twins" episode at La Pitchoune. They demonstrated *pâté pantin aux épinards*—a turnover made with a *pâte brisée* (pastry dough) that enfolds a mix of puréed spinach, mushrooms, and ham; is decorated on top with pastry strips; and glazed with egg yolk. It was a simple, earthy recipe that Simca had devised.

The lights were hot enough to melt an igloo, Paul observed, yet *La Super Française* looked cold and severe. She stared down at the table as she pounded and rolled out a pastry crust, leaving minutes of dead air. Attuned to the camera, Julia kept talking, then appeared to goad Simca, saying of the pastry, "You could even use a piecrust mix, couldn't you?"

Simca stopped and glared. "I'm French. I *hate* ready mix."

Julia laughed, and said, "Oh, Simca, you're going to get them in France, you'll see."

"Even if they come in France, I won't use them—"

"How about dehydrated potatoes?"

"*Ugh*, awful! For me it's awful. To be good, plenty of eggs and plenty of cream, then you can eat it. No, I think it's interesting, but that's my own opinion. I'm old-fashioned. I'm an old-fashioned—you know that!"

The two friends smiled, as Simca's strong fingers folded the pastry and sealed it tight.

v. Rigor Mortis

On Saturday, May 30, the crew piled into their rented white Peugeot wagons and drove west to Marseille, France's second-largest city after Paris. For the Childs it was a homecoming. In 1953, Paul was transferred from the U.S. Embassy in Paris to the U.S. Consulate in Marseille, where he would spend a year and a half as the public affairs officer (PAO). At the time Julia, Simca, and Louisette were deep into the sauce chapter for what would eventually become *Mastering the Art of French Cooking*. Julia was devastated to be uprooted from Paris, but within a month of arriving in Marseille she had adjusted to the Mediterranean climate and its flavor base of olive oil, garlic, onions, tomatoes, herbes de Provence, and fish. She sipped pastis, made gallons of *soupe de poisson*, and researched the many versions of *bouillabaisse à la Marseillaise*. By the time they were transferred to Germany, in October 1954, the Childs had been seduced by Marseille's rough charms. Paul seriously considered quitting the Foreign Service in order to stay in France. He would work as a freelance photographer, while Julia taught cooking classes and finished her cookbook. But the more they discussed it, the more they realized that this was a romantic dream. With a decent government job in hand, Paul decided to stick with what he knew.

As the Childs drove into Marseille in 1970, they were sad to see that what had once been open countryside was now crowded with multistory housing blocks. But once they'd pushed their way into the loud, smelly, crowded heart of Old Marseille, their mood lightened. "It comes over us again what a meaty, down-to-earth, vicious, highly seasoned old city this is," Paul noted. "It has its own atmosphere, part African, part oceanic, reverberating with the rhythms of the whole Mediterranean littoral, from Turkey to Spain, and from Morocco to Egypt."

The streets were jammed with people of every hue, and the stalls sold a dizzying variety of foods. One shop displayed sixteen different kinds of olives. At a fish stand, Julia met a *beldam* who had been selling fish in that spot for sixty-one years. When Julia asked who would take over when she retired, the woman snorted, "Nobody wants to *work* anymore! The young people are afraid they might get dirty hands. Not everybody can be driven around town in a golden bathtub, name of God!"

This was the kind of vital Gallic earthiness that the Childs had hoped to capture on film. Years later, Daniel Berger recalled in a blog post:

Julia and Paul were guided by their memories. With an applied and joyful gluttony, they revived in Eastmancolor [film] . . . a France of music, markets and auctions, roads, and squares of chocolate, brave men in berets. [Julia did not give] real briefings before [shooting began, but] rather imagined how each story would restore the atmosphere of a neighborhood, the light of a shop or kitchen, the colors of a dish . . . [She never gave] orders or instructions, not even suggestions. She told a story and nobody in the team posed questions, everyone knew what he had to do.

Their first stop was a small fish market in an oblong *place* amid a knot of slim, twisting streets. A flood of people swirled around bins filled with fish of every size, color, and shape, and shouted at one another—not because they were angry, but because that is how they like to communicate in Marseille.

Daniel, dressed in a bright red shirt, led the way into the melee, yelling in French as he attempted to clear a path for the "FCiF" team. Hoving followed him closely with the bulky camera on his shoulder. Atwood, dressed in yellow, tucked behind him, then Morton, with his tape recorder and microphone. Behind them were Nancy, dressed in green; Julia in pink and pale blue; and Ruth in navy and white stripes. Paul popped up in a window to shoot a panorama over the fish market, vanished, and reappeared close by to capture Julia's hands buried wrist-deep in a vat of Niçoise olives.

The taciturn fishermen and the extravagant fishwives were not immune to the charms of Julia and her camera, and a few seemed to compete for the most outrageous, compelling, or quintessentially French interview. The winner was a weathered, long-faced salt with a smoldering Gauloises jutting from his mouth, unloading just-caught fish.

"*Bonjour, m'sieur,*" Julia said, eyeing the rigid fish approvingly. "Is that rigor mortis?"

"*Non, madame,*" he answered with a straight face. "It's a mackerel."

"That's marvelous!," she chuckled.

At 4:00 on the morning of Tuesday, June 2, Willie Morton swigged a bottle of Pepsi-Cola for breakfast, while the rest of the team tucked into cafés au lait and croissants. Then they trooped into the dawn and made their way to the city's large central fish market, La Criée aux poissons. In a building the size of a train station, the Criée was already roaring with wild energy. Tuna carcasses lay on the concrete floor. Big men dressed in heavy sweaters and yellow sou'westers speckled with silver fish scales used metal hooks to haul plastic boxes of fish across the floor. They weighed, hosed, shoveled ice, cursed, argued, laughed, and smoked. Women the shape of stevedores, with hair flying and dressed in thick black rubber aprons, hawked their fish shrilly, laughed like hyenas, and screamed like fiends.

By 6:30 a.m. it was all over. Julia was exhilarated and declared it one of the best days of shooting yet.

THE SCHEDULE ALLOWED for two days off before the next shoot. Paul and Julia wandered Marseille, socialized with old diplomatic friends, and ate rich *bourride* (thick fish stew) at a tiny restaurant. Ruthie and her husband, Arthur Lockwood, hired a guide and toured the Château d'If, the island fortress made famous by Alexandre Dumas's *The Count of Monte Cristo*. (In a nod to the local drug trade, a key scene from the thriller *The French Connection* was shot there in 1971.)

The trouble began innocently enough. The crew's next stop was Paris: the Childs and Lockwoods took the overnight Train Bleu north, but the "kids" decided to fly, instead. This would give them extra time in Marseille, and the freedom to spread their wings.

The film crew spent the afternoon shooting background footage, and that night treated themselves to a wonderful seafood dinner with plenty of wine. The moon was nearly full, and it seemed like a good idea to drive up the hill overlooking the harbor, to take in a panoramic view of the Mediterranean. Atop the hill, the moon glittered on the sea far below. It was warm and dark. Along the sweeping coast, the city buzzed with golden light, like an electrified beehive. It was mesmerizing, and as they tumbled out of the car nobody thought to lock the doors. Half an hour later they returned to discover that Nancy's purse, which held all of their plane tickets, money, papers, and passports, had disappeared.

Panic set in.

Tires squealing, they rushed back into the city, where they filed a police report. The detective in charge was a square-jawed tough guy who modeled himself after Dick Tracy in a fedora, trench coat, white shirt, black tie, and big wristwatch. Astonishingly, he had already apprehended the thief: a wretched little man, who quaked in a cell. One of the *flics* had noticed the thief "acting queer" in a side street, and it turned out he was stuffing $400 worth of francs into his socks.

By now the WGBH crew was worn out, and wanted only to return to the hotel. But French bureaucracy required they fill out a pink slip, a brown slip, and a white slip. A description of every item in Nancy's purse had to be noted, as did the time and place of the crime, and their reason for being on Marseille's highest peak at midnight. Plus there was age, nationality, home address, Marseille address, passport number, et cetera, et cetera. After several hours of this, the Americans befriended the thief and felt sorry for him. "If he hadn't been poor and desperate, he wouldn't have stolen the money," they reasoned. But the police wouldn't allow the man to leave his cell or to contact his family. Nancy thought his wife must be worried sick. When Daniel finally persuaded Dick Tracy to allow the WGBHers to leave, they drove into the bowels of old Marseille with no map. Finally, at 3:00 in the morning, they found the thief's wife in an Armenian neighborhood. She was frantic about her missing husband. Daniel explained what had happened. She cried and thanked them profusely. As they left, the Americans handed her a fistful of the formerly stolen francs.

After two hours of sleep, the team rushed off to catch their flight. But a slowdown strike at Orly airport caused them to depart late and to circle over Paris. In the terminal, the bedraggled filmmakers lost the key to their rented car, and a replacement had to be brought from the head office in Paris. At 7:00 p.m., they slumped into the Hôtel Samur, on the Left Bank, "half dead."

VI. PARIS: "AN APPETITE FOR WINE"

Paris was Julia's favorite city in the world. She had a long list of scenes, foods, characters, and storylines she hoped to document for the "FCiF," but deciding which to shoot, and where, required some hunting and pecking.

Couscous, a North African wheat dish that had become a staple of Parisian kitchens, was high on her list. But the grain was not widely available in American supermarkets, and rather than send her viewers on "a wild couscous chase," Julia decided to save it for another time.

Then there was the matter of wine. Living in Paris in the late 1920s, Paul had become a passionate oenophile and had passed his enthusiasm on to Julia. By 1970, wine was becoming popular in the States, thanks to vintners such as Robert Mondavi, who had introduced his Sauvignon Blanc—dubbed Fumé Blanc—to California in 1968. Daniel Berger wrote appreciatively: "Paul always knew what to drink with each dish. He had a taste for white as an aperitif, [which was] pretty cool [at the time, and has become] institutionalized since—it was not yet fashionable . . . and a predilection for red Rhône with red meat, and Burgundy with simmered dishes and cheeses."

Julia wanted to demonstrate the pairing of wine with food. The obvious place to demonstrate this was at a classic restaurant like Le Grand Véfour, a gilded three-star tucked behind the Palais Royal park. Built in 1784, the dining room featured a painted ceiling, crystal, ornate rugs, and a grand sommelier named Monsieur Hénocq. The Childs had relied on him for twenty years, but Hénocq was now eighty-seven, and slipped into tedious philosophizing. Julia embraced him warmly, but it was clear that Hénocq would not translate well to American television. "Sentiment and professional standards, alas, cannot be teammates in this instance," Paul acknowledged regretfully.

Their next attempt at filming wine led the Childs up an ancient, steep street called Rue de la Montagne-Sainte-Geneviève, where they entered the *caves de Monsieur Besse* (the wine caves of Mr. Besse). Besse was a jolly fellow with a gap where his front teeth once stood, who owned a legendary wine collection. Although numerous print journalists had chronicled Besse's *caves*, no one had yet managed to record their murky depths on film. For Julia, this was an irresistible challenge.

Besse's cellars dated to the twelfth century and contained some thirty-five thousand bottles. The *caves* receded deep underground, connected by rotting ladders and tunnels that grew darker, dustier, moldier, more cobwebbed and claustrophobic as they went. Wine bottles had been dropped in great heaps, flung in random corners, or stacked precariously along staircases. Glass shards jutted out of the shadows menacingly. The *caves de M. Besse* were emblematic of the kind of hidden treasure that the Childs intended to show their audience: a moody, thrilling, scary, fabulous repository of ancient vinology that was thoroughly un-American. It required a deep knowledge of Paris to find, and there was no logical, business-oriented, market-tested reason for it to exist (Besse ran a collection, not a store); yet it did exist, thanks to the passion of the half-crazed wine miser. Julia worried that in the rush to modernize, not only would France cast aside the rubbish of the past, but also gems, like Besse's *caves* or the Les Halles marketplace, and other tools, skills, and places that defined France's culinary heritage.

Julia's plan to film inside the *caves* was stymied in a very French way.

When the "FCiF" team rented a small camera and battery-powered floodlights from a cinema-outfitting store, Daniel Berger asked for a receipt. The request sent the store owner into a rage. He grabbed the equipment and locked the door. Perhaps there was a misunderstanding, but, Paul wrote, any American who has lived in Paris has "had some experience which has created in his breast a point of frustration, despair, even dislike, so that in the end—even if one loves living here, as Julia and I do—he ends up having a sort of love-hate relationship with the French."

June 4 was the sixteenth day of filming, and Julia declared it Cheese Day. Like wine, cheese is an essential part of the French diet. To explicate it, Julia invaded Androuët, a noted restaurant-store on Rue d'Amsterdam devoted entirely to *fromage*. As Julia inspected trays holding at least a hundred different kinds of cheese, Monsieur Androuët bobbed his bald dome fringed with curly hair and led the crew into his cellar. There, shelf after shelf was filled with cheese: hard, soft, crumbly, rocky, runny; blue, goats' milk, cows' milk, ewes' milk; heart-shape cheese, moldy lumps, powdered pyramids, enormous wheels of Emmentaler and tiny squares no bigger than a matchbox. The *caviste* (one who oversees aging cheese in a cellar), Monsieur George, was the spitting image of the farmer-husband in Grant Wood's *American Gothic*. It took all of Julia's charm to extract the information from him that her audience would want. After four hours of close-ups, long shots, and repeats, she prevailed. Yet, after all of this effort, the cheese sequence was not used on television, and the films have disappeared. Such is the uncertain nature of a project like "The French Chef in France."

On Friday, June 5, Paul and Julia took the crew to Prunier, the famed restaurant near the Arc de Triomphe, to document the cooking of frogs' legs. Julia was certain this would cause a sensation when it aired in the States, where frog is not a typical comestible. Inside, the kitchen was narrow, dark, and hot, and the chef was unsmiling. With little space for his camera, Hoving positioned himself to shoot through a slot between the stove and countertop. He worried that the heat from the coal-fired stove and his floodlights would destroy the sensitive color film. But they had just a short window to get the job done, and Julia would not be deterred.

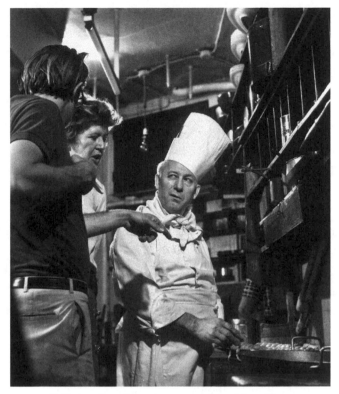

Julia inquires about the preparation of frogs' legs
in the Prunier kitchen.

The camera rolled and the chef deftly rolled the frogs' legs in flour, salt, and minced garlic; laid them neatly in a cast-iron pan; and fried them in gobs of fresh butter.

There was not enough room for Daniel Berger in the Prunier kitchen, so he waited alone in the dining room. A young waiter appeared with silverware and a plate of a half dozen frogs' legs. Then he poured a glass of pale yellow Chablis. Daniel took a sip and felt his life change. The Chablis was "a sensual wonder . . . like a crystal punch in the mouth: the point of harmony between the delicate and slightly garlicky flesh of the frogs' legs and the [wine's] smell of windfall, and its barely noticeable acidity," he wrote. "I still remember the emotion all these years later, the first of its kind [for me], like the first kiss of love. My first real encounter with wine happened on that day at that location."

When Daniel wrote these words in 2009, he was married with children and had left cinema to become a wine merchant and commentator. He pointed to his lunch at Prunier thirty-nine years earlier as the precise moment he found his "appetite for wine."

VII. FRENCH BREAD TWO WAYS

After their months of research and numerous failed experiments, Julia and Paul considered their clear explanation of how to make French bread in an American home oven the most important element of Volume II and the "FCiF" shoot.

There are many types of bread made in France, and Julia would demonstrate the making of various loaves in two episodes: the first showed the traditional, handmade approach, which dated to the Middle Ages; the second showed the latest, mechanized techniques used in Paris.

On June 8, Paris was hot and steamy. It felt cruel to stand in front of a bread oven. But there was Julia, by the ovens at Chez Poilâne on Rue du Cherche-Midi. A chic bread store at street level, Poilâne baked its loaves in two cast-iron ovens in a small basement with rough stone walls. Down there two bakers dressed in only stained shorts worked feverishly, like a pair of goblins.

As Julia stooped in the low space and asked questions, the men demonstrated the ancient system of making bread—from the development of the *levain* (a leavening agent used in place of yeast to rise bread dough) to forming the loaves by hand and shuttling them into the wood-fired oven, and sliding them out on long wooden paddles. Julia sniffed the aroma, cocked her head attentively, and smiled as the *boules'* crusty skin crackled as the loaves cooled.

The next day, the crew shot an episode about modern baking in a large, bright, air-conditioned bread laboratory with a sleek stainless-steel oven with a conveyor belt attachment. Julia's tutor was Raymond Calvel, the esteemed *professeur de boulangerie*, École Française de Meunerie, who had guided the Irving Street baking research.

A handsome man, and a master bread maker, Calvel rolled, kneaded, slashed, and pinched the dough. Julia followed suit, tentatively at first, then with growing confidence. She was surprised to discover that his lessons had never been captured on film before, and so she asked him to repeat the process to be sure every step had been documented. "It is a very earnest and somehow fundamental scene, the passing of one of mankind's oldest life-sustaining techniques from one person to another," Paul wrote. "I wish our records were on clay tablets, or bronze, or granite. Films, like people, are so evanescent."

IN THE MIDST OF a prickly-hot, thundering deluge in Paris, another kind of storm arrived in the form of Ninette Lyon, a French food writer who had materialized at Simca's apartment. *McCall's* had deputized Lyon to oversee the creating and photographing of food from the recipes in Volume II, and Lyon enlisted Simca to summon the Childs away from the bread laboratory.

It was in Julia's and Knopf's interest to cooperate with the magazine, which would generate valuable publicity for the book's launch. But Julia was filming Calvel's baguette-making technique. Time was of the essence. She had already said *"Non!"* to posing for *McCall's*, but to Paul's mounting frustration Julia was reluctant to stand her ground. With Simca's pleading, and with Judith Jones and Alfred Knopf in the back of her mind, Julia reluctantly agreed to cut the bread sequence short.

Ninette Lyon was neither a cook nor a photographer, but she was amiably pushy. She had ostensibly called the meeting to choose which dishes from Volume II to photograph, but, Paul suspected, the decision had already been made by someone in New York: Lyon's real agenda was to convince Julia to participate in the photo shoot with Arnold Newman.

Angry that *McCall's* was manipulating Julia and had chosen the celebrity lensman over himself, and concerned about the time and energy required of Julia, Paul fiercely resisted Lyon's entreaties.

A boxing aficionado, he saw his role as being akin to Julia's manager and "cornerman." An important aspect of a manager's job is to keep his fighter fit, pace her, and conserve her energy to ensure she will last the entire contest. Paul was growing worried about Julia's stamina. Over the winter she had worked nonstop on Volume II, rising at 6:30 every morning and going all day, every day, without a break. As soon as the book was finished, she began preparing for "The French Chef in France." Now they were in midshoot, with many scenes left to film in Paris and Normandy, and Paul feared the "attacking battalions of *McCall's* Army" would exhaust his charge. The dilemma was further strained by Simca's increasingly vocal calls for attention.

Julia waffled. While she agreed with Paul in theory, she understood the pragmatic need for book publicity and Simca's emotional need for inclusion and validation. It was a quandary.

Paul wrote a script for Julia, which she more or less stuck to in a phone call with Lyon: "I am finished with the book. My time and energies must now be devoted entirely to television. I therefore will NOT cook anything" for *McCall's*.

Lyon responded with charm, telling Julia, "You are like Brigitte Bardot: you do not need publicity . . . I myself am dying to see you perform in front of the camera. I hear you are stunning!"

Paul smirked at such transparent cajolery: "How pitifully far they are from judging the kind of woman Julia is! As though these puerile appeals would mean anything to her . . . But still they will keep pushing."

VIII. Artisanal Miracles

The oppressive heat continued to wilt Paris on June 10, but Julia was perfectly comfortable in the large, well-lit, air-conditioned supermarket Suma (for *"supermarché"*) in Parly 2, near Versailles. There, a "fish professor" named Madame Pasquet cleaned trout and lectured insightfully about cooking technique. A thin, self-contained woman of about forty-five, she had the aspect of a schoolmarm. In fact, this *professeur* had lectured about fish for twenty-seven years. Even slicked with fish blood and slime, Madame Pasquet kept her dignity. Julia, dressed in pale green, asked questions and smoothly translated Madame Pasquet's answers for the camera. "Watching those two expert women cooperating . . . was as exciting as watching a computer read out ten thousand bits of accurate information," Paul wrote in his diary (this was 1970, after all). "And we have it all on ever-living film, ladies and gentlemen, an artisanal miracle, preserved forever."

Julia turned from the fish counter to the meat department. Concerned that French butchers were giving up the hand carving of meat in favor of *"la coupe américaine"* ("the American cut")—or band-saw transverse cutting—the Childs spent the afternoon documenting the butchering of a steer. "In our culture when hand-work competes with machine-work the latter usually wins," Paul wrote, as if documenting the contest between John Henry and the steam-powered drill. "There is no question that for speed and ease the band saw licks the knife." But Monsieur Guyon, Suma's master butcher, demonstrated the value of skilled knife work. His sharp blade didn't cut across the grain, but flowed sinuously along the muscles of a veal leg, creating beautiful pieces of meat that would cook and eat well.

On June 12, the crew jammed into Claude Deblieux's petite workshop on the Rue de l'Étoile in Paris. It was a nook ten feet wide by fifteen feet long, stuffed with stoves, sinks, shelves, refrigerators, a table, and a long marble slab. Deblieux was a *pâtissier* (pastry chef) and a *maître sucrier* (sugar master) who sold handmade desserts. A compact man of perhaps sixty-five, Deblieux had white hair, gold-rimmed spectacles, a toque, and a soft voice. He had been awarded an MOF, a Meilleur Ouvrier de France, or "Best Worker in France." And he took the same childlike delight in making pastry as Professor Calvel had in the making of a perfect loaf of bread.

With patience, Deblieux guided Julia through the making of chocolate "cigarettes," chocolate leaves, palm trees, camels, and fish. But the pièce de résistance was a "gateau in a cage," an amazing creation made of three round layers of sponge cake; each layer was slathered in whipped cream, cut strawberries, and sugar syrup. It was topped by three white doves made of sugar, and surmounted by a magnificent golden "cage" made of spun sugar.

"We do feel that a lot of what we are filming is historic," Julia wrote to Avis DeVoto, "that much of the artisan skills will die out with the passing of the present generation, like the hand-forming of French bread, the hand-cutting of meat, and the *pâtissier*'s decorative skills."

Julia had saved the best shoot in Paris for last: Dehillerin, a century-old, family-run cookware store that she had patronized since 1948. She called the store one of her favorite places on earth, "my addiction." Paul called it "crazy." Dehillerin would not be out of place in Harry Potter's Diagon Alley: a long narrow space, in which every centimeter was festooned with copper pots, cheese graters, bread pans, spoons, ladles, whisks, mortars and pestles, and every other kind of culinary gewgaw imaginable. To film this pirate's treasure, Peter Hoving took the heavy camera off its tripod and perched it on his shoulder, to rove through the aisles, ducking under, over, and around utensils in the crowded store. There were three Dehillerin brothers, but Julia chose a good-looking salesman named Gaston as her on-camera guide, and they discussed the merits of copper versus aluminum pots, the care of wicker breadbaskets, and the best way to sharpen steel knives.

It was now mid-June, and "The French Chef in France" shoot was nearing its end. A few days in Normandy—to document roast duck, tripe, and Camembert cheese—were left. The "FCiF" had gone better than anyone could have hoped. "We have, like Pollyanna, the Glad Girl, much to be thankful for, but particularly that we have really excellent footage on certain classical techniques [that] have never before been filmed in this intimate and fascinating way," Paul wrote. "Most of them will die out within 25 years. So our films . . . will be all that's left to show how food was once processed by human beings rather than machines."

IX. THE BATTLE OF THE DUCK

On June 16, Julia, Paul, and Ruth Lockwood climbed into one of the white Peugeots and drove northwest to Rouen to film the scene Julia had been looking forward to for months: Monsieur Dorin and his silver duck press. Twenty-two years after her first meal in France—the life-defining lunch of *sole meunière*—Julia was returning to La Couronne to learn how to prepare *Canard à la Rouennaise*.

The plan was to eat dinner at 9:30, then start filming at midnight, after the last customer had left. Once they started they wouldn't be able to stop. As the Childs strolled to their hotel, the junior members of the "FCiF" team rolled to a stop. They looked shaken. Peter Hoving was buckled in pain, his left leg immobilized. "I'm not sure I can carry on," he said. "I've had this pain on and off the whole time we've been in France, but never anything like this . . ."

"We're going to the hospital," David Atwood said.

Julia was concerned but remained calm. Paul was aghast: the cameraman was "the beating heart and center of this whole expedition . . . and only now he tells us he has been having recurring pains."

Paul, Julia, and Ruthie decided to eat dinner and mention nothing to Monsieur Dorin until they knew more about Hoving's status. Finally, the restaurant's phone rang: X-rays showed that one of Hoving's vertebrae had been dislocated—probably by the heavy camera on his shoulder—which pinched a sciatic nerve and sent an excruciating charge down his leg.

It was a moment of crisis. The doctors told Peter to "lay off all camera work for six months." But the "FCiF" team was out of time. Paul and Julia decided to proceed with "The Battle of the Duck," come what may.

At 2:00 in the morning La Couronne's rustic dining room was sweltering from the summer heat, the roaring fire, a half dozen bright camera lights, and the crowd of anxious filmmakers, chefs, and waiters. Dorin had built a large, visually dramatic fire for the camera: as the heat

M. Dorin and the duck press at La Couronne

rose, it spun a fan that turned a gear and rotated the ducks, which had been basted in butter.

Suddenly, Peter Hoving, who had been given antipain injections at the hospital, appeared. Toting the heavy camera, he sat, stood, panned across the dining room, kneeled below a table, and gazed down on the fire from a ladder.

Julia and Dorin talked, cooked, and ate duck through the black night and into the blue-pink dawn. As Le Gros Horloge, the clock in the center of town, chimed 5:00 a.m., roosters crowed. The crew rolled up cables and placed their cameras and lights into padded travel cases. Their faces—flushed by the fire, the exertion, the wine and food—were cooled by a light breeze.

"Everybody feels great," Paul noted. "It may well be one of the most successful filming sequences we've done."

They slept until 11:00. Then, basking in the afterglow of the night's work, Ruthie, Julia, and Paul drove toward their final destinations. First, to the town of Thury-Harcourt, for "All About Tripe," and then to a Camembert cheese maker in Aunay-sur-Odon. On Friday, they would hold a wrap party in Caen, the famed capital of Lower Normandy, which was founded by William the Conqueror in the eleventh century and largely destroyed during the Allied landings in 1944.

Arriving in Thury-Harcourt, they were told to call the team in Rouen: "Peter has a hideous pain in his leg," Atwood reported. "He can't continue. He's flying to the hospital in Amsterdam this afternoon."

Boom! With that, "The French Chef in France" adventure ended. There was not enough time or money to find a replacement for Peter; and while the tripe and Camembert segments would have been instructive, they were not essential.

The exhausted crew had no energy for a wrap party and quickly dispersed. Ruthie Lockwood would arrive on Cape Cod by the morning. Willie Morton and his wife, Jane, would take a belated honeymoon through Europe. David and Nancy had plans to sightsee in Denmark. As for Paul and Julia? "We will be off at once, driving slowly southeast for the next five or six days, and will stop finally when we reach our little house. There we hope to have a fortnight's peace, though that is unlikely . . . damn it," Paul wrote, anticipating a showdown with *McCall's*. "I fear there will be little rest for us."

5

That's It

I. CLICK, CLICK, CLICK

The sudden loss of momentum from the pell-mell "FCiF" production left Julia and Paul in a disoriented limbo. But they didn't have the luxury to worry about it, for 527 miles to the south *McCall's* magazine had established a base camp in Plascassier manned by a half dozen staffers. Pressure was building for the Childs to return to La Pitchoune as soon as possible. The magazine, Knopf, and Simca were growing increasingly anxious about Julia's cooperation, or lack thereof, with Arnold Newman's photo shoot.

The Childs were resentful. When Paul suggested they avoid Plascassier altogether, and spend the next two weeks driving slowly and anonymously through the remote Massif Central, Julia snapped: "I am not going to be put out of my own house by any bunch of magazine people!"

They drove south, and when they arrived at La Pitchoune, they were dismayed to discover that Simca was uncharacteristically wan and despondent. She had visited the doctor for the first time in eight years, only to discover she was losing her hearing, suffered "valve trouble" in her heart, and had been recommended for a pacemaker.

Patrick O'Higgins, a charming and flamboyant *McCall's* editor, managed to talk his way into La Pitchoune. Almost the moment the Childs put down their bags, Arnold Newman and his assistants arrived and began setting up tripods, light boxes, reflectors, and cables in their living room.

"*Non!*" Julia declared. "No photos."

O'Higgins began to wheedle, but Paul shut him down: "Julia has been very clear about this from the start—"

"*Augghhhhh!*" The air was rent by a loud cry.

It was Simca. From a corner, she glared at Julia with a wounded look and tears streaming down her face. "I had my whole heart set on this picture of you and me together, and now you say '*no more photos,*'" she shouted. "How can you treat me like that?"

Julia stared at her old friend, dumbstruck. In two decades of collaboration Simca had never said anything like that before.

Perhaps Simca's outburst was due to worries about her health. Or maybe it was due to the illness itself, which can make people act in unpredictable and emotional ways. Or maybe it was Simca's belated discovery that her old friend had become a superstar in America, achieving a level of success that Simca would never achieve. Or the outburst might have been a delayed response to Julia's 1967 demand for a greater share of their royalty income from *Mastering.* Whatever the reason, Simca had put her two-decades-long collaboration with Julia on the line in front of a room full of journalists on the eve of the publication of their new book.

Julia glanced away and marinated in silent rage for a few minutes. Seeing no graceful exit, and trying to take the long view, she agreed to pose for Arnold Newman.

Sputtering with rage and hurt feelings, Paul sequestered himself in the little *cabanon* across the driveway, where he slashed paint across a canvas.

For the rest of the afternoon, Julia and Simca posed for photographs in the dining room and kitchen at La Pitchoune—*click, click, click.* In the resulting photos, Julia sits at the kitchen table with a weary half smile on her face, her head and body leaning away from Simca, who holds a sharp pencil up and tilts her body toward Julia. Arranged on the Peg-Board behind them is a row of knives.

The next day, *McCall's* took over the dining room in Rancurel's farmhouse down the hill, and turned it into a stage set for a *fête champêtre,* a "festival of rustic food." Rancurel, the farmer, and Boussageon, the butcher, cooked dishes—green herb soup, lamb in a brioche crust, potatoes Anna, sautéed zucchini, strawberry shortcake—from Volume II, and O'Higgins arranged them in platters on large tables. A dozen local

Julia and Simca posing for Arnold Newman

characters—including Jeanne, the cleaning lady; Laurent, the gardener; Lerda, the carpenter; Ceranta, the electrician—were recruited to pose as celebrants. As Newman shot roll after roll of film, the "patrons" ate and drank copiously, roared with laughter, and told lewd jokes. At the end of the feast, kids dabbed fingers into the fresh whipped cream, while the elders sang traditional songs in gravelly voices.

II. Volume II: Stepping into Contemporary Life

When *Mastering the Art of French Cooking*, Volume II, was published in October 1970—nine years after the original volume—Knopf printed one hundred thousand copies and mounted a major publicity campaign.

By that point *Mastering* had sold more than seven hundred thousand copies, and the publisher had high hopes for the follow-up book.

Food-world allies such as James Beard and Craig Claiborne trumpeted the arrival of Volume II. *McCall's* ran Patricia Simon's three-part series in their October, November, and December issues. And early reviews were mostly rapturous: "It is without rival, the finest gourmet cookbook for the non-chef in the history of American stomachs," Raymond Sokolov declared in *Newsweek*. "No serious scholar of the kitchen will want to function without it," Gael Greene wrote in *Life*. "Volume I was mud-pie stuff. With Volume II it is no longer mere Child's play."

But some found the book overly complicated. Volume II would appeal to those "who learn to drive a car by having the workings of the internal combustion engine explained to them in full detail," quipped Nika Hazelton in *The New York Times Book Review*.

In the foreword, the authors laid out their case for the second volume and contrasted it to the first: "Mastering any art is a continuing process . . . While Volume I was a long introduction to French cooking, [Volume II] is a continuation." *Mastering* had been a reflection of France in the 1950s and was written, the authors admitted, with "a rather holy and Victorian feeling about the virtues of sweat and elbow grease—that only paths of thorns lead to glory . . . and all that." But beating egg whites in a copper bowl, or pushing fish paste through a fine sieve for quenelles can be tedious and take the fun out of cooking, while a machine can do the same job much quicker. "Volume II, like France herself, has stepped into contemporary life," the authors wrote. Times had changed and so had Simca and, especially, Julia, whose distinct voice clearly emanates from the page.

The new book was written in a looser tone than the original. Child and Beck expanded on their idea of "theme and variation," encouraging their readers to apply basic approaches and techniques across a wide range of dishes. Occasionally the authors strayed from orthodoxy, adding curry to beef tongue here, or advocating the use of broccoli (almost unknown in France) there.

As with *Mastering*, the publisher regarded the second volume as a major work and lavished attention on design, type, and appendices crammed with arcana, such as three pages on "Stuffings for Meats and

Vegetables" and thirty-eight pages on Julia's *batterie de cuisine* (a "roundup of the kitchen equipment we find useful . . . solid, practical, professional equipment designed by people in the chef business who sell to chefs"). There is even a disquisition on bottle openers, corkscrews, and types of wineglasses ("the brandy snifter will release after-dinner esters").

The book was illustrated with technical drawings by Paul Child and instructional drawings by Sidonie Coryn, who produced thirty-four drawings just for French bread, and twelve for *pâté en croûte*. To ensure that the recipes in Volumes I and II reinforced each other, Knopf devised an index that tied the two books together, referencing items in Volume I in boldface and those in Volume II in plain type.

By the time Volume II was published, Julia and Simca had put their differences aside, and joined for a well-financed, carefully orchestrated book tour that took them from New York to Washington, D.C., and Virginia, then out to Portland, Oregon. In New York, they were celebrated at the Ford Foundation, where 250 "very swish" guests included Governor Nelson Rockefeller, the writer Ada Louise Huxtable, and other notables. It was a long way from the launch of *Mastering*, which Julia and Simca had promoted with a self-financed trip, during which they had stayed with friends across the country.

III. "The French Chef Faces Life"

Two weeks after Volume II was published, Season Two of *The French Chef* debuted in color on PBS stations, to produce a cross-promotional juggernaut of Julianalia. The first episode to air was the show on bouillabaisse, including the documentary footage shot in Marseille's Criée aux poissons marketplace. The early reviews were positive, which helped to boost book sales. Writing in the *San Francisco Chronicle*, Terrence O'Flaherty enthused:

> I really don't know how to explain Julia Child's appeal. She wasn't even cooking something I like. It was that loathsome assemblage of fish carcasses called bouillabaisse. Yet Mrs. Child has a wonderful way of catching the attention and holding it because she is doing something she likes to do and she does it better than anyone else around . . .

In the past seasons Mrs. Child's culinary adventures have been in black-and-white. Home viewers just had to take her word for it when the lobster bisque got the right shade for serving. The addition of color this year is a great help. The parsley is green, the cook's cheeks are a healthy pink, and her fingernails are orange. But I could be wrong. I'm on Cablevision and . . . its colors are never the same.

"Hoooray!" Julia crowed in relief.

The first problem cropped up two months later. As was revealed in *My Life in France*, Judith Jones met a doctor from Mount Sinai Hospital who was researching the suspected link between asbestos and cancer. Recalling that Volume II instructed readers to bake bread at home on "asbestos-cement tile," Jones immediately alerted the Childs, who were alarmed to think they might be endangering their readers. But the taping of Julia's two bread shows was just days away. While Julia was busy preparing her TV scripts, Paul rushed to experiment with a half dozen kinds of tiles. When Julia taped the bread shows, she suggested that people use basic red floor tile instead. Jones quietly altered the text in later printings of Volume II, and no one was the wiser until Julia told this story in her memoir.

Despite all of the authors' research on fish, the entire piscatory chapter—save a few fish soups—was cut from Volume II, to save time and space. This caused some heartache for Julia and Simca, especially over the loss of *Loup de Mer en Croûte*, the sea bass they had tasted at L'Oasis in 1969 with Patricia Simon. Both writers would return to that dramatic dish later in their careers. Nevertheless, the idea of wrapping protein in pastry stuck with them, and was evident in Volume II dishes such as *Filet de Boeuf en Croûte* (Tenderloin of Beef Baked in Pastry—Beef Wellington Brioche). "That whole idea just grew out of that experience that day" at L'Oasis, Julia recalled, explaining how one gastronomic experiment often led to another, and another.

Indeed, with Simca's tremendous productivity and Julia's doggedness, there were many recipes that did not make it into the pages of Volume II or onto television in 1970. The question hung in the air: What would happen to those orphaned ideas? After their rapprochement, Simca broached the idea of writing *Mastering the Art of French Cooking*,

Volume III. Judith Jones raised the same issue, writing to Julia: "Who knows, we may have a tetralogy before you are finished!"

It was a dilemma that weighed on Julia.

In the meantime, she continued to work on television. WGBH described Season Three of *The French Chef*, which aired from 1971 to 1972, as "a tour of the French classics": twenty-six half-hour programs designed as "a refresher course for experienced cooks and as a jet-assist takeoff for beginners." When Polaroid hesitated to fund Season Four, a public outcry helped convince them to underwrite the 1972 to 1973 season. Here Julia explained how to cope with the "demands of society," such as planning family dinners, getting kids excited about cooking, having unexpected company, or preparing three-course sit-down dinners. The title of this final season was, aptly enough, "The French Chef Faces Life."

IV. THE END

In June 1971, *Réalités*, a French magazine, sent a writer and photographer to La Pitchoune to interview Julia over lunch. Mindful of Simca's tender feelings, and intent on showing the world that they remained a harmonious team, Julia insisted that her co-author be included. She loved Simca as a friend, respected her as a talented cook, and remained grateful for the use of La Pitchoune. She promoted Simca's Parisian cooking classes, and coached her on public speaking (perhaps a bit too insistently: "You must polish up your English constantly . . . Listen to American radio programs, and read as much American as possible," Julia advised. "You just have to follow your recipes exactly, or your audience gets terribly confused . . . I know you are always saying you can't cook and talk at the same time—but YOU CAN, and YOU MUST . . . Practice looking happy . . . SMILE.")

For years, Julia had staunchly defended Simca against Paul's criticism—"I would strangle her if I were in Julia's position," he groused. But now Julia worried about her friend's increasing deafness and chronic heart problems, and was frazzled by her abrupt mood swings.

Even those who adored Simca, such as Richard Olney, an Iowa native who had become an exquisite Provençal cook, noted that her itchy restlessness, and affinity for *lutte* (strife), could be "irrational" at times. Simca had "a respect for French tradition coupled with a fascination for all that is new, a formal correctness of speech often seasoned with rather astonishing expletives, a fierce loyalty to friends, a determination that knows no bounds and sometimes irrationally refuses to recognize any barriers," Olney wrote. But, he added, Simca's drive could tilt into unhealthy, compulsive behavior. One day, "Simca slipped on the icy steps leading down from her house and broke a leg. She was found some time later, apparently indifferent to the pain but furious at the inconvenience, trying to pound the splintered and protruding bone back into place with the heel of her shoe so that she could get on with her business." Olney's story sounds apocryphal, except that Simca included it in her "memoir with recipes," *Food & Friends*, without comment.

"Julia and Simca had a very good partnership for twenty years," observed Judith Jones. But under the strain of producing Volume II, and Simca's growing resentment of Julia's celebrity, financial success, and bullheaded Americanness, the creative friction that had worked so well in the past was reduced to mere friction. "It began with the fight over cassoulet, and got worse," Jones added. "For Simca, it was unbearable to have Julia become a star of French cooking in America."

For her part, Julia resented being the workhorse and main salesperson for the *Mastering* franchise, and bridled at Simca's French dogmatism. "She wouldn't listen," Julia said. "*She* told *you* what was what."

Jones was discreet and respectful of the two cooks' friendship, but she could plainly see that their collaboration was in trouble. She encouraged Julia to prepare to go out on her own. "I warned her: 'It's going to happen,'" Jones recalled.

There was another factor at work. While Simca continued to teach cooking classes in her Paris apartment, Julia was chafing against what she called "the straitjacket of classical French cuisine." She was feeling an almost primal urge to stretch out in new culinary directions, to keep learning and pushing forward into terra incognita. But she had conflicted feelings about this, and was reluctant to bring it up.

The tipping point arrived on a hot day in July 1971. Jones sat at the Childs' kitchen table in Cambridge while Julia read a seven-page tirade from Simca aloud. "At a certain point, Simca's condescension grew unbearable," Jones said. "You could hear the tension rising in Julia's voice. It was remarkable."

Attacking a recipe that she herself had contributed to Volume II, Simca wrote, "*Ce n'est pas français!* You Americans cannot possibly understand that we French would never baste with beef drippings!"

Reaching the end of the letter, Julia stood up to her full six-foot-two-plus-inch height. Her eyes flashing with anger, she threw the letter to the floor and stomped on the pages with her size-twelve sneaker, shouting, "That's it—end of collaboration!"

JULIA AND SIMCA NEVER DISCUSSED the demise of their collaboration. They understood that after more than two decades, it was time for each to go her own way professionally. They were two strong-willed women with different styles in different countries who were moving at different speeds and in different directions with different goals. In retrospect, the split appears inevitable.

Jean-François Thibault, one of Simca's nephews, recalled that *La Super Française* had seen only a few minutes of *The French Chef,* and did not comprehend the power of television. "I was the one who relayed to her how famous Julia was, how important she was," said Thibault. "But she didn't really understand it." Thibault was close to both Simca, who "was like a cinema star—overbearing and elegant," and Julia, "the funniest, most lovable person in the world." As for the end of their collaboration, he said, "I wouldn't dare discuss it," but "there was not any tension. I think Simca understood." She "never expressed anything but love for her American 'sister,' even when she expressed regret at their parting of ways. When I inquired if she was sad about the many successes of Julia, she only replied: '*Oui, mais maintenant c'est une femme d'affaires*' ('Yes, but now she is a businesswoman')—which, in her mouth, sounded like a compliment."

Others saw the split in a different light. "Simca was hurt," said Judith Jones. "She just didn't understand what Julia had become. She expected to be treated with attention and a grand book tour, that sort of thing."

The hard truth was that Simca's star did not shine as brightly as Julia's. Simca would continue to teach and write cookbooks, but never repeated the success of the two *Mastering* books. And, arguably, neither did Julia, for those two volumes remain her most famous and best-selling books—though later works, such as *The Way to Cook, Julia and Jacques Cooking at Home*, and *My Life in France* were best sellers.

Simca declared that she wanted to slow down and devote herself to her husband, her garden, and cooking classes. But she was not really the slow-going type. Judith Jones helped to ease her out of Julia's direct orbit and into a solo career when Knopf published many of the recipes Simca had developed but not used in Volume II in a book published in 1972. Called *Simca's Cuisine* it was a mix of autobiographical stories and recipes from three regions of France that had shaped her cooking: Normandy, where she was raised; Alsace, where the Fischbachers originated; and Provence, where she and Jean had found their "greatest inspiration." Eager for Simca's culinary wisdom, but wary of Simca's lack of authorial discipline, Jones hired the *McCall's* writer Patricia Simon to help massage the text, test its recipes, and ensure the project was completed on schedule.

Julia was relieved, and grateful, that her colleague had landed on her feet. *Simca's Cuisine* "should be a very nice book, I would imagine, and I am so happy to have nothing whatsoever to do with it," she wrote Avis DeVoto. "It will be good for Simca, I think also, not to be associated with me, and to be quite on her own."

In the book Simca wrote her version of the breakup: "We had vowed, Julia and I, to terminate our collaboration—she to pursue her television program and other work, and I to devote myself to my private life. At the age of sixty-six, and after twenty-two years in the professional practice of the cuisine, I wanted a rest! But during the tour of cooking demonstrations . . . it seemed that a great many people were urging me to do one more book, a book all my own. I ended by taking the course of least resistance (and undoubtedly giving in most of all to my own real desire) in undertaking to write this little book—which would, finally and in truth be my last."

In fact, Simca would go on to publish two more books—*New Menus from Simca's Cuisine*, written with Michael James and published by Harcourt Brace Jovanovich in 1979; and *Food & Friends: Recipes and Memories from Simca's Cuisine*, written with Suzanne Patterson and published by Viking in 1991.

"After Julia, Simca never found the right collaborator," Jones sighed. Though *Simca's Cuisine* had sold about twenty-six thousand copies by 1977, Knopf had printed many more, and the editor had decided not to publish a second volume. In a carefully crafted letter, Jones explained to Simca: "I was struck by how little emphasis there was on new and different and somewhat experimental ideas; rather, I felt the recipes [in Simca's proposal for a second volume] were almost interchangeable with those in the first book . . . I just have serious doubts about how well we would do with it . . . So do pursue the Harcourt offer and know that you have my blessings."

What is remarkable about this difficult transition is that while Julia and Simca would never write another book together, they preserved their friendship. They continued to post a steady stream of letters across the Atlantic, and remained devoted neighbors in Provence until the end.

V. OUT OF STYLE, OUT OF STEP

On May 4, 1971, Julia narrated a version of *Tubby the Tuba*, accompanied by conductor Arthur Fiedler and the Boston Pops Symphony Orchestra. It was a glamorous affair before a live audience, and was taped for a PBS special. But after months of taping the final episodes for Season Two of *The French Chef*, Julia was worn out. The next day, she and Paul flew off to their quiet French retreat. Then Julia checked into a *clinique* in Cannes, where the skin on her fifty-eight-year-old face was tightened a bit (to preserve a youthful appearance for TV), far from America's prying eyes.

Stuck in bed without much to do, Julia took stock of her career, which had hit a perplexing juncture. In early June, she typed her thoughts out in letters to her confidants. While *Mastering*, Volume II, was doing well—Knopf had sold two hundred thousand copies by then—public reaction to Season Two of *The French Chef* had been muted, and she couldn't understand why. The new show had all of the right elements to make it a hit: it was shot in color for the first time, was expansive in scope with more episodes than ever, and it featured the novel "French Chef in France" documentaries. She had worked hard on those shows, and was proud of them. Yet the public seemed indifferent.

"Actually Paul and I are both a bit disappointed . . . the new series has really provoked little or no comment," Julia wrote to Ruth Lockwood. "Apart from the reaction to our very first show, there seems to have been no reaction whatsoever. We did engender some small amount on the bread shows, in the provinces, but nothing on the pressed duck, the puff pastry, or on really anything else—with or without the [French] inserts."

Julia puzzled over the dilemma as she typed: "Perhaps we aren't quite getting across. So why? This we must try and find out, because if we don't do better, there won't be another year. Are we trying to be too technical or booky? Are we losing the fun because we are too picky? Are we too complicated and talky? Or are we just getting out of step? (I will NOT do macrobiotics and vegetarianism, however.)"

She wrote a similar letter to Judith Jones: "I don't feel this year's shows have been particularly successful, at least they haven't raised even a ripple of comment, praise, or blame . . . The unifying force is the same old cook in the same old kitchen. That is perhaps why we have aroused no more interest, in spite of color and French inserts—essentially the same, so why talk about it."

Here Julia seemed to confront a previously unthinkable possibility: that the culture was shifting beneath her feet and America's infatuation with French cooking—and *The French Chef*—was becoming passé, in part because of forces she had unleashed. Though Julia remained a brightly shining star, she worried that the response to Season Two was a harbinger of professional mortality.

"I am quite aware that there comes a time when one is frankly out of style, out of step, and had better fold up and steal away," she wrote Jones. But then she seemed to catch herself sounding maudlin, and stiffened her spine: "However, I shall certainly hang on with full vigor for the time being."

Julia was restless and, perhaps unconsciously, preparing to shift her career in what Jones called "new and different and somewhat experimental" directions.

JULIA WAS NOT the only one whose restless energy was shifting in experimental directions that June. Just up the road a darker spirit prevailed in Villefranche-sur-Mer, a seaside resort between Nice and Monaco, where the Rolling Stones had "exiled" themselves to record a new album. On the run from British tax authorities, Keith Richards had rented Villa Nellcôte, a stately mansion twenty-five miles east of La Pitchoune, and turned the basement into a studio. A growing tribe of musicians, engineers, producers, drug dealers, writers, and hangers-on—Gram Parsons, Bobby Keys, Mick Taylor, William S. Burroughs, Terry Southern—along with the wives, girlfriends, and children of the band, turned Villa Nellcôte into a den of Fellini-esque debauchery. Playing loudly through the night for months on end, the Stones created their seminal double album *Exile on Main St.*, which was released in May 1972. Mick Jagger called it "fucking mad" and "not good," but others have deemed *Exile* one of the greatest rock 'n' roll albums ever. While Julia Child characterized one aspect of the seventies, the Stones embodied another—the manic, dangerous, sexy, hallucinogenic weirdness of the time—a few miles away.

VI. A Summation

In December 1972, Julia finished taping Season Two of *The French Chef* and began to contemplate her first solo project since *The French Chef Cookbook*. Perhaps, she thought, it was time to shift her focus back home. After all, she was living in Massachusetts, and had family roots stretching back to colonial days; her audience was American; and she was cooking all kinds of foods at home. But how best to give form to this vague idea?

One of the first ideas the Childs pitched to WGBH was a TV cooking show before a live audience. For years Julia had given demonstrations for crowds that could swell to more than a thousand people. She loved the electric energy of live performance, the back-and-forth banter, using real knives and flame and producing real smoke and smells, to teach flesh-and-blood people who liked to cook and eat real food. Things could, and often did, go wrong onstage. Audiences were thrilled as Julia recovered from mistakes—adding a dash of olive oil to save a separating sauce, or plastering a delaminating cake together with extra frosting—to make everything turn out right, more or less, in the end.

But director-producer Russ Morash wasn't sold: "We can do it," he wrote. "The question really is, should we?" He didn't think a live cooking show would make consistently compelling television, and he worried there were too many ways it could go wrong.

When Julia suggested a program in which she would cook with well-known professional chefs, David Ives, president of WGBH, turned her down: "I have doubts that such cooks could come up to your standards as television personalities," he wrote. (Julia moved on, though her instinct about this would be validated: in 1993, her show *Cooking with Master Chefs* was nominated for an Emmy Award; the 1996 follow-up series, *In Julia's Kitchen with Master Chefs*, won Julia her second Emmy.)

Feeling stymied, the Childs put their heads together and composed a list of ideas they labeled "10 Possibilities for a New Julie-Special Show." A close reading reveals the Child team's preoccupations in midcareer. It included: a look at their life at La Pitchoune, with a peek at Julia's kitchen "laboratory," Paul's photography, and guests such as James Beard, M. F. K. Fisher, and Richard Olney; a visit to Charlie and Freddie (Fredericka) Child's cabin on the coast of Maine, featuring Julia on a lobster boat, Paul and his twin building an art studio, and a view of local maritime history; life in Cambridge—its history and food, and the Childs' remarkable group of neighbors; a tour of the SS *France*, with an emphasis on the liner's haute cuisine; a behind-the-scenes look at The Four Seasons Restaurant in New York, a gastronomic mecca; "From Ocean to Gullet," a documentary about the procuring and eating of fish, from the Grand Banks cod fishery to fly-fishing for trout in a Wyoming creek; "The Beef Cycle" (aka "From Range to Range"), in which Julia would follow a single cow from a ranch in Montana to cattle train, slaughter, processing, selling, buying, cooking, and eating (an idea that presaged contemporary endeavors, such as Michael Pollan's celebrated article "Power Steer" in *The New York Times Magazine*); and "How a *French Chef* Program Is Made," in which Julia would take her audience behind the scenes at WGBH as she shopped, cooked, taped, ate, cleaned up, publicized, and fund-raised for a typical episode.

Most intriguing to Julia was the notion of a "Cross-Country Culinary Tour," which, in the spirit of "The French Chef in France," would follow her on an adventurous tour of regional cooks and specialties in the United States: from John Bennett's restaurant in Oklahoma City to a streamside lunch on a Rocky Mountain pack trip; from a chitlin-and-hog-jowl dinner in Harlem to a poolside party at a Pasadena mansion. It was to be an ambitious and expensive idea, which is probably why it was never green-lighted.

Each of these ideas had potential, but none of them gained traction at WGBH. Yet such brainstorming had been the Childs' modus operandi for years, and they trusted that it would eventually lead them to an answer. "We put down *anything* we could dream up because any one of these might strike a spark in somebody else's mind that could lead to the kind of spectacular blaze we want," Paul wrote.

BY THE SPRING of 1973, Julia was honing the conception of a new book. It would be a transitional work: starting with a handful of recipes from Season Two of *The French Chef* not used in Volume II of *Mastering*—including dishes such as pressed duck and chickpea pancakes that she investigated in the "FCiF" documentaries—she would expand her vision beyond classical French cuisine to encompass dishes from the United States and around the world. To some, this seemed a radical shift, but to Julia it was a natural evolution.

In a 1966 *Life* profile, Julia said, "I personally will never do anything but French cooking. There are so many marvelous French recipes, I don't think I'll ever live long enough to do them all." But with the benefit of a dozen years of experience, she said, "I'm tired of French cooking. It's too limiting."

The more she widened her gastronomic scope, the more she delved deeply into "tangents, comments, anecdotes, personal trials and discoveries," until her new work became a "rather large and rambling book—a summation, really, of my 25 years in the kitchen . . . a personal meander."

With this notion in mind, Julia began to pitch potential titles for the book to Knopf, including: *The French Chef, Book II; From the French Chef's Kitchen;* or *Straight Talk from the French Chef's Kitchen.* She told Ives—"rather cavalierly," she'd later admit—that she aimed to publish her latest work in the fall of 1974. This delivery date was off by months. But the resulting book would prove a major turning point in Julia's career: the most difficult and personal cookbook she would ever write.

It was called *From Julia Child's Kitchen,* and its publication in 1975 marked a watershed. It seemed to release Julia from Phase One of her career and herald Phase Two. In the second half of the seventies, she broke from classical French cuisine to embrace foods of the world, examined the recipes of her colonial forebears, and intentionally re-Americanized herself. Julia Child was sixty-three years old and was at last discovering her true voice.

Part II

The French Chef in America

"The destiny of nations depends on the manner in which they nourish themselves."
—JEAN BRILLAT-SAVARIN, *The Physiology of Taste*, 1825

6

From Julia Child's Kitchen

I. An American Point of View

In her new book, *From Julia Child's Kitchen*, Julia broadened her repertoire to include a few French classics, like *salade niçoise* and *madeleines*, in
a multicultural cornucopia of hamburgers, coleslaw, New England fish
chowder, turkey, pizza, curried beef, Bombay duck, Oriental chicken,
spiced Belgian cookies, and so on.

Aside from the recipes, the most obvious departure was the author's
voice. Judith Jones suggested that Julia tell personal stories in her new
book. This would have the dual effect of distancing her from the past
with Simca and *The French Chef*, while bringing a new energy and a
warmer, more intimate tone to the work.

But writing about herself in the first person singular—as "I"—did
not come naturally to Julia. She was congenitally modest, and preferred
to deflect questions than to crow about herself. This trait was endearing, though it could be challenging for her collaborators—as I learned
in working on her memoir, when she would deflect my questions about
her life to ask about my life. In a typical note, Julia wrote to Judith Jones
in 1981: "For our next book it would be nice to have . . . *no photo of cook*,
except perhaps a small one on the back cover. I'm tired of such photos,
and would rather see food for a change."

"She didn't like the me-me-me-ness of celebrity," Jones explained.

In general, writing did not come easily to Julia. While she used
expressive language—*"plop," "wham," "OUF!"*—she did not have the
intuitive and fluid way with words that Paul did. She and her siblings

were affected by a set of mild learning issues related to dyslexia, which they referred to as "the family curse." Julia worked hard to make her writing clear and distinctive, and she relied on Paul and Jones for editorial assistance. Her struggle to find a comfortable first-person voice "was difficult," Julia admitted to the *Chicago Tribune.* "But Judith coaxes the writer out of you."

The voice Julia settled on was genuine and unpretentious but also, in turns, knowledgeable, humorous, opinionated, self-confident, occasionally revealing, and always encouraging. She wrote:

> Where the other books are almost entirely French in their inspiration, this one has burst out into other directions . . . Although my formal culinary training was entirely French . . . I always look at French cuisine from an American point of view: How can we make that pastry here? . . . How can we make that French bread, or that chick-pea pancake? . . . I've gone into experiments with the pressure cooker . . . the micro-wave oven, and the electric super-blender-food-processor . . . I am, in other words, putting my cooking vocabulary to work in all directions. I hope, in turn . . . to encourage the same attitude in you, my fellow cook.

Julia spoke to her audience directly in these pages, as if through the fourth wall: "The only way to begin cooking is to start right in, and *Mousse au Chocolat* is a small treasure of culinary basics," she wrote. "This recipe, then, I am directing at those of you who are new to cooking . . . Mastery of this operation opens up endless vistas of soufflés, cakes, *mousselines*, *roulades*, and even *bûches de Noël*. What better way is there to learn five fundamentals of *la cuisine universelle*, and to eat them too?"

Julia had done a tremendous amount of research into cooking basics: how to make hamburger taste like something more than random beef scraps molded into a patty (grind your own chuck, and cook it with shallots and cream); how to Americanize a *bûche de Noël* (decorate it with American flags and a mini ax for George Washington's birthday, or sparklers for the Fourth of July); the proper method of consuming spaghetti Marco Polo ("It's more fun with chopsticks, and they truly eat spaghetti that way in China; I've seen them do it."); or how to deal with a snob who frowns on pairing wine with eggs (give him a carafe of chilled

"*Château la Pompe*," or plain pump [tap] water, and there will be more Pouilly-Fuissé left for you).

She could wax lyrical about foods she adored, but made sure to circle back to earth: "A touch of aspic is a touch of magic. It can turn a plain poached egg into a glittering *oeuf en gelée*, a naked chicken into a *poulet en chaud-froid* . . . and a modest poached fish into a glistening poem . . . The effect is so dazzling you would think only a professional could execute it until you realize that the complex-looking whole is but an assembling of standard parts."

Julia was not afraid to state blunt opinions: "If truth in packaging were truly enforced, frozen spinach would be labeled 'Branch Water & Leaves.'" Or, "The greatest block to the self-teaching of meat cuts . . . has been the fanciful nomenclature used by markets . . . This [is a] ridiculous, confusing, and frequently deceptive state of affairs."

Julia's enthusiasm steeled the nerves of thousands of readers. To make French bread in the home oven, she noted, required the dough to rise over a minimum of seven hours: "That sounds horrendous to the non-cook—7 hours! Ye gods!" she wrote. "But you're not standing around holding it by the hand all this time. No. You are out shopping, but remembering to come back on time; or you are teaching a course in croquet, or you are playing the flute—and the dough takes care of itself . . . In other words, you are the boss of that dough."

One of Julia's most endearing traits was to admit her own mistakes. She bemoaned her aptitude for collapsing apple desserts, acknowledging that "every one of them has been my own fault because I chose the wrong kind of apple." This led to a recitation of her "sad" errors. A beautiful apple charlotte sagged because she had "stupidly" used juicy apples that did not hold the dessert upright. On another occasion Julia made a tarte tatin, a gorgeous upside-down, caramelized-apple confection, on TV. Feeling chuffed that she had developed a new method for preparing the dish in a cast-iron pan and dramatically unmolding it on a platter, she ignored Ruth Lockwood's suggestion to practice the dessert before taping the show. "No tricks," she declared. "I want people to see the whole tart just as it would be at home. There won't be any problems!" But when she flipped the pan too soon, she produced a puddle of beige mush. To save the day, she scooped the apple mess into a pile, sifted powdered sugar over it, and browned it under the broiler. "*Voilà!*" she

"Cooking up a storm": Julia and Simca make a sole mousse with crawfish butter sauce for *Vogue*, December 1968.

trumpeted—though, in truth, she was annoyed with herself for appearing unprofessional.

Sometimes Julia "failed" on purpose, to make a teaching point. When she demonstrated mayonnaise, for instance, she would allow the sauce to thicken but then add a large dollop of olive oil. This thins out the mixture; if allowed to sit, the soft yellow mass turns into broken curds separated by rivulets of oil—"a dreadful sight that looks particularly fine in a close-up view on color television," Julia chuckled. To save the mayo, she explained, you need only to beat teaspoons of the turned sauce with Dijon mustard in a warm mixing bowl. "The contrast of those miserable curds side by side with the thick yellow reconstituted sauce coming into being beside it, is sheer drama."

When Julia's grocer said that long, thin, female eggplants taste the best, and that one can tell the female by its smooth bottom, she "confidently gave this bit of lore over the air, and was roundly scolded by letter afterward," Julia acknowledged. "There is no such thing as sex in fruit." Yet when she informed her grocer of the mistake, he shrugged and said, "Maybe so. But the long, thin eggplants with the smooth bottoms are still the best. We call them female." To which Julia added, "So there!"

There were times when Julia found herself nonplussed by fans, like the "nutty woman" she met, appropriately, in the fruitcake section of the supermarket. "I love the way you cook your green beans," the woman said, "but I only do it your way on weekends [because] I want to be sure of getting all my vitamins."

Then there was the couple who could not wrap their heads around Julia's instruction to "fluff the rice lightly with a fork." "What does that mean, 'fluff with a fork'?" he asked. "It's in *Webster's Collegiate*," Julia responded. "'Fluff,' a verb." "I don't think you should use words like that," he said. "Well," Julia replied, "if neither you nor your wife can find out how to fluff with a fork, you'll never be able to cook rice."

And she poked fun at scolds. When she dared stray from classical French cooking into curries or paella, she was attacked by "angry nationalistic chauvinists." Her most vociferous critics were the "Italian anti-defamation league," who, with "blood in their eye and fury in their ears," called her an ignoramus and demanded a public apology for suggesting that lasagna could be made in a French way. In such cases, Julia resorted to form letters: "We should be thankful to the Italians for having invented lasagna-shaped pasta, and to the French for their fine cooking methods that make such a splendid dish possible." Then she slipped her lasagna recipe into the envelope. Pleased by her "masterful rebuttal," Julia never received a reply.

Like her shows about cooking rabbit, roasting a whole pig, or preparing calf's brains, veal, or tripe, Julia's lobster "murder" raised a hue and cry from aggrieved humanitarians. "I saw your show where you were cooking a lobster and I couldn't believe your cruelty when you cut it up alive and struggling," read a typical complaint. "Don't be so cruel to an animal, and don't tell me that he died within a few seconds so what does it matter? It matters plenty!" Julia found herself sending out dozens of form letters in response: "That was not a live lobster . . . we killed him 2 hours before the show," she wrote. "The only alternative to killing animals for food is to be a complete vegetarian; just because one has not personally participated in the assassination of a steer for one's beefsteak does not mean one is free of guilt. And now it appears that plants have feelings."

She consulted the Massachusetts State Lobster Hatchery to get to the bottom of proper crustacean dispatching, "with no shillying around the murder aspects." Plunging a knife into the lobster's brain or tail causes suffocation, she learned, while setting the cephalopods in cold water and slowly bringing them to a boil led to drowning. *The most humane way to deal with live lobsters,"* Julia concluded, "is to plunge them headfirst and upside down into boiling water. Since their circulatory functions are centered at the back of the head, they die within a few seconds."

From Julia Child's Kitchen wasn't all bubbly comedy or cold-blooded instruction: for the first time, Julia told personal stories, including a reminiscence of one of her earliest taste memories. In 1926, when Julia was fourteen, the McWilliamses took a family trip from Pasadena to Tijuana, Mexico, just south of the border. It was a place where Americans could drink forbidden beer and cocktails during Prohibition, listen to marimba, and "gamble wickedly" at the casino. Word had spread to Los Angeles, and soon Hollywood celebrities were driving down to enjoy the good life in Tijuana. One of the allures was Caesar salad.

Caesar Cardini was an Italian immigrant who owned a restaurant in Tijuana. On July 4, 1924, a crush of tourists depleted his pantry, and Cardini made do with whatever leftovers he could find: romaine lettuce, olive oil, lemon juice, eggs, Worcestershire sauce, croutons, garlic, Parmesan cheese, and black pepper. He carefully composed a salad, using only the best leaves, and then—with a flourish—tossed the ingredients together tableside, turning them over and over, "like a large wave breaking," Julia wrote. When the McWilliams family visited, "Caesar himself rolled the big cart up to the table [and] tossed the romaine in a great wooden bowl," Julia recalled. "I can see him break 2 eggs over that romaine and roll them in, the greens going all creamy as eggs flowed over them." He encouraged his guests to pick each romaine leaf up by the stem and eat it with their fingers. "What a great idea!" enthused Julia (who instructed her nieces and nephews to eat asparagus with their fingers). "What fun for television."

Julia championed "modern machines" in this book, especially mixers of various ilks. Referring to the old French recipes that instructed pastry chefs to beat butter and sugar with a wooden spoon, then add eggs, one by one, and beat each one to create a sweet froth, Julia—who had once aspired to becoming a famous novelist—slipped into a fictional reverie. She imagined a cook's exhausted helper, "sitting on a stool in a dark corner, her bowl between her knees, her poor little arm beating, beating, beating, a wisp of hair escaping from her mussy white cap. Every once in a while cook gives her a contemptuous look and orders her to beat even faster and more vigorously."

But then she snapped back to the present: "Those cakes took grueling hours to make, while a mixer does the same work in a few minutes." Julia dismissed those who quavered that "a cake is just not the same when made with an electric mixer," and diagnosed them with bramble bush syndrome: "It's no good unless it hurts." In her all-American mode, Julia teased, "Let these romantics make their cakes by hand, then, while we go to heights unheard of, by machine."

Yet, wary of romanticizing the "new," Julia admitted to her mechanical misadventures: "I used my microwave a lot for cooking when I first got it . . . Now I rarely cook in it. I defrost frozen bones, stocks, egg whites, and bread; I warm a chilled glass of milk . . . I use it for melting chocolate and softening butter, for drying out wet newspapers . . . I have learned . . . to never leave the oven in operation when I am not right in the kitchen, since . . . an overcooked fully dried-out newspaper will catch fire. That latter lesson cost me thirty-five dollars in oven repairs."

Julia reflecting on her most personal cookbook

In keeping with the personal tone, Jones wanted to call the book *From Julia's Kitchen*, but the author demurred: "People won't know who 'Julia' is," she said. "Of *course* they will!" the editor retorted, trying not to laugh. In the end, they opted for the more formal *From Julia Child's Kitchen*.

Julia's great hope was that readers would use this book as a "private cooking school." She structured each recipe as a class, and included personal anecdotes and bits of advice, as if she were standing next to you, kibitzing. "No one is born a great cook, one learns by doing," she assured readers. "This is my invariable advice to people: Learn to cook—try new recipes, learn from your mistakes, be fearless, and above all have fun!" Julia wrote those cheerful words in 1974 to encourage her readers, and herself. For it had been a significant and trying year.

11. Good Food Is Also Love

In April 1974, Julia wrote Simca a gloomy letter about the state of the world: Simca's gardener, Jeanne, was in poor health; the popular president of France, Georges Pompidou, had died in office; wars raged in Vietnam and the Middle East; President Nixon's scandals had led to a loss of public trust in the U.S. government; a photograph of Patty Hearst holding a machine gun had scandalized Julia's California friends (many of whom knew the Hearst family); overpopulation was a problem; and she worried about the "general aura of nameless terror."

In June 1974, after nearly eleven years of performing as "the French Chef," Julia had decided to retire that persona and move on to a new stage in her career. The decision had been a long time coming. WGBH was shocked, and tried to talk her back into the studio: "Your decision . . . came as a surprise. I had understood you were open to considering diverse possibilities," wrote the station's vice president and TV manager, Michael Rice. But Julia held firm: "We wish to terminate *The French Chef* series as far as new programs are concerned," she wrote. (Season One of the show aired from 1963 through 1966, when it went into reruns; Season Two aired from 1970 through 1973. Season Three ran from 1971 through 1972. And Season Four ran from 1972 through 1973. In total, *The French Chef* encompassed some three hundred episodes over a decade.) In the meantime, Julia devoted herself to polishing *From Julia Child's Kitchen*.

In August, the Childs took a working vacation at La Pitchoune, and invited Jim Beard to join them. It was the first time they had visited their little house at the height of the Provençal summer, and they suffered in the hundred degree heat. Beard, who was overweight and had a weak heart, looked pale, felt terrible, and medicated himself with iced Champagne.

Early one morning, Paul was awakened by a suddenly gushing nosebleed that spattered the white sheets with ruby splotches. This was odd and inconvenient, but he didn't pay much attention to it; everyone gets a nosebleed, after all. Just to be safe Paul spoke to a local doctor, who advised him to apply ice to his nose and keep his head tilted back. He did, and the bleeding stopped.

Perhaps his nasal gusher had been unleashed by the revelations in Washington, D.C., of President Nixon's "dirty tricks" campaign against Democrats. On August 9, after the Watergate hearings and facing imminent impeachment, President Richard M. Nixon became the only U.S. president to resign from office. This kind of news got Paul exercised.

A week later, Julia celebrated her sixty-second birthday with a dinner party on the terrace at La Peetch. The nine guests that night included Beard, Richard Olney—the irritable American writer who lived on a nearby hillside and was an expert on Provençal cuisine—and Simca, whom Olney regarded as a truer French chef than Julia. Julia made a birthday feast of roasted leg of lamb, and a dessert she had been trying to get right for weeks, a *tarte au citron* (lemon tart), which she deemed "marvelous."

It was a festive party and everyone was genuinely at ease, a fact worth mentioning only because of the Childs' private homophobia. Beard and Olney were gay; so was the *New York Times* restaurant critic Craig Claiborne; and the Childs' Provençal neighbors, the writers Sybille Bedford and Eda Lord, were a couple; M. F. K. Fisher was bisexual. So it is surprising that Julia and Paul had privately denigrated homosexuals as "fairies" and *pedals* (or *pedalos*, crude French slang for homosexuals) for years. Such language strikes a bafflingly discordant note from a couple who had few prejudices. Julia wrote to Simca that a mutual friend was "distressed that good cooking seems to be the province of the *pedals* to too large an extent, and that will discourage other people—including real male men. I agree with her. It is like the ballet, filled with homosexuals, so no one else wants to go into it."

There is no simple way to explain Julia and Paul's homophobia, except as a function of their generation, their ignorance, and their experience. Paul was trim and fit, a natty dresser who favored a turquoise ring, spoke fluent French, wrote poetry with a fountain pen, and was a gourmet. Some observers considered these attributes effeminate. When Senator Joseph McCarthy's henchmen accused Paul of being homosexual in 1955, he laughed off the question, and Julia wrote Avis DeVoto: "Homosexuality. Haw Haw. Why don't they ask the wife about that one?" Yet, the accusation left the "taste of ash" in Paul's mouth, and was part of the reason he took an early retirement from the diplomatic service. Julia, meanwhile, was a tall, loud, self-confident woman who was attractive but not classically beautiful. She wielded a Thor-size mallet and used a serrated "fright knife" the size of Excalibur to pound, cleave, and eviscerate her work. To some she appeared manly, and they suspected she was a lesbian.

According to family members, Paul and Julia were very much in love and had a healthy physical relationship. I knew the Childs to be tolerant, generous people who embraced unconventional friends wherever they went, and had great empathy. (I witnessed Julia speak to a homeless man on the street one day and an official from the George W. Bush White House the next: she treated them in exactly the same way, peppering each with questions and listening intently to their answers.)

Julia was a flirt who liked "red-blooded men," as she put it. She admired not just male physicality, but the "mental male," by which she meant the self-confidence and clear thinking of men, as opposed to the emotional changeability of women—herself included. "Thank God there are two sexes!" she wrote Avis. Julia rejoiced at macho foreign correspondent/food writers, such as R. W. "Johnny" Apple Jr., at *The New York Times*. When William Rice was named *The Washington Post*'s food editor in 1972, she wrote, "I'm all for having MEN in these positions; it immediately lifts it out of the housewifery Dullsville category and into the important things in life!"

Sometimes Julia's weakness for male charm and machismo blinded her to discomfiting realities. When her lawyer, Bob Johnson—who aggressively pushed Knopf and WGBH for more favorable contracts— died of pneumonia at age forty-five, in 1986, Julia was shocked to learn that he had lived a closeted gay life and had, in fact, succumbed to AIDS.

It was AIDS that led Julia to a change of heart. She was heartbroken when beloved friends suffered "months of slow and frightening agony." At an AIDS benefit in Boston, she said, "But what of those lonely ones? The ones with no friends or family to ease the slow pain of dying? . . . Food is of very special importance here. Good food is also love."

III. A Lion on Mouse Feet

Over the summer of 1974, Paul, now seventy-two, was quietly suffering chest pains on a daily basis. He didn't bother to mention them to Julia right away. Looking back, he realized they had started in 1967 as slight moments of pinching discomfort that would come and go. He mentioned them in passing to his doctor, who congratulated Paul on having "the heart of an athlete in his thirties," so he had ignored them. But then he had suffered the nosebleeds of August. When he returned to Cambridge in October, Paul scheduled a checkup at Mount Sinai Hospital.

When the doctor learned of the nosebleeds and chest pains, he immediately sent Paul to the intensive care unit. Was Paul suffering a heart attack? No one could say for sure: his cholesterol was fine, and so was his blood pressure. But after a series of tests it became clear that two of his major arteries were blocked.

"It wasn't a roaring lion of a heart attack, such as you see in the movies," Paul wrote to his twin. Rather, it was an infarction, a slow but steady blockage of the blood vessels leading to his heart that snuck up "on tiny padded feet, like a field mouse."

In 1974 the heart bypass was a relatively new procedure. The doctors removed veins from Paul's leg and used them to replace the clogged veins around his heart. The operation was deemed a technical success. But it came at a cost.

"WHAM," Julia reported to Simca. "Recovery is slow, but if he had not had this operation he would probably be dead, or at least moribund . . . It will take 6 months at least to get him back on his feet, but when that occurs, he should be just fine. Thus we are making no plans at all."

It is unclear exactly what happened during the surgery, but it appears that Paul suffered a lack of oxygen to his brain. He was kept in a hospital bed, trussed in tubes, for weeks. Julia visited him daily, sometimes twice a day. She remained strong and patient in public, but alone in their big house she lamented that Paul had lost much of his dexterity, confused numbers and names, could no longer speak fluent French, and that his beautiful flowing script had deteriorated into jittery scratches and inkblots. This was an agonizing state of affairs for a physical man, an artist who had devoted himself to "the clarity of perception and expression." My mother, Erica Child Prud'homme, recalled: "I wore a yellow shirt one day, and Paul said, 'Oh, I love that shirt that is . . . the color of daffodils.' He couldn't remember the word 'yellow.' It was alarming."

Julia kept hoping against evidence that Paul would have a miraculous recovery and life would go on as it always had. There were weeks when every letter she wrote sounded a hopeful, upbeat theme: "Paul is a little better . . . ," she'd say, or "he's regaining strength slowly . . ." But eventually Julia acknowledged that his recuperation was slow, "like a snail," and that he might not recover soon, if ever.

Paul spent more than a month in the hospital recovering from his ten-hour bypass surgery in October 1974. His voluminous correspondence stopped cold for weeks, and resumed only as short, meandering notes to immediate family members. Julia was heartbroken. "It was a *very* difficult time," Judith Jones remembered. "Julia didn't like to talk about it."

IV. The Team

Julia was always careful to use "we" rather than "I" in talking about her career. Paul had been her original inspiration and mentor, and was essential to her success. In *The French Chef Cookbook*, Julia thanked him thus: "Paul Child, the man who is always there: porter, dishwasher, official photographer, mushroom dicer and onion chopper, editor, fish illustrator, manager, taster, idea man, resident poet, and husband."

Later, she'd say, "Not everybody realizes that Paul and I are a team, and that we work together on developing menus and dishes."

When they hosted dinner parties, Paul and Julia would plan a menu and shop together; she would cook, while he chopped vegetables, set the table, made cocktails, poured wine, and helped with serving; at the end of an evening, they would share pot scrubbing, floor-mopping, and trash removal. "We always finished our individual tasks at the same time—because, I suppose, we did everything that was to be done together," Julia said. "Two are so much faster than one."

He was always there for her, and she for him, but they also knew when to give each other space. "We each need long, silent times by ourselves, and it's worked out awfully well," Julia said. "We agree on just about everything. I think I'm more social than Paul. I enjoy big parties, he doesn't. But we don't fight about it. We like the same friends."

Julia described the institution of marriage as a "lovely intertwining of life, mind, and soul," and asserted that she was content as a housewife: "I think the role of a woman is to be married to a nice man and enjoy her home. I can't think of anything nicer than homemaking." She fondly recalled that in all their years of living abroad, she and Paul were rarely apart: "We had a happy marriage because we were together all the time."

These are appealing sentiments, and they were genuine. But once Julia became a celebrity the day-to-day reality of the Childs' marriage

Dinner at La Pitchoune, July 1967 (*left to right:* Ruth Lockwood,
Jean Fischbacher, Arthur Lockwood, James Beard, Simca Beck)

Judith and Evan Jones in front of the fire at La Pitchoune
in the early seventies

grew more complex. There was a tension inherent between her wish to be a good wife and her professional ambitions. The first required selflessness while the latter required selfishness; maintaining a balance wasn't easy.

Beneath her modest exterior, Julia was a very determined person who loved to work hard and was energized by success. Cookery was not merely a pastime to her: it was a vocation and a nearly religious calling. She had found her raison d'être in Paris and never deviated from it, though she denied she was goal oriented. "I'm not driven. I'm enjoying what I do, and I don't have any great ambitions," she said. "I'm lucky to be in this profession that I just adore."

With all due respect, she *was* driven and ambitious. She had to be. One doesn't stumble into the kind of remarkable career she had in books, television, magazines, newspapers, and live performance, or invent and reinvent oneself as often and as successfully as she did—especially as a woman of that era—unless one is focused on doing so.

Julia's professional obligations dictated how and where she and Paul spent their time. This could mean working twelve to sixteen hours a day at home or in the TV studio, rising before dawn to perform live cooking demonstrations in far-flung cities, or undertaking cross-country book tours, transatlantic cruises on the *Queen Elizabeth*, or visits to the White House. She felt guilty about ignoring Paul, and made sure to include him and take care of him as much as she could. The two of them occasionally slipped away to "recharge the batteries" in Maine or California or France. But most of their time was devoted to the care and feeding of Julia Child, Inc.

Paul was content with this arrangement. He was proud of Julia's success, and happy that she was the public face of the team while he remained in the background. This is one of the most remarkable aspects of the Childs' marriage. While Julia was naturally social, Paul was a quiet observer who trained himself to be an effective public speaker, writer, and editor. "My whole life has been concerned with communication," he explained. "Communication is the glue that holds people together . . . it's the mortar of civilization's structure."

While in the Foreign Service, Paul was the "senior" member of the Child team; after his retirement, he took care of the less glamorous side of things. He was a dedicated gardener and was handy with broken lamps, leaky toilets, or caulking around the furnace. He had a sophisticated eye, and helped Julia—who was not an especially visual person—style her dining tables and the sets of her TV shows. "'Paul,' was my frequent plea, 'this platter of vegetables just doesn't look right,'" Julia recalled. "And with a few deft movements he'd almost always manage to transform it."

At home, Julia could be found in the kitchen on the first floor, or in her office on the second floor. While she loved the "big, rambling Victorian house" on Irving Street, she did not care for vacuuming, bed making, or other non-culinary housework. She liked to have cut flowers on the table, particularly roses, but had a brown thumb in the garden. (Julia complained bitterly about Simca's habit of buying lots of plants for Bramafam, then leaving for Paris and expecting Julia to water them. Julia couldn't be bothered, so Paul did the job.) Julia loved animals, especially *"poussiquettes"*; while she kept a cat named Minette ("Pussycat" in French) in Paris in the fifties, she was too busy thereafter to keep a permanent feline in residence; she would temporarily adopt local farm cats while at La Pitchoune.

There were times when Julia grew wistful about not having a child and grandchild, as her siblings did, and commiserated with Simca about their lack of progeny. Yet, Julia acknowledged that had she conceived she would have devoted her energy to her children and would not have had the career that she did.

Paul was Julia's first reader and toughest critic. He pushed her to write clearly and originally, without cliché, and to say exactly what she meant. For most of his life, he was a prolific writer of letters, journals, date books, and poetry. Paul wrote hundreds of words a day, usually in longhand, in a clear flowing script, in blue, black, or green ink. He recorded mundane details and globally significant events with equal fervor: noting the pink socks on a clothesline in Paris, the price of Champagne on a Wednesday in 1952, the internal politics of the U.S. Consulate in Marseille, the impact of the Cold War on German civilians, the subtleties of Norwegian humor, and the sounds of Julia cooking—as if to fix each moment in time. In this accretion of journalistic detail, he seemed to be writing for the ages; it was as if he hoped that one day someone might use his notes to write about his and Julia's remarkable lives.

Paul and Charles Child in Maine

Julia saw his epistolary output as a way for Paul to bring order to his exciting but often chaotic existence—"a curry of a life," he called it. His father, Charles Tripler Child, was an electrical engineer who died of typhoid fever when Paul and Charlie were six months old. Their mother, Bertha Cushing Child, was a beauty, a singer, a theosophist, a wonderful cook, and a distracted single mother. His older sister, Meeda, was an attractive and fiercely intelligent woman who grew dissolute and died young. As boys, Paul and Charlie bounced around various schools and jobs, such as carting supplies in a munitions factory during the First World War, mostly around Boston.

Julia noted that much of Paul's writing was to, or about, Charlie. Like many twins, they were mutually supportive and rivalrous. While Charlie "opted for chaos," Paul preferred the "fortress-castle-square" of calm and control. When they were seven, Charlie accidentally blinded Paul's left eye with a sewing needle. Paul never complained about it, and managed to earn a black belt in judo, could drive a car, and taught perspective drawing.

Known in the family as "Cha" or "the Eagle," Charlie was brawnier, louder, more charismatic, and less sensitive than Paul, who was called "P'ski." Charlie was apparently the favored twin. One of Bertha's paramours—said to be Edward Filene, the founder of Filene's department store in Boston—paid his tuition at Harvard; Paul was given tuition for one year at Columbia. When the money ran out, he worked on ships, at odd jobs, and traveled across the country. Yet Paul was a voracious reader and autodidact, and for much of the 1920s and 1930s he worked in Italy, France, and the United States as a private tutor and teacher. As mentioned earlier, he fell in love with Edith Kennedy, and they lived together unmarried in Cambridge, until she died in 1942. Charlie was a professional painter, while Paul made art in his spare time, but was arguably more talented. In his letters, Paul went to great lengths to appraise, analyze, and critique Charlie's artwork, and frequently suggested techniques, exhibits, or readings to his brother. Charlie was an evocative writer, but he rarely returned the favor; he ignored Paul's questions, and preferred to write—and talk—about himself, a habit that grated on Paul and Julia.

Though she was very fond of his wife, Freddie (Fredericka), "Charlie brings out the absolute worst in me," Julia confided to Avis DeVoto. "He is inclined to holier-than-thou statements . . . I become crass, violent, materialistic, gluttonous, mean. Paul finds his ancient twindom animosities rising to the fore, though is far nicer than I. It is probably really much better not to see one's intimate family for more than 2½ days at a time."

Charlie would pout, or yodel *"Ohhh, Juuuullliaaa!"* in exasperation, rolling his eyes, when he felt that she was being pushy or intrusive— which she could be, though some would say she was merely being enthusiastic or watching out for her husband.

Paul needed Julia. She was strong, enthusiastic, funny, and smart. She provided the emotional love and humor that he did not have as a boy, and the intellectual and physical love that he needed as a man. He did not want children as much as she did. I suspect Paul wanted Julia all to himself, and she was happy to have him. She made sure to tell interviewers how intelligent and supportive he was, and how she admired his "EOT" ("Eye on the Target") ability to get things done.

"Without Paul Child," she said, "I would not have had my career."

v. *L'âge*

Finally released from the hospital on November 24, Paul returned to 103 Irving Street, where he worked with a speech therapist and learned to walk again. As his brain was stimulated, his physical health began to improve. "It is the fact of DOING something, I think, that is especially useful," Julia noted. "He is still having reception trouble, but that is very gradually improving. That also annoys him because, being better, he is more aware of it."

We fidgety children learned to tiptoe around the grumpy old man who slumped in his chair like a smoldering volcano. Occasionally, he'd erupt in public—demanding to be seated at the head of the table in a restaurant, or pointing theatrically to his watch and shouting, "Julie! Time's up!" while she performed onstage. My sisters and I were mortified by these awkward outbursts. But Julia handled them with great patience and empathy. "Yes, dearie, just a minute," she'd say with a smile, before getting back to work.

She tried to include him, and wrote to friends: "He was even on radio talk shows, and if he answered quite other things than the questions posed, it made little difference. So we shall just go on as usual, as long as he is able."

While the doctor said Paul was "just fine physically, the mental picture will not improve, and there is nothing to do but hope for the best," Julia confided to Simca, whose husband Jean was also beginning to decline. "We must be thankful for each day, I have come to believe, and to *remember* that every day—I tend to forget my credo, but it does make each day sweeter. *L'âge, ma chérie.* Suddenly it is there, staring at you."

Julia faced a poignant quandary: while Paul was confused and needed her help, she was brimming with energy and ideas for new books and TV shows. She was constantly invited to events, but declined most of them to care for her husband.

Characteristically, Julia poured her energy into completing the seven-hundred-page manuscript for *From Julia Child's Kitchen* in a few months of highly focused industriousness. She found that working without Simca's suggestions, or Paul's input, for the first time gave her a new sense of freedom and purpose. She drove herself to the point of exhaustion. "And thank heavens I did!" she'd say. "Without a challenging project like a cookbook to work on, I could well have gone cuckoo in those dark months."

On January 19, 1975, Julia put the finishing touches on *From Julia Child's Kitchen*. Then she sat back and typed a letter to Simca: "I have nothing more to say—I'm writ out . . . NO MORE BOOKS!"

VI. "1,000 CACKLING WOMEN"

From Julia Child's Kitchen was published on October 6, 1975, and Julia departed Cambridge on a book tour. Once again she was in her element. She found cooking, signing books, talking to her admirers, and trying new foods across the country invigorating. For help at the stove, Julia hired Elizabeth Bishop—a pragmatic, tart-tongued Boston food and wine expert. At one of their first stops, on Long Island, Julia reported "1,000 cackling women" appeared to watch her every move with rapt attention. She was deeply grateful for their warm reception, and stayed for hours that afternoon, talking to nearly every person in the room, whether they bought a book or not. Most did, and *From Julia Child's Kitchen* sold more than a hundred thousand copies by 1977.

Paul accompanied her for part of the tour, but it was not a happy experience. He tired easily, and resented the large, noisy crowds she attracted. Had he been at full strength, Julia would certainly have traveled more extensively. She went on alone, and did special events, such as a televised "Noodle Jamboree" with Jim Beard and Barbara Walters. But it was neither practical nor desirable for Julia to be away from her husband for long.

"We are going to take a 'sabbatical' next year," she wrote to Simca. "We've been on deadline basis for some 15 years or more, and that is enough . . . No more trips . . . And this is thinking of Paul—were it only me, that would be a quite different matter."

SO HERE WAS Julia Child in 1975, with a new persona, a new book, a large audience, plenty of energy, but with no TV show. Though she had dedicated *From Julia Child's Kitchen* to her producer Ruth Lockwood, it was the first of Julia's cookbooks not to be turned into a series by WGBH. (*Mastering*, Volumes I and II, inspired much of *The French Chef*, Seasons One and Two.) Of course, some of the blame for this can be assigned to Paul's condition. But there might also have been a feeling in the halls of WGBH that Julia's new book was built on recipes left over from *The French Chef*. To prod WGBH, and perhaps to inoculate Julia from charges of padding her book, her attorney Bob Johnson went so far as to write up an estimate that just a third of *From Julia Child's Kitchen* contained material previously aired by WGBH.

The lesson Julia took from the modest response to *Mastering*, Volume II, and Season Two of *The French Chef*, and to the strong response to *From Julia Child's Kitchen* was that her audience was splintering, or distracted, or perhaps was hungry for something more distinctly American. Sensing this shift in public mood, and feeling itchy to get back on the air, Julia began to root around for a new television special.

7

The Spirit of '76

1. THE BEARDED CHILD MANIFESTO

In advance of the American bicentennial celebration of 1976, Julia envisioned a TV series and book about pre-Revolutionary cooking, and she wanted to collaborate on it with her good friend James Beard, whom *The New York Times* called "the dean of American cookery."

She named the project "Thirteen Feasts for Thirteen Colonies." Its conceit, Julia wrote, was that "in the 200 years since Independence, Americans have been enjoying—without knowing it—many dishes of the Revolutionary period." Now the two best-known cooks in the country would "acquaint Americans with their great national dishes and how to prepare them."

With the combined strengths of "Julia and Jim," as the publicists called them—or "the Bearded Child" ("*l'enfant barbu*"), as they called themselves—it was an idea perfectly suited to its bicentennial moment.

James Beard, a six-foot two-inch, rotund, twinkle-eyed cook, culinary historian, and author, was born in 1903, in Portland, Oregon. His father, John, worked at the Customs House, and his mother, Mary Elizabeth, was a strong-willed Englishwoman who loved to cook and ran a boardinghouse. The Beard family liked to camp and grill outside, and Jim was raised on the Pacific Northwest's salmon, grains, and berries. He grew into a large boy who loved theater. He attended Reed College, in Portland, but was quietly expelled when he was exposed as a homosexual.

His mother arranged for Jim to take a European tour, and in 1937 he moved to New York to study acting and opera. But he soon found his calling backstage, where he prepared elaborate cast dinners. That led Beard and a partner to open a catering company, Hors d'Oeuvre, Inc. Beard began to teach cooking classes, and in 1940 published a cookbook, *Hors d'Oeuvre and Canapés*. It was the first of what would become a Herculean outpouring. Between 1940 and 1983, he authored thousands of recipes in more than twenty books, including *Fowl and Game Cookery, How to Eat (and Drink) Your Way Through a French (and Italian) Menu, James Beard's Fish Cookery, How to Eat Better for Less Money, Beard on Bread, The Casserole Cookbook, Delights and Prejudices*, and the posthumous *Love and Kisses and a Halo of Truffles*.

Julia first met Jim Beard in 1961, at a publication party for *Mastering*. By then, Beard was America's most famous cook: he taught classes across the country, and from 1946 to 1947 hosted the nation's first network cooking show, *I Love to Eat*, on NBC. Upon the publication of *Mastering* in October 1961, Julia and Simca, who were complete unknowns, arrived in New York to promote their book (Louisette Bertholle remained with her family in France). Judith Jones—who "rather cheekily" cold-called Beard—asked him to read their new book. He did, and was so impressed that he offered to host a book party at Dione Lucas's restaurant, the Egg Basket. The evening featured everyone of note in New York's small food and publishing worlds, including Craig Claiborne; Helen McCully, the powerful food editor of *House Beautiful*; and her protégé, a young French chef named Jacques Pépin. Jim and Julia hit it off right away. "After the party he said, 'I wish *I* had written that book,'" Jones recalled. "High praise indeed."

By 1975, Jim and Julia were great pals, and he was a frequent guest at La Pitchoune. They loved to cook together, and made a natural and charming duo in their live performances onstage. So hopes ran high for the pilot for "Thirteen Feasts for Thirteen Colonies."

The title referred to the British colonies along the East Coast, stretching from Virginia to Georgia to the New England enclaves. In 1776, those colonies declared their independence from Britain and later banded together as the United States of America. The colonists had arrived in the New World bearing tastes, sensibilities, and utensils from the Old World. They settled in rugged areas, some of which had short growing seasons. As the Europeans adapted their recipes and cooking styles to local clams, lobster, cod, venison, pheasant, wild turkey, corn, cranberries, wheat, and the like, the combination of Old World techniques and New World ingredients led to a distinctly American cuisine.

As Julia put it, "The persecuted Puritans came to New England 'to serve their God and to fish.'"

"As Massachusetts is the mother of American cooking, so Boston is the mother of American cookbooks," wrote José Wilson, a South African English editor hired to research "Thirteen Feasts." The first cookbook authored by an American was Amelia Simmons's *American Cookery* (1796), which led to Mrs. D. A. Lincoln's *Mrs. Lincoln's Boston Cook Book* (1884) and Fanny Merritt Farmer's *The Boston Cooking-School Cook Book* (1896). The food lore of Massachusetts had a strong influence nationwide, "unlike the Southern states, what they cooked in the northeast translated easily to the Midwest and west."

To set the scene, Wilson quoted from *America Cooks:*

When young daughters who trekked across the mountains recovered from the first hardships of setting up housekeeping in their own log houses, they wrote back home asking mother how she did this and that, and pasted mother's recipe in a blank book along with father's directions for killing potato bugs and curing the horse of heaves. Many a fine old dish, like the original Pan Pie which one of our great-great-grandmothers wrote down as a popular Michigan recipe of her day, might have been lost to posterity had it not been preserved in the Midwest. Thus, as many Massachusetts recipes, modernized and adapted, of course, turn up in the other states as have survived in the Mayflower Colony itself.

Julia loved this kind of history, and "Thirteen Feasts" gave her an excuse to return to one of her favorite subjects: her family's roots, and the foods they ate as they migrated across the country from East to West.

JULIA'S MOTHER, Julia Carolyn "Caro" Weston, was a tall, orange-haired, warm-spirited native of Massachusetts. Her father, Byron Weston, traced his lineage back to eleventh-century England, and to

Edmund Weston, a Plymouth Colony settler. The family were Congregationalists, Republicans, and, as heirs to the Weston Paper Company fortune, New England gentry. Byron founded the company in 1863 to produce high-quality paper. In 1865, he married Julia Clark Mitchell, who was descended from Plymouth Colony settlers and a Massachusetts governor. Byron and Julia Weston had ten children, and he served as the state's lieutenant governor.

He was also an enthusiastic hunter, who liked to serve the rabbit, goose, duck, and partridge he shot for dinner. This was in stark contrast to his neighbor, the Reverend Sylvester Graham, a zealous Presbyterian minister and temperance leader who inveighed against meat, preached that vegetarianism would quell alcoholism and sexual urges, and is remembered as the inventor of graham crackers. Weston's granddaughter, Julia McWilliams Child, would inherit Byron's love of meat and disdain for fervent preachers of ascetic diets.

Julia's paternal grandfather, John McWilliams, was descended from a line of tall, strong, quick-minded, thrifty Scottish Presbyterians who had settled in Illinois. In 1849, when he was sixteen, stood six feet two inches tall, and weighed only 121 pounds, he became a forty-niner, running off to join the gold rush in California. He panned for gold in the Sacramento Valley for three years, gained thirty pounds, and returned home with a gold nugget in his pocket.

Back in Illinois, he married and then parlayed his gold into successful investments in Arkansas rice fields and land in the California Central Valley. One of his sons, "Big John" McWilliams Jr., was Julia's father. Big John graduated from Princeton in the class of 1901, moved to Chicago, where he married Caro Weston, and then to Pasadena, to manage his family's properties.

On August 15, 1912, Caro gave birth to her first child, Julia Carolyn McWilliams, in Pasadena. From her father, Julia inherited drive, intellect, and organization; from her mother, she inherited the "Weston twinkle," an exuberant and accepting nature. Julia (known in the family as "Juke" or "Juke the Puke") was followed by her brother, John, in 1914, and sister, Dorothy (called "Dort"), in 1917. The children attended the local Montessori school, where they practiced hand exercises—ringing bells, buttoning buttons, opening and closing latches—which Julia credited with teaching her the dexterity she relied on as a cook.

The McWilliams family had a driver, gardener, and cook at their large house in Pasadena. Caro rarely stepped to the stove, but when she did it was to make classic New England dishes: baking-powder biscuits, codfish balls, and Welsh rarebit. To young Julia, the kitchen seemed "a dismal place."

DESPITE HER CALIFORNIA UPBRINGING, Julia was proud of her Yankee lineage. Researching "Thirteen Feasts," she spent hours leafing through old American cookbooks and developed a good understanding of how our national cuisine evolved. She began to tinker with American ingredients and recipes in the kitchen, and naturally felt the urge to share her discoveries with her audience.

Julia planned thirteen episodes of the show, one per colony. She and Jim would begin every program with an overview of a state's eighteenth-century landscape, buildings, kitchens, furniture, and cookware. Then they would move into a period studio kitchen to demonstrate two principal recipes. Each episode would end with a dramatic finale, in which the dishes were served in a period dining room.

Julia carefully worked out the details of the collaboration in what she called the "Bearded Child Manifesto" on a yellow legal pad. In a note about important elements for the show, she listed: "local ingredients, inventiveness, frugality, visual fun, rediscovery of American roots, and pride in our heritage."

She would show oysters and clams heaped in woven baskets, Boston baked beans bubbling in a traditional bean pot, corn and bean succotash in a rough iron pot, bread sliced on a wooden cutting board, red flannel hash served in a cast-iron "spider" (a metal pan with three stubby legs, which held it steady just above the fire coals), and pumpkin pie on a brown-glazed hand-potted plate.

In one program, Julia and Jim planned to visit Monticello, where they would show the ingenious kitchen mechanisms Thomas Jefferson invented, tour Jefferson's garden, and demonstrate the making of traditional Virginian dishes, like Smithfield ham and beaten biscuits. In another episode, they would go to the nation's oldest operating inn, the three-hundred-year-old Longfellow's Wayside Inn, in Sudbury, Massachusetts, to explore the history of New England through specialties such as fish chowder.

Julia loved hearty French fish stews like bouillabaisse, and was excited to discover the word "chowder" originated with "*chaudières*," the giant cauldrons used to cook fish caught by French Canadian fishermen. She decided to use a recipe that came from England to Camden, Maine, to Boston, to Paul Child, via his sister, Meeda. This simple formula called for chunks of fish simmered until tender, potatoes cooked in milk, salt pork, onions, and crumbled crackers.

Each recipe was designed to tell a larger story about the exigencies of early American life. Within the basic narrative of chowder, for instance, they found numerous substories that they could banter about on air: Cape Cod was named for the fish, and a golden cod hangs in the State House in Boston; codfish was known as "Cape Cod turkey," and salted cod (or *bacalao*) was traded to the West Indies and led to great wealth among the "codfish aristocracy." But cod fishing on the Grand Banks was dangerous, and many coastal houses were equipped with widow's walks, small porches on which wives waited for their husbands to return from the merciless sea.

Boiled salmon with egg sauce was another intriguing recipe, a "Thanksgiving-in-spring" dish that took advantage of the raw materials available in season: the salmon spawning in rivers, hens laying eggs, cows producing milk, and gardens producing new potatoes and green peas. Pork cake was an economical dish that allowed Julia and Jim to talk about the use of cured salt pork in cakes and chowders in wintertime. Hedgehog pudding was based on a German *Rehrücken*, a cake baked in a rounded form, then studded with almonds to look like a larded saddle of venison. It was an evocative-looking dish that could lead to a discussion about German immigrants in the colonies.

In a note to herself Julia scribbled: "12 recipes for 13 states=156 recipes" for the companion book.

There were many factors to take into account when choosing which dishes to feature. Each one should be authentic, economical, worth doing, and capable of being made by viewers across the country. Each should also use balanced ingredients (that is, not overrelying on staples such as cornmeal), provoke conversation, and be visually interesting.

Julia learned that the Dutch brought coleslaw, pancakes, and doughnuts to New York; the Swedes brought meatballs to Delaware; and the Germans brought sauerkraut and scrapple to Pennsylvania. The English enjoyed giving their foods funny names—like toad in the hole (sausage in Yorkshire pudding batter), spotted dick (a suet-and-dried-fruit pudding), and bubble and squeak (fried leftover vegetables). Julia and Jim would demonstrate such evocatively named dishes as soup in your pocket (from Rhode Island); apple Jonathan (New York); pigeon stew and scripture cake (New Jersey); slump, buckle, and grunt (New Hampshire); and limping Susan and hopping John (North Carolina).

There would be eel stifle (New England eel chowder), pork cake, salt pork and cream gravy, pickled pork and cabbage, and fried dough. Julia and Jim would also consider Charleston shrimp and Carolina rice pudding from South Carolina; funnel cakes and sticky buns from Pennsylvania; fried chicken, Sally Lunn, and crab cakes from Maryland; peach cake from Georgia; and election cake from Connecticut. But, José Wilson discovered, it wasn't always easy to connect the historical dots: "No one could think of one dish that was Delaware's alone, except for slippery dumplings, which are some form of noodles that no one admitted to liking," she wrote.

As any storyteller knows, stirring up controversy helps draw attention to a project. In this spirit, Wilson suggested that "people feel very strongly about Indian pudding, which makes it a good choice" to highlight. "We should get some fascinating reactions."

In February 1975, Craig Claiborne wrote an article in *The New York Times* entitled "The Great Indian Pudding Controversy." He noted that while Americans are not generally ardent epicures, there are a few dishes that people care so passionately about they are willing to take up forks and cleavers and do battle over the "real" recipe. These battle-worthy dishes include clam chowders (white, red, or clear), chili con carne, Boston baked beans, mint juleps, oyster stew, and, on the eastern tip of Long Island, clam pie.

But Indian pudding seemed to exist in a food-fighting category of its own. When he included a recipe—essentially Native American cornmeal added to traditional English pudding and saturated with molasses—based on a two-hundred-year-old recipe from Connecticut, it provoked such "good-natured wrath" from readers that he followed up with a second column. In the latter piece, he included another traditional recipe for the dish, which inflamed his correspondents further. "Why all the talk about the proper Indian pudding, and then nothing but a non-traditional recipe?" wondered Dorothy Kamen-Kaye, of Cambridge, Massachusetts. "Traditionally, Indian pudding was composed solely of corn meal, molasses, milk and spices with no eggs, raisins or anything else," wrote Mrs. Ivy Dodd, of Rockland, Maine.

"I will mercifully withhold comments on the use of tapioca—and non-use of eggs," sniped Mrs. Lewis Cage, of Rowayton, Connecticut. But John R. Cole, a professor of anthropology and sociology at Hartwick College, responded: "The heretical tapioca recipe is certainly 'Indian' since Indians 'invented' tapioca—the first domesticated manioc, the source of tapioca, 6,000 or more years ago in South America where it is still the staple food in many areas."

Julia enjoyed such gustatory donnybrooks, both for the sheer drama and because they got people to think and talk about food in a new way. She and Beard knew that the history of American food raises other, far more sensitive issues than the role of tapioca. While they didn't delve

Julia and James Beard prepare to cook together.

into white settlers' exploitation of Native Americans, they fleetingly acknowledged the ghosts of slavery. In one script Julia said, "Within a generation after their arrival, the industrious settlers of Massachusetts Bay were engaged in a brisk trade with the West Indies, exporting salted codfish in exchange for much needed cotton . . ."

To which Beard added: "By the early 1700s a network of international trade called the Golden Triangle was in bloom. With cash in their pockets from selling codfish in Europe or rum in West Africa, Yankee captains bought slaves. This human cargo they sailed to the Indies, where they loaded on stores of sugar and molasses to distill into rum and sell as seasonings to spice up the menus back home."

Having done all of this preparatory work, it was time for Julia and Jim to film a "Thirteen Feasts" pilot, which would be used to entice public television stations across the country to support the program.

11. The Birth of American Cooking

"This is the colonial kitchen of the Wayside Inn, which was immortalized by Henry Wadsworth Longfellow, who slept here. It's on the Boston Post Road. And by *law*, in Massachusetts, if you come with a horse, or a pig, or a dog, the inn *has* to put it up!" Julia said in an excited, slightly breathless voice. "So there's a barn to put things in."

"I'm going to try it with my pig someday!" chortled Jim Beard.

Julia laughed, saying, "That would be lovely."

It was October 1975, and the two were standing in a dim, wood-paneled, eighteenth-century kitchen in Sudbury, Massachusetts. Before them spread the inn's large brick hearth with a fire burning inside. A metal "crane" attached to the fireplace wall suspended a large cauldron filled with burbling, creamy codfish chowder. A metal "spider" hunkered in the coals. As the camera zoomed out, a long table was revealed, groaning under a feast of colonial-era foods—roasted wild turkey, silver cod, red lobster, gray oysters, yellow corn bread, chunks of Boston brown bread, a heap of beets, carrots, and onions, a terra-cotta pot of Boston baked beans, and sweet desserts like hedgehog pudding and apple pudding pie. The table was lit by green, hand-dipped candles.

The screen showed a dozen men and boys dressed as Revolutionaries, in britches and tricorn hats, playing flutes and drums as they marched along a road. Then the scene shifted to show Julia and Jim in a modern kitchen. She was dressed in a purple-hued shirt with the sleeves rolled to her elbows, the familiar blue apron tied around her waist. Beard—as tall as Julia, but far wider, entirely bald, with a mustache—was dressed in a mustard-yellow shirt and a red bow tie, and wore a blue apron around his neck.

"Julia and Jim will take turns leading the recipes, one leading the way, the other kibitzing," the narrator said. "The climax of each show will be the cooking and presentation of the principal dishes."

Julia looked into the camera with eyes humorously agleam. "Today we're going to make Indian pudding—it sounds *awful*, but it's *very good!*" She put her left hand on her hip and cocked an eyebrow at Beard. "It's a cornmeal mush that is flavored with molasses and spices, and baked a long, slow time."

"Hours and hours and hours and hours . . . ," Beard said in a monotone.

Julia goaded him: "The whole two continents of America were nourished on nothing but corn!"

"I know," Beard mumbled. "Rather amazing."

"Corn," she added, "has everything but *niacin* in it."

"Everything in the world. And of course it won't leaven."

"No. But who wants that? OK!" Julia turned to grin into the TV. "We can say the Indians gave us *meal* and the English gave us *pudding*. Everything that is dessert, the English call 'pudding.'"

"Alas and alack, yes." Beard sighed.

Julia and Jim loved to cook together whenever they could, so it was surprising that their on-screen chemistry was . . . *flat*.

It came down to personality, style, and the very particular skills required for TV. While Beard was eminently knowledgeable about colonial food, technique, and cookware, his voice went from a deep baritone to a high pitch; sounding like an exasperated schoolteacher, he broke into rapid-fire, fact-crammed bursts that were hard to follow. Even a seemingly minor detail—his bright yellow shirt with red bow tie—which looked good onstage, appeared jarring on the screen.

For her part, Julia had a wild energy that day. She had a frizzy new hairdo and grew so excited about cod, venison, maize, and molasses that she sometimes talked over Beard, or pleasantly bossed him around, while cracking jokes and weaving double entendres as she played to the camera.

"It's truly a most beautiful wild turkey—doesn't it look beautiful, Julia?" Jim said in his deep voice, nodding at the bronzed fowl with baked apples that glistened enticingly on a platter. "They taste very turkey."

"Not like the artificial breasts" of modern supermarket turkeys, Julia chuckled, "those old *fatsoes!*"

As Beard explained how Native Americans ground corn between stones—"just like the Mexicans do, in a metate [a stone mortar, used for milling corn]"—Julia began to play with various corn-grinding contraptions. She instructed Beard to grind corn by hand in a silver device screwed to a stool. "It takes a little muscle, but it does very well," she encouraged him. In a mischievous tone, she added, "Let's do it with*out* the little cover and see what happens . . ." She removed the splatter shield while Beard dutifully ground away. A great spray of cornmeal flew out of the machine and scattered across the floor. Delighted, Julia put her head back and roared with laughter. "Well, you see how it goes all over the kitchen!"

Beard looked at her with a tolerant, slightly worried expression, unsure of what she'd do next.

After trying out a modern corn-grinding attachment on a rotary mixer, which smoothly ground fine cornmeal and stored it cleanly in a glass jar, Beard said, "I think I'll take this against the hand one."

"*Hmm!*" Julia said, turning her attention to a copious New England seafood platter: an Essex lobster, Cotuit oysters, Annisquam mussels, and Ipswich clams.

In a reverential tone, Beard announced, "*Gloucester codfish cakes . . . with egg sauce . . .*"

"I was brought up on that because my mother came from the Berkshires." Julia sighed. "Oh, I *love* egg sauce."

Later, as she dolloped spoonfuls of cream onto the viscous brown "Injun pudding," Beard said, "What a lovely feast it 'tis. A feast of Native American things prepared according to the English rules."

"You can say it's the birth of American cooking," Julia noted.

At the end of the segment, Beard explained that the term "wassail" signified "the pledging of health," a New Year's custom among the Saxons. Upon drinking in honor of a friend, they would salute him with the phrase "Wes hal," which meant "Be hale," or "Health be to you." The modern version of the drink is made from warm beer, sugar, nutmeg, ginger, sherry, and slices of lemon. It is served with slices of toasted bread, set afloat in the brew, whence comes the origin of "drinking a toast."

Beard dipped a piece of toast into a tankard of ale, and in a fine voice sang, "We'll wassail, and wassail, all over the town."

Julia held up a piece of toast and hoisted her tankard heartily toward the camera: "Let's say 'Wassail, to the Spirit of Seventy-Six!'"

III. OUR DECISION IS FINAL

"Our great week of TV trials with Jim is finally over," Julia wrote to Simca in March 1975. "He does not seem well, is fat as ever, and has lost some of his verve—which, I suppose, is to be expected. But his schedule is as busy as ever, including classes twice a day . . . Eh bien . . . it sounds nutty to me, but that's what he loves to do."

In the summer of 1975 the bicentennial loomed just a year ahead, and WGBH was fully supportive of the colonial food project. The station had changed the show's working title from the puckish "Thirteen Feasts for Thirteen Colonies" to the statelier "Revolutionary Recipes," and then the more generic "Julia and Jim: Classic American Cooking." The latter reflected the fact that "we're presenting great American cuisine, not just history," a station executive noted.

Television production is expensive, and funding public TV shows, even Julia Child's, was a perennial struggle. Henry Becton Jr., WGBH's program manager for cultural affairs, was pitching "Julia and Jim" to public television affiliates across the country (if enough of them agreed to purchase the series from WGBH, it would help defray production costs) and potential corporate underwriters, such as Safeway Stores: "I'm confident this series will be one of the most talked-about new television projects of the 1976–77 seasons," Becton wrote. "We're already getting many inquiries from the press. Although it's got a bicentennial emphasis, its value is timeless."

But the commitment and cash did not materialize. "Nothing at all has come of that pilot TV program Jim Beard and I did, and I have given [WGBH] a deadline of July 1st . . . and after that we shall be free to do what we wish," Julia wrote to Simca. "I pray I shall NOT hear because I really am *not* at all anxious to get back into that rat race. Tant pis about less exposure for our books—life is too short!"

She was newly pragmatic, out of necessity. While Paul had regained some muscular strength, he still had trouble processing information. "There is still some brain injury there that has not healed. Perhaps it never will, and he will just have to live with it," Julia said philosophically. "If he were 54 or even 64 rather than 73, he'd have bounced back faster. It is a shame, is it not, that we shall not all go on forever!"

Jim Beard's health was worsening too. While teaching cooking classes at the Gritti Palace, in Venice, he contracted a kidney infection. The combination of Paul's ill health with Jim Beard's struggles and WGBH's challenge in landing an underwriter for the colonial food show gave Julia pause. As the weeks of inaction turned into months, she confided to friends that she was thinking of pulling the plug on her treasured colonial cooking special.

When he caught wind of Julia's change of heart, Michael S. Rice, WGBH's general manager, pleaded: "Please give us a little more time before closing the door on the 1976 series . . . I know the delay and difficulties are frustrating. I know how disruptive they can be to your heavily committed schedules. But please reconsider and bear with us . . . Everyone here on staff has felt the excitement and rightness of a series with you on American cooking for the Bicentennial year. It would be WGBH's most fitting contribution, given your part and our own in Public Television's short but remarkable history."

In a note scrawled across the letter, David Ives, the station's president, wrote, "Oy!!!!! Is there something that doesn't meet the eye here? Julia mad at Beard or feeling that he isn't right as a partner for her?"

Michael Rice responded in another note: "Am very puzzled. Sometimes I think she's annoyed that we don't just go ahead, w/ or w/out funding. Sometimes I think she's just tired. Hope this letter will smoke out any problems hitherto unspoken of."

Julia replied in a terse note: "I'm sorry but our decision must stand. This is really concerned with Paul and his health—a long television siege is really too much for him . . . I understand Jim Beard is still right there and willing to go. And there are numerous other people who could do the series with him, if, indeed, anyone is really needed besides that large and charming personage."

While Julia's rationale was legitimate, Ives may have intuited something that Julia could not bring herself to voice. There *was* something else, a difficult truth behind her decision: Jim Beard was simply not very good on television.

Admittedly, this seems odd. One would think that after such a long TV career Beard would have gained a workable set of skills, and that Julia would have been aware of his shortcomings. But Beard was a dear friend, a masterly cook and culinary historian, and he *seemed* like the perfect partner. Perhaps Julia's devotion blinded her to Jim's lack of telegenic charm, or perhaps she chose to ignore the facts until she no longer could. Indeed, in 1972 Julia had warned Simca: "We all (including Jim B.) tend to look rather grim when we are concentrating, and . . . it is really a matter of getting into the habit of showing a sunny smile at almost all times."

While Julia was cheerful and dynamic on camera, Jim was glum, static, and mumble-mouthed.

"It's true." Judith Jones sighed. "He was terrible on TV." It was sad, because "Jim was such a wonderful resource, and a very good friend of Julia's. She couldn't go on with the program. She wanted to protect Jim. She was very sensitive to this sort of thing."

Despite this significant setback, the American bicentennial was not a historical moment that Julia Child intended to miss. As she scrambled to regroup and find a replacement for "Classic American Cooking," her mind slipped back to past successes, foremost the *White House Red Carpet* special of 1967. Would it be possible, she wondered, to return to the White House kitchen almost a decade later? And if so, what would she find there?

IV. THE INSTANT PRESIDENT

In 1976, 1600 Pennsylvania Avenue was occupied by Gerald and Betty Ford, and their guests of honor for the bicentennial would be Queen Elizabeth II and Prince Philip of England. They would celebrate with a white-tie dinner for more than two hundred VIPs at the White House.

The more she thought about it, the more Julia recognized this as an opportunity well suited to her professional talents and personal enthusiasms. It would allow her to celebrate America's emancipation from "the Old Sod," as she called Britain, while further examining her family's English roots and celebrating the queen, the rare celebrity who genuinely fascinated her. And Julia had an ace in the hole: her friend Henry Haller remained the White House's executive chef. The only problem, as far as she could see, was the president himself.

Gerald Ford had not been elected to office. In October 1973, the Michigan Republican was minority leader of the House when he was suddenly thrust into the spotlight. His party was in chaos: Vice President Spiro Agnew was forced to resign for allegedly accepting more than $100,000 in bribes as governor of Maryland. Ford replaced him for a year, until President Nixon resigned in August 1974. At that point, Ford was named president, and New York governor Nelson Rockefeller was elevated to vice president.

Gerald Ford is the only man in history to serve as both vice president and president without having been elected by the electoral college. But that didn't change his eating habits. Nixon liked to eat cottage cheese slathered in ketchup, and so did Ford. "Day in and day out, Mr. Ford eats exactly the same lunch—a ball of cottage cheese, over which he pours a small pitcherful of A.1. Sauce, a sliced onion or a quartered tomato, and a small helping of butter-pecan ice cream," John Hersey reported in *The New York Times*. " 'Eating and sleeping,' he says to me, 'are a waste of time.' "

In a speech to the Grocery Manufacturers of America, Ford said that he preferred instant coffee and instant oatmeal to the real thing, adding, "I happen to be the nation's first instant Vice President. I only hope that I prove to be as pure, digestible, and as appetizing to consumers who did not have a chance to shop around for other brands of Vice President when I was put on the market."

Julia had little faith in Ford, and referred to him as *a tête de lard* ("fathead"). Yet he was presiding over the White House at a signal moment in American history, and he had invited Julia to join him in celebrating the bicentennial with the queen.

8

The President, the Queen, and the Captain

1. Just Two Lucky Girls at Dinner for the Queen at the White House

On July 5, 1976, Julia ate dinner with the public television producer Martin Clancy in Washington, D.C. He had run coverage of the Watergate hearings and other major stories, and explained his meticulously planned telecast of the queen's White House visit. (It was produced by WETA, Washington, D.C.'s public television station.) Most of the show would be live, except for a few pretaped segments. Julia would provide commentary with a multicultural cast: Robin MacNeil, a Canadian working for American public TV, was the anchorman; Jean Marsh, a British actress best known in the States for the period drama *Upstairs, Downstairs*, would discuss royal etiquette and fashion; and Frank Gillard, a BBC correspondent who had covered the Second World War and helped launch *Masterpiece Theatre*, would add historical gravitas.

Washington was in a tizzy. The presidential primaries had just concluded, and now the bicentennial celebration was under way, bringing throngs of tourists to the capital. There were so many official events scheduled that the White House could barely keep up. Betty Ford worried they'd have to close the People's House to the public for months, but then she hit on a solution.

Inspired by a party at the French Embassy—where a large tent decorated with crystal chandeliers and red velvet walls hung with paintings had provided extra space—the first lady had a tent erected over the Rose Garden. "Just a great white tent which would also enable us to invite more guests than we could have served indoors," she recalled. The tent would have a wooden floor and carpet. "I'd been thinking of an outdoor party the Nixons had given for some newly released prisoners of war and their wives. It had been raining for three days, and the chairs just gradually sank into the ground. And all those poor wives, who'd gone out and bought beautiful new shoes, ruined them in the mud." To forestall such a disaster, Mrs. Ford decreed, "We'll have a floor and a carpet. It will be just like a room."

On July 6, the day before the feast, the White House lawns were clipped, and the vast white tent was assembled, hung with paper lanterns, and equipped with an air-conditioning unit. The doorways to the White House were given a fresh coat of paint.

Nine years after Julia's first visit, Executive Chef Henry Haller was fifty-three and at the top of his game. Highly professional and usually discreet, he had suddenly become "unavailable to the press" as of 1970, when he volunteered more about the Nixon family's food and beverage habits than they cared to share, including that President Nixon liked to mix his own martinis before dinner. Julia and a public television crew were given a two-hour window to film chef Haller preparing the bicentennial dinner.

Thanks to a renovation, the White House kitchen seemed even smaller than it had nine years earlier. Now it could contain only three cooks and two helpers. The food was still transported from the basement to the dining rooms by rickety dumbwaiters and a zigzag staircase.

Julia noted there would be 224 hungry guests for dinner, and Haller explained his strategy. After consulting on the menu with the first lady, the State Department gave notice of the royal couple's single dietary restriction: no raw fish. "That's not much of a problem for the Queen *here*, of course," Haller cracked. "But I guess it is when he [*sic*] visits the Japanese or the Eskimos. With Prince Philip, it's not a problem at all—he's an old Navy man, and eats everything. But I guess these people who go to such dinners all the time learn to eat a lot of things they don't like.

"First of all, you use what is seasonal. You do not adjust the seasons to the menu, it should be the other way around. Then it should be possible to do some of the preparation in advance."

The meal would begin with a spectacular dish, New England Lobster *en Belle Vue, Sauce Rémoulade. Belle vue* is French for "a beautiful sight," and it was. "It's a very queenly, beautiful dish," Haller said. Escorting Julia into the walk-in refrigerator, Haller beamed with pride at a collection of enormous four-pound lobsters, each nestled on a bed of pink aspic. They had been boiled in a bouillon, and their tail meat had been removed and sliced into thick medallions; the medallions were laid out along the tops of the shells, decorated with red pimiento and black truffle, and glazed with jelly. Thus decorated, the crustaceans were arranged on oval platters, twenty-five servings to a platter.

This spectacular centerpiece was surrounded with a mix of carrots, peas, celery, and apples, topped with the meat of boiled baby lobsters. "*Apples:* that's my touch in vegetable salad," Chef Haller explained. As he garnished a lobster plate with parsley and lemon, he grumbled, "I wish someone would invent lemons without seeds."

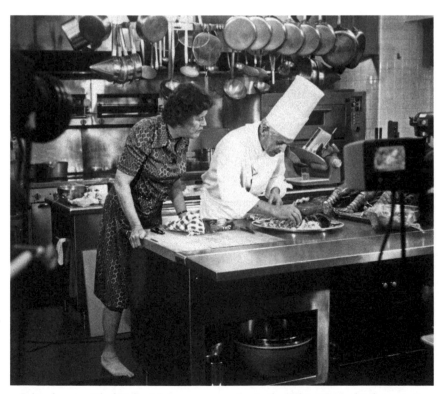

Julia observes Chef Haller's lobster preparation in the White House kitchen, 1976.

To start, each guest would receive several lobster medallions, a serving of the vegetable-apple-lobster salad, dressed with a rémoulade sauce (mayonnaise mixed with lemon, mustard, gherkins, capers, tarragon, and chervil).

The entrée was saddle of veal, a choice cut that makes for a large and expensive roast that is rarely served in home kitchens. "But if you're going to have a fancy party like this one, and entertain *the queen of England*, you've got to spend a little money for it," Julia quipped.

On a counter, twenty-six saddles of veal (total cost: $1,000) had been boned. Haller cut the veal on the bias, not crosswise, which makes for a slightly larger serving—"a very attractive way of serving it that I hadn't seen done," Julia observed. The meat was tender and "just beautiful, a lovely pale pinky whitey color." Haller used a pastry bag to stuff each piece with a mixture of ground veal, bread crumbs, garlic, herbs, cognac, egg, cream, and Worcestershire sauce; then they were rolled, tied, and roasted in a 350-degree oven for fifty minutes.

With the veal, the chef would serve rice croquettes and broccoli. The croquettes—compact balls of rice (cooked in veal stock) with ham and parsley—were chilled, then made into *panées à noblesse*, and rolled into sausage-shape rolls. These were dredged in flour, coated with egg, and rolled in bread crumbs, then deep-fried.

The sous-chef, Hans Raffert, made little "baskets" of interwoven strands of noodle dough, which were glazed with egg and baked in the oven. Each basket contained a croquette of rice.

For a side dish, Chef Haller peeled and blanched his broccoli and served it with a *sauce Mornay*—a hollandaise sauce combined with a cheese-flavored *velouté*, and lightened with whipped cream—then sprinkled with grated Parmesan cheese and broiled golden brown. "A very, very fine dish," Julia declared.

The meal would be rounded out with a fresh garden salad and a selection of Trappist cheeses.

"I'm not at all nervous about this [dinner], but there are too many people in a little kitchen," Haller grumbled, his hand shaking slightly as he downed five glasses of water in twenty minutes.

For dessert, the pastry chef, Heinz Bender, had created fluted bombes of vanilla custard with fresh pale golden peaches spiked with brandy, and surrounded by fresh raspberries, whipped cream rosettes, and green "leaves" made of marzipan. "Very pretty," Julia judged. "Nothing sensational, but a really good kind of American cooking."

As he passed a plate of petits fours, lemon wafers, sugar cookies, and macaroons, Bender observed, "Washington is not a cookie town. There's too much humidity and they get soggy. I have to bake them fresh every day."

"They don't taste at all like soap to me," joked Raffert.

"How would you know about *taste*?" Bender grinned. "You are a painter who only cooks when he gets mad."

Chef Haller was Swiss, and Bender and Raffert were German; Bender was married to one of the housekeepers. They had been hired by the Johnsons a decade earlier. At the prompting of Mimi Sheraton, of *The New York Times*, the chefs reminisced about presidential food preferences. "Nixon didn't eat many things. He didn't like lamb or calves' liver or a lot of things, and it was hard to make up an interesting menu," Haller said. "The Fords like almost everything—even liver and red cabbage cooked with wine, the French way."

Bender recalled that "the Nixons liked plain sponge cake with lemon filling and coconut meringue. Real plain. President Johnson—now he really had a sweet tooth but had to watch his weight, so I made everything with Sucaryl [sodium cyclamate, an artificial sweetner]."

Upstairs, the producer Martin Clancy checked a four-page schedule, in which every minute of the dinner had been precisely choreographed. At 8:02 p.m., the queen and prince would leave the official guest accommodations at Blair House and drive by limousine to the Rose Garden, where they would arrive at 8:06. They were allotted twelve minutes to visit the first family's private residence upstairs, where they would enjoy a quick cocktail and exchange gifts. At 8:18, they would descend and walk out to the white tent in the Rose Garden for dinner.

Among the constraints that night was that "one does not show the queen eating," Julia noted, nor does one show the president eating, for that matter. She decided not to mention this on air, as it would "only disappoint the audience." The White House would concede to one or two TV cameras taking general footage of the crowd entering and being seated in the tent, but once the first course was served, no further filming would be allowed.

The dinner was scheduled to last for ninety minutes. To fill that time on air, Clancy would use pretaped segments, such as a profile of Queen Elizabeth, an interview with Prince Philip, scenes of the royal couple arriving at the White House, and a series of vignettes showing Julia's visit to Chef Haller's kitchen and a tour of the White House.

Ruthie Lockwood had blocked out Julia's segments as best she could. She allotted six minutes to show the first course, the lobster; five minutes for the veal entrée; and another four or five minutes for Chef Bender's ice cream bombe and cookies. But much would be left to on-the-spot decision making, improvisation, and luck.

AT 5:00 THAT EVENING the sky over Washington, D.C., turned dark gray, winds whipped off the Potomac, thunder boomed, lightning crackled, and the city was drenched in a violent, torrential downpour. The cloudburst nearly washed the white tent out of the Rose Garden, and Julia was soaked to the bone. She rushed back to the hotel, re-dressed, fixed her makeup, and had her hair redone.

The storm knocked out six of eleven television cameras and the audio link between the presenters and the remote truck, where the program's director and crew sat. Without audio, Julia and the other announcers didn't know the extent of the damage.

While technicians scrambled to fix the cameras and audio link, Robin MacNeil, the anchor, had to carry the show by himself. A steady hand, MacNeil was armed with a stack of three-by-five cards filled with facts about the White House, the queen, the bicentennial, and the like. "I hope that the viewers didn't turn it off at that point," Julia said. MacNeil "is very attractive, but half an hour of just talk when you are told that you are going to see the queen of England doesn't go off very well."

Martin Clancy's neat schedule was in shambles. It was thrown even further off when the queen and Prince Philip inexplicably loitered in the first family's private quarters for an extra twenty minutes. (Perhaps they were fearful of more rain, or were just in need of a relaxing cocktail before the festivities, Julia surmised.) The delay allowed the technicians to shift cameras around, but the talent had gone missing. Finally, Jean Marsh and Frank Gillard were discovered mingling with guests on the lawn.

The announcing team was reunited in the East reception room, where they shared one small black-and-white monitor, in which they could dimly see Lady Bird Johnson and Cary Grant entering the party, English nationals curtsying before their queen, and a beehive of activity inside the white tent. Viewers at home with large color TV sets saw far more than the announcers did.

The 224 guests were seated in groups of 8 or 10 at tables covered with mist-gray cotton tablecloths printed with sprigs of daisies and bands of pink ribbon. Each table had a centerpiece made of summer flowers, "adding a soft impressionistic touch to the garden setting, as will, undoubtedly, the women guests in their long summer dresses," the *Times* noted.

Guests at the head table included Queen Elizabeth and Prince Philip, President and Mrs. Ford, Vice President and Mrs. Rockefeller, Secretary of State and Mrs. Kissinger, and British foreign secretary and Mrs. Anthony Crosland. Other guests included Lady Bird Johnson, Willie Mays, Ella Fitzgerald, Julie Harris, Helen Hayes, Barbara Walters, Dorothy Hamill, Bill Blass, Alistair Cooke, Yehudi Menuhin, Secretary of Defense Donald Rumsfeld, and Assistant to the President Dick Cheney.

The announcers had hoped for a sandwich, at the very least, to keep them fueled during the broadcast. Instead, they were left to squint at

Queen Elizabeth and President Ford at the White House bicentennial reception

their little monitor from 7:45 until 11 p.m., trying to sound upbeat while their stomachs growled. "That was not very well planned out," Julia objected. "We were treated like trained animals."

To add insult to injury, she was unable to show, or taste, a final version of Chef Haller's magnificent veal roast. Indeed, she was unable to taste any of Haller's food. The closest she got was in talking to a woman leaving early who said it was "an absolutely superb dinner, and everything was absolutely scrumptious." With that, Julia sighed. "She seemed like a very intelligent woman, so I believe that they did have a marvelous meal."

Nor was there much to drink. Julia had specifically asked to taste one of the wines being consumed by the chosen few in the presidential tent. This, she thought, "would bring a note of gaiety and relaxation" to the proceedings. Jean Marsh also pined for "just one glass." But it was not to be. (For the record, the Fords served a Sterling Chenin Blanc, 1972; a Beaulieu Vineyard Cabernet Sauvignon, 1968; and a Schramsberg Blanc de Blancs, 1973.)

"For some reason, they thought there would be public criticism of seeing us drink wine—'Oh, you are wasting the taxpayers' money!'—so we never got a taste, and I have no idea if it was any good or not. That was a silly and spineless point of view." Julia fumed. "Bureaucrats are terribly afraid of any kind of criticism at all. And if they really had convictions about things, they would brush the criticism aside and do what they felt proper."

The party was forty minutes behind schedule when the toasts began. Julia found them "dull" and "full of platitudes." While Queen Elizabeth's speech was "rather stilted and careful," Julia detected glimpses of humor. "I found her delivery quite a bit easier than the other times I have heard her, when her voice was rather high and girlish. But as Frank Gillard pointed out, she has been queen for twenty-five years and had matured in the role."

The evening ended with entertainment and dancing in the White House. "The Queen was easy to deal with," Mrs. Ford recalled. "She was very definite about what she wanted and what she didn't want. She loves Bob Hope and Telly Savalas, so we invited Bob Hope and Telly Savalas. Both came, and if I hadn't kept mixing up Your Highness and Your Majesty (he's His Highness, she's Her Majesty), I'd give myself four stars for the way that visit went off."

In contrast to the lupine Tony Bennett, who prowled the stage as he crooned at the Johnson White House in 1967, Ford chose the pop duo Captain & Tennille as the musical act for 1976. The Captain was Daryl Dragon, who had sung backup for the Beach Boys (and was known then as Captain Keyboards), and Tennille was Toni Tennille, also a onetime backup singer. They were thirty-three years old and married. They played a number of their bubbly hit songs, including "Love Will Keep Us Together," and ended the night with "Muskrat Love," a treacly tune about amorous rodents.

Prince Philip tapped his feet to the song, Nancy Kissinger yawned, and Lady Keith (an American once married to a British knight) sniped that the song's sexual overtones were "not suitable for the Queen."

"Only a person with a dirty mind would see something wrong," Tennille responded later. "It's a gentle Disneyesque kind of song."

Julia was unimpressed. "I don't know why they picked something like *that*," she told *McCall's*. "It didn't seem to be that it came up to the glamorous occasion of the Queen of England having dinner at the White House. I would like to have seen a marvelous musical comedy, or a bit of ballet, or Beverly Sills. 'Muskrat Love' just didn't seem to be the kind of music that fitted into that kind of an evening . . . [Maybe] because it is an election year, the president decided that he had to show that he wasn't highbrow—not that anyone has ever accused him of being highbrow. But I just do not care for that very jarring sort of cheap note in the otherwise quite elegant evening."

She repeated the criticism on television, and it gained almost as much attention as the official proceedings. "I agree with Mrs. Child," wrote several fans. Asked years later if she felt slighted, Tennille replied, "I laughed through the whole thing. We were told to turn the music volume down. In front of us were the Kissingers, and the look on his face! Queen Elizabeth was sleeping, and the Fords were lovely. I see them in Palm Springs, and all they remember is I sang a song about mice. The whole thing is ridiculous. Why would you ever hate a song?"

At the tail end of the evening, the United States Marine Band struck up a Rodgers and Hart medley in the State Dining Room. President

Ford danced with the queen, who wore a yellow dress, a blue sash around her shoulder, and a sparkling diamond tiara on her head. (Upon reviewing the PBS tape, the Marines noticed that the queen and the president were dancing to the tune "The Lady Is a Tramp." The band cut the medley from their repertoire.)

When the camera swung to show the first lady, in a pale green dress, dancing with the tall, tuxedoed Prince Philip, Julia purred: "I thought it was about time they showed him because he's such a handsome fellow." Gillard noted that Prince Philip always managed to hide in plain sight: "He is there but then he isn't there, unless somebody really seeks him out." Julia decided to seek him out, and was greatly satisfied to meet the handsome prince.

At the end of the night, Julia and her colleagues were given limp tuna fish sandwiches and soggy hamburgers with fried onions. "I just wish someone would give me a tiny glass of wine," Jean Marsh croaked. "It would be so nice . . ." Instead, they sipped warm Coca-Cola.

Despite the inclement weather, bureaucratic bumbling, political conventioneering, "Muskrat" melodies, and lack of food and wine, Julia told *McCall's* that it had all been "a great deal of fun." To take part in a big, historically meaningful celebration like that "is the kind of thing that I love to do. I feel extremely lucky to have had a part in something that is a *real event*. Ruthie Lockwood and I just felt that we were two lucky girls to join in a dinner for the Queen of England at the White House."

II. *Starsky and Hutch*

The press was not so kind, and generally lambasted the "Quaint Spectacle" of the broadcast. "It Wasn't Much for White House TV," brayed a *Washington Post* headline. And then the letters began pouring in to WGBH. A few people enjoyed "the wonderful coverage" of the bicentennial, though even those fans wondered why Jean Marsh couldn't find her glasses and was therefore unable to comment incisively about the ladies' dresses.

Many more watchers, like April Oray, wrote to say, "Dear Channel 2, your program . . . was a fair imitation of 'Monty Python's Flying Circus' (in fact we were sure it *was* MPFC), but as a 3 hour . . . effort it was pitiful . . . You all looked so uncomfortable, unprepared, unprofessional we nearly wept for you." Archibald Murphy wrote: "Your coverage of the State Dinner for Queen Elizabeth has raised the presentation of *Starsky and Hutch* to the level of creative programming."

Julia generally fared well, with Mrs. Eugene Klein noting that "Julia Child . . . was the one bright spot in the otherwise dreadful telecast."

In a postmortem on July 8, the White House Press Office lamented an opening shot obscured by a tree limb, the misnaming of important guests, Bob Hope's unfunny jokes, the Muskrat-themed music, the fact that Julia was not allowed to taste the wine, and the general chaos wreaked by the rainstorm: "It appeared the White House didn't know what was going on."

"I simply cannot understand why we went to the effort to arrange this live coverage and then have it turn out in such a way that the President could be described as 'lumbering through a clumsy toast' and other similar observations," a senior White House official wrote to Robert Mead, the television adviser to the president. "I want . . . an explanation of why your office . . . screwed up."

Mead vigorously defended himself and the telecast. But by the end of the day he had submitted his resignation.

III. A Thoroughly American Dinner

In her mostly approving article about Chef Haller's bicentennial menu for the queen, *The New York Times* food writer Mimi Sheraton included a strongly worded caveat: "Through it all, one could not help wondering if a really imaginative, thoroughly American dinner might not have been more interesting and appropriate to the occasion than this menu which, though elegant and appetizing, was all-purpose international."

Julia rose to the defense of Haller and Mrs. Ford's choices in an article for *The New York Times Magazine* the following January:

> There was a lot of public caterwauling at the time of the Queen Elizabeth menu . . . why could it not have been an American dinner? Isn't American cooking grand enough? Does it need to be rejected as too homey? And so on and so forth. Why not have pineapple upside down cake, apple Betty, sweet potatoes, beaten biscuits, sourdough bread, pie à la mode, three-bean salad, turkey and so forth? Well, why not? To

some extent, it's just a matter of packaging and public relations. All you have to do is change the names of the dishes from international French to national American, and everyone is happy.

Sheraton was playing to the gallery, Julia felt, and promoting a false controversy over what was "French" versus "American." After all, Julia had pointed out many times that *"boeuf bourguignon* is just beef stew with a French name."* It drove her mad when people said, "Oh, I can't make *boeuf bourguignon*, it's too heavy and complicated." To that she'd reply, "Balderdash!"

She illustrated her point with a bicultural menu, in which a French *quiche aux crevettes* becomes an American "open-faced tart of Louisiana shrimp," a *filet de boeuf* becomes "a prime tenderloin of Texas steer," and truffles and foie gras are replaced by homemade liver pâté and wine-flavored *duxelles*. "You can take almost anything in the French repertoire and turn it into plain old American, and vice versa," Julia explained.

She translated the bicentennial dinner like this:

FRENCH	AMERICAN
Homard en Belle Vue	Cold Boiled Lobster from the Coast of Northern Maine—in Fancy Dress
Macédoine de Légumes	A Salad of Fresh Vegetables from Maryland Gardens
Sauce Rémoulade	The White House's Own Green Mayonnaise
Selle de Veau Farcie et Braisée	Stuffed Boned Saddle of New Hampshire Veal
Brocoli Mornay	Fresh Blue Mountain Broccoli Sauced the Wisconsin Way
Croquettes de Riz	Arkansas Rice Croquettes
Salade	Native Salad
Fromages des Trappistes	Trappist Cheese
Glace Crème aux Pêches	Fresh Georgia Peach Ice Cream
Sauce aux Framboises	Rose Garden Raspberry Sauce

By the time Julia's article about the bicentennial dinner ran in *The New York Times Magazine*, the Democratic governor of Georgia, Jimmy

Carter, had defeated the Republican Gerald Ford in the 1976 presidential election. Julia used the changing of the guard to address the myth that food at the White House was "dreary." Not only was Haller "a splendid chef," she wrote, but "ultimately, it is the First Lady who is responsible for the nation's gastronomic image."

Perhaps, Julia added, Rosalynn Carter would "do something about improving it."

Julia had been impressed by the "deep-South flavor" of a meal the Carters had served visiting members of Congress in Georgia—fried chicken, country ham, baked cheese grits, candied apples, turnip greens, corn bread, and biscuits. "That sounds mighty good to me," Julia wrote, "I am all for trotting out American regional cooking for official visitors."

Though she questioned the practicality of cooking fried chicken for 150 people at a formal White House event, and wondered if serving peanut soup would be considered a conflict of interest for the Carters (a peanut-farming family), she encouraged the First Lady to look deeply into her larder and consider its symbolic importance—and her role in emphasizing "the good in American cooking."

Sensing that authentic "down-home" cooking "just has to be born and bred into one," Julia encouraged Mrs. Carter to fly her cook from Plains, Georgia, to Washington, D.C., to bring the "authentic deep-South flavor" to her banquets. And she should fly in chefs from other regions, as well, Julia suggested. "We most certainly must act to preserve our culinary heritages, and what better way to encourage them than at the White House."

In France, the press reports the menu of virtually every official function, from a sparsely attended book award held at a country inn to a crowded state dinner at the Élysée Palace. The practice emphasizes the importance of food, and, Julia noted, "we should certainly do likewise.

"Whatever our new First Lady does to make White House entertaining more American, let her vigorously publicize it. The good news about good food at the White House should be trumpeted far and wide."

9

The New French Revolution

1. "Adventures in Eating Are In"

After the bicentennial celebration of July 1976, Julia Child once again found herself at the top of her game but drifting in professional limbo. While *The French Chef* continued to play in reruns, she told journalists that she was swearing off TV: "It's gotten much more expensive to do, and it involves a 12-hour day and a 7-day week, and we've had it," she said.

Julia loved television, and never shied from hard work, but she simply needed a break. She was about to turn sixty-four. She worried about Paul's health. And after the flurry of sometimes frustrating activity over the past two years, she wanted to spend some quiet time at home with him, tinkering at the stove, reading books, and writing letters. It was time to recharge her batteries. But just as she declared "No More Books!" after nearly every volume, so this would prove a temporary hiatus from television.

While she enjoyed the domestic nurse role at first, it grew predictably tedious, and Julia became restless and unhappy. To ease the strain, she hired her old friend Liz Bishop (the Boston cook who had assisted on the *From Julia Child's Kitchen* book tour) to help clean the house, discard old clothes and books, and pack box after box of Julia's letters to and from the likes of Simca, M. F. K. Fisher, and Judith Jones. "I am not sentimental," Julia liked to say, though she was a pack rat who kept nearly every letter, date book, receipt, expired passport, driver's license, and scribbled note she'd ever had. Once the clutter was exhumed and neatly boxed, Julia was happy to donate the lot to the Arthur and Elizabeth Schlesinger Library at Radcliffe.

Julia was nearing her wit's end at 103 Irving Street when an unlikely savior appeared: *McCall's*. Back in the spring of 1970, Julia had resented the magazine for bullying her into posing for Arnold Newman, and Simca's teary recriminations had hastened the end of their collaboration. But the magazine had bent over backward to smooth things over: the three-part series about Julia and Simca cooking in France helped promote Volume II, and the magazine arranged for Julia to record her impressions of the bicentennial bash at the White House. Now, *McCall's* was offering Julia a monthly food column. It was tempting. The magazine had a circulation of several million readers every month, was offering her a creative outlet, a way to generate income and keep her name in the public eye, and would be a welcome distraction from the home front.

Not one to harbor grudges Julia gladly accepted the assignment. As it happened, she reentered the media stream just as America's interest in food and dining was reaching critical mass.

BY THE MID-SEVENTIES, the food business, and food journalism, were experiencing a renaissance. A *Newsweek* story hollered that "adventures in eating are in." Kitchenware stores offered vegetable steamers, earthenware roasters, casseroles, whisks, spoons, spatulas, and carbon-steel knives. Between 1970 and 1975, Crate & Barrel tripled its revenue and couldn't keep up with the demand for Cuisinarts, crepe pans, and porcelain mortars and pestles. "Americans," observed Gordon Segal, the chain's owner, "are showing an increased seriousness about food."

Across the country, markets carried previously unheard-of specialties, such as escargots, pâtés, and Reblochon cheese. Restaurants served giant snails from Normandy steamed in Pernod, or smoked haddock mousse topped with caviar on a nest of fresh dill. Knowledgeable patrons felt empowered to tell the waiter what was in a sauce, and some knew "more about wine than we do," admitted a French chef.

Chinese food was all the rage, and in New York, Shun Lee Palace employed master chefs versed in Peking, Hunan, and Szechuan cuisines. Novelty eateries appeared in former bank vaults, railroad cars, or abandoned warehouses. La Potagerie in New York and Stone Soup in San Francisco served only soup; The Brewery in Chicago served only salad; Dante's Down the Hatch in Atlanta specialized in fondue. And regional American cookery was having a moment: in Kansas City, for instance, The American restaurant served Minnesota turkey, Montana elk, and Columbia River salmon.

Enrollment at cooking schools like the Culinary Institute of America (CIA) spiked. "There is a growing appreciation for the dining experience as an art form," said Henry Ogden Barbour, president of the CIA. "And besides, you can get a job. There were 3.5 job offers for every graduate."

In a parallel movement, Americans became increasingly focused on health. We grew enamored of marathon running, bottled waters like Perrier, vegetarianism, and the calorie calculations of *Dr. Atkins' Diet Revolution*. In revising *The Good Housekeeping Illustrated Cookbook*, food editor Zoe Coulson said, "We really noticed the changes in eating habits. Too many recipes asked for heavy cream or oil."

In response to these converging trends, newspaper editors and food magazines scrambled to meet the demand for restaurant news, information about food, and stories about chefs. *Gourmet* had been founded in 1941, and *Bon Appétit* first appeared in 1956 (well before Julia brought her signature sign-off, *"Bon appétit!,"* to television in 1963), but in the seventies, the category blossomed. In 1978, the Batterberry family, with funding from *Playboy*'s Hugh Hefner, published *Food & Wine*. They witnessed "a big changeover at the moment we founded" the magazine, from a time when "it was 'the little wife in the kitchen' to a period in which more men developed an interest in cooking," recalled a spokesperson. *Cook's* magazine, edited by Christopher Kimball, first appeared in 1980: after selling the magazine to Condé Nast, he launched *Cook's Illustrated* in 1993, and built a mini food-media empire of his own.

Julia was surprised and delighted by Americans' surging interest in food. "There are now so many people in this country, teaching and writing, who have had wonderful training such as working in restaurants in France, taking courses at Lenotre, etc. I can't pretend to keep up with them," Julia wrote to Louisette Bertholle. "It is amazing what a revolution in cooking has taken place in this country—I wonder if young people in France are that much interested? Or as expert? It has perhaps not yet happened there as it has here."

It was against this backdrop that one of the most hyped, confusing, and impactful food trends to hit the United States in years arrived from France: *la nouvelle cuisine*, or "the new cooking." Rooted in French culinary experiments of the 1950s and '60s, nouvelle jumped the pond to America in the early 1970s, where it led to simultaneous cries of delight and gnashing of teeth.

More of a philosophy than a strictly defined regime, nouvelle cuisine was difficult to codify. It was "a bit like pornography . . . people knew it when they saw it," one wag observed. In essence, nouvelle was a style of cooking that emphasized fresh seasonal ingredients, personal creativity, healthfulness, and artistic presentation. It inspired American chefs such as Alice Waters, Wolfgang Puck, and Larry Forgione. Craig Claiborne lauded nouvelle as "the greatest innovation in the world of food since the food processor."

Thanks to chefs like Paul Bocuse, and food journalists like André Gayot, who popularized and promoted the "culinary French Revolution," nouvelle cuisine revolutionized traditional butter and flour–reliant French cooking. Then it had a similar impact in America, where the reverberations of the movement are still felt today. Yet nouvelle was controversial. Julia dove into the fray, enthusiastically questioning whether the new cuisine was as "revolutionary" or as "healthy" as its promoters claimed.

The fight over nouvelle energized Julia, and ushered in a remarkable period in which she engaged American pop culture as never before. In the latter half of the seventies, Julia became more outspoken, used sharper humor, and was willing to use her bully pulpit to promote her agenda in new, sometimes disconcerting ways.

"The older we get," she declared in 1976, "the more American we get."

II. Down with the Old-Fashioned, Up with the New

In order to understand Julia's resistance to nouvelle cuisine, it helps to look back at where nouvelle cuisine came from and why it caught on. At the turn of the nineteenth century, the master chef Auguste Escoffier created *la grande cuisine*, a luxurious style of cooking based on high-quality ingredients and made possible by a wealthy clientele. Escoffier concocted extravagant dinners of ten or more courses for kings, emperors, and czars across Europe. The menu of a 1903 state dinner in Paris, for instance, included: crème Windsor, oxtail soup, crayfish Nantua, salmon trout with morels, baron of lamb, grouse in sherry, duckling, sherbet, fowl, foie gras, salad, asparagus, peas, tarts, ice cream, and fruit, accompanied by wines at least twenty-five years old.

But *la grande cuisine* was ill suited to the twentieth century. By the early 1970s, the world was grappling with the effects of war, recession, social and political turmoil, the OPEC oil embargo, and jet and space travel. In France, young chefs turned away from Escoffier's excess to focus on nouvelle cuisine's seasonal ingredients prepared in a simple, straightforward way. In America, meanwhile, the public had discovered "natural" foods, meaning healthful dishes with fewer calories and more nutrition at a reasonable cost.

The term "nouvelle cuisine" was coined by the French food critic Henri Gault in 1972, but the movement began with Fernand Point, the three-star chef at La Pyramide, in Vienne, in the 1950s. Trained to cook à l'Escoffier, Point grew bored with the classics and began to tinker with them. Vowing to "protect the integrity of the raw product," he emphasized simple, fresh ingredients and elemental techniques. One of his sous-chefs, Paul Bocuse, embraced this approach and took it several steps further after Point's death in 1955.

Bocuse was raised in Lyon—which many aficionados believe is the true culinary capital of France, rather than Paris—on regional specialties such as rabbit stew, pork sausages, tripe, and offal. During the Second World War, he dropped out of school to work in the canteen of a Vichy youth camp, learned to butcher calves and pigs procured on the black market ("excellent training," he'd say), and joined the Free French against the Nazis. After the war he apprenticed under Point at La Pyramide, and admired him for being "a little mean" in the kitchen, a practice Bocuse was proud to continue.

By 1962, Bocuse had opened his own restaurant and was awarded two Michelin stars. His career as a classical chef took off, but, inspired by Point, Bocuse began to innovate. He drastically cut the use of butter and intensified the taste of fresh ingredients. He seared fish quickly and served it "pink at the bone." He flash-cooked green beans, to preserve their crunchiness because he liked the taste. He abstained from using flour in sauces and substituted crushed tomatoes as a binding agent. (Bocuse wasn't always so abstemious: he had a weakness for foie gras, and one of his best-known dishes was *Loup de Mer en Croûte*, the sea bass in a buttery brioche crust that Julia, Simca, and Patricia Simon feasted on in 1969.) "A chef, even a bad one, can never go wrong if he has good raw materials," he said. "The point is to render unto a chicken that which is its due, and nothing more."

Bocuse's approach was deemed heretical by traditionalists, but the public gobbled up his creations and demanded more. By the early seventies, he was a culinary superstar, as adept at publicity stunts as he was at creating signature dishes, like his famous truffle soup or chicken cooked in a pig's bladder. He called himself "the Lion of Lyon," erected a gigantic "Paul Bocuse" sign atop his restaurant in Collonges-au-Mont-d'Or, cooked for President Valéry Giscard d'Estaing, and was awarded the Légion d'Honneur, France's highest decoration.

Jean Didier, of the *Guide Kléber*, wrote: "If Point was God, Bocuse is his prophet." The prophet and his colleagues were labeled *la Bande à Bocuse* (Bocuse's gang), and included Roger Vergé, of the Moulin de Mougins; the Troisgros brothers; Alain Chapel of Chez la Mère Charles; Paul and Jean-Pierre Haeberlin of Auberge de l'Ill; Jean Delaveyne of Le Camélia; Louis Outhier of L'Oasis; and Michel Guérard of Les Prés d'Eugénie.

"It is a cuisine of friendship," Bocuse said of nouvelle. "In my father's day, the chef was a slave. He lived in a stinking hot kitchen underground. He never saw customers. He became a cretin. And, invariably, he began to drink."

In contrast, the "nouvellers" shared recipes, socialized with their guests, and proselytized their new cooking at every opportunity. And, importantly, they were comfortable with journalists and worked hand in glove with a brash new group of media entrepreneurs.

IN MARCH 1969, André Gayot founded *Le Nouveau Guide*, a monthly magazine devoted to a "new era" of food and wine in France, with Gault and his colleague Christian Millau. They believed that "an evolution seemed necessary" in French cooking.

At the time, every top restaurant served virtually identical menus of Escoffier's coq au vin, *sole dieppoise*, and *homard cardinal*, while the *Guide Michelin* awarded the same restaurants three stars year after year. This irked younger chefs, who felt the game was rigged against them. "The profession was contained within the yoke of rules established more than a century ago and nobody thus far had dared to question it," Gayot wrote. In response, the *Nouveau Guide* championed unacknowledged chefs and risky, creative cooking. In the magazine's first issue, the editors wrote:

> Down with the old-fashioned picture of the typical bon vivant, that puffy personage with his napkin tucked under his chin, his lips dripping veal stock, *béchamel* sauce, and *vol-au-vent financière*. Singer of mighty drinking songs, pincher of pretty party girls, festooned with medals and knighted by every wine and food society in Christendom, it is his very image we want to wipe from memory.
>
> Up with the new French cuisine. It is bursting with health, good sense, and good taste! . . . No more of those terrible brown sauces and white sauces, those *espagnoles*, those *Périgueux* with truffles, those *béchamels* and *Mornays* that have assassinated as many livers as they have covered indifferent foods. Down with meat glaze! Down with veal stock, and down with red wine, Madeira, pig's blood, roux, gelatin, and flour in all sauces, and with cheese and starches. They are forbidden! The New Wave should have essences of fresh fish and game, along with lemons, truffles, fresh herbs, and clear sauces that marry with their foods, that exalt them, that sing, that leave the spirit clear and the stomach light.

The nouvelle cuisiniers were inspired by the French New Wave in cinema. After the "spring fever" of 1968, when massive protests essentially shut France down, *"les copains"*—a group of avant-garde filmmakers led by Jean-Luc Godard, François Truffaut, Louis Malle, and Alain Resnais—shook up the movie industry with fiery articles in their journal, *Cahiers du Cinéma*. They advocated replacing conventional equipment and narratives with lighter, handheld cameras and inventive free-flowing films that expressed a "more truthful reality." The movement, known as *la nouvelle vague* (the new wave), changed French cinema and had an impact on moviemaking around the world. Similarly, the *Nouveau Guide* advocated for simpler, more creative and naturalistic foods presented on elegantly composed plates.

To these firebrands, the *Guide Michelin*—the annual, red-covered guide to Europe's best-known hotels and restaurants published by the Michelin tire company—was public enemy number one. The *"Guide Miche"* is a highly regarded, if occasionally capricious, arbiter of taste. The *Guide*'s anonymous reviewers have tremendous power to make or break careers, and have at times been accused of cronyism, lax standards, or, as *The Guardian* put it, of being "a tool of Gallic cultural imperialism." (The three-star chef Bernard Loiseau, of La Côte d'Or, committed suicide in 2003, when it was hinted he would lose a Michelin star. It was later revealed that he was distraught about mounting debts, and the restaurant did not lose a star.)

The cover of *Le Nouveau Guide*'s first issue proclaimed, "Michelin: Don't forget these 48 stars!" It was a challenge, or plea, for the public to pay attention to forty-eight accomplished but relatively unknown chefs that the editors considered rising stars.

To counter the mandarins of the *Guide Miche*, Gault and Millau published their own directory, *Guide de la France*, known as "GaultMillau," or simply "GM." While Michelin awarded chefs one to three stars and black toques (a chef's hat symbol), GM used one to four bright red toques, plus a numerical rating from 1 to 20. And while the *Guide Miche* simply listed a starred restaurant and three of its culinary specialties, the *Guide de la France* included lengthy descriptions of décor, atmosphere, wines, and foods in its listings. Rarely did the two guides agree. In 1973, Michelin anointed the celebrated Parisian restaurant Taillevent with three stars, while GM rated it 17/20 (very good)—meaning, Julia wrote, that "it is clearly too old-fashioned for the tastes" of the nouvellers.

Julia thought each camp had merit. Agreeing with the *Guide Miche* about Taillevent, she wrote that it "excelled in service, comfort, and welcome" and eschewed nouvelle cuisine dogma. But, more generally, she approved of GM's flexible rating system and in-depth commentary. And she criticized Michelin for continually awarding three stars to restaurants like Maxim's in Paris, L'Oustaude Baumanière in Provence, and the Pyramide in Vienne, when "none of [them] seems the glorious temple of gastronomy it once was." While she acknowledged the "terrible responsibility" of adding or subtracting stars, Julia prodded Michelin to maintain consistent standards or risk becoming meaningless.

In the "Manifesto of Nouvelle Cuisine," published in the October 1973 *Nouveau Guide*, Gayot, Gault, and Millau laid out the "constitution" of the movement in the manner of the Ten Commandments. To qualify as nouvelle cuisine, they declared, a restaurant's food had to be fresh and high quality; dishes should be prepared without flour or butter, to promote health and "reveal the true taste of the food"; chefs should be adventurous and use the latest kitchen tools; each plate should satisfy all of the senses, "starting with sight," meaning that food should be presented like works of art, with compelling colors and forms.

The manifesto set off a heated debate on both sides of the Atlantic. In France, newspapers heralded "The French Revolution of the plates." In America, the press had a field day trumpeting the rift between the nouvelle upstarts and traditional French chefs.

AS IT TURNED OUT, the "new cooking" had a similar impact in the States. In the early seventies, the movement blew across the Atlantic like a spore, took root, flowered, and propagated across America. When chefs like Paul Bocuse, the Troisgros brothers, and Michel Guérard published cookbooks in English and demonstrated nouvelle techniques in the United States, they inspired similar innovations here. First with the California cuisine of the mid-1970s; and then, under the influence of "fusion" cooking—which incorporated Pacific Rim, Latin American, and European food—in the New American cuisine in the 1980s.

For Americans, nouvelle cuisine reconciled several conflicting imperatives: our growing enthusiasm for fine food, a focus on healthful cooking, and a heightened concern about fat and cholesterol. Nouvelle's light, eye-catching style was perfectly suited to the cultural moment.

As Craig Claiborne described it, nouvelle cuisine expanded into "an accordion-pleated affair that affects amateurs and professionals alike [and] can be expanded or contracted—for better or worse—according to the whims and imagination of the cook or chef." He would later elaborate: "Nouvelle cuisine is the greatest innovation in the world of food since the food processor and, like that machine, it has opened up and broadened horizons in the world of cooking that slightly more than a decade ago were unthinkable."

But not all Americans were ready to embrace lighter, snazzier fare. René Verdon, who had cooked for President John F. Kennedy at the White House, grumbled: "When people go to a French restaurant, they want to eat very well." And Jack Lirio, a San Francisco cooking teacher, sniped, "Without butter, cream and foie gras, what's left of French cooking?"

Julia sided with the dissenters. She did not care for blood-rare quail or pink-at-the-bone turbot, which "does not develop the essential taste." To her palate, the loss of flour in sauces resulted in thin, plain, and unsatisfying reductions. "Humph!" she declared to *The New York Times*. "Vegetables astringently crisp, indeed. Why, that's from people who've never had a properly cooked green bean, just those limp frozen ones." To cook a proper green bean, Julia said, one drops very fresh beans into rapidly boiling water, snatches them out after exactly four minutes, and refreshes them in an ice bath, which fixes the color and texture, then shakes them in a hot pan with plenty of salt and butter.

Simca concurred: "Nouvelle Cuisine was debased when every hash slinger started trotting out pretentious dishes in big plates, and now it's almost a dirty expression," she wrote. "That horror nouvelle . . . if some hapless cook should happen to serve me crunchy, half-cooked vegetables, I say, 'Cook it some more, please. I'm not a rabbit.'"

Paul had another take: nouvelle's supposedly radical chefs were "just doing the same thing that's been done for years," he said; their cooking was an *evolution* not a *revolution*. While nouvelle chefs tinkered with the details—using new types of herbs, say, or familiar ingredients in different combinations, or plating their food in a new style—they had nevertheless stuck to the basic tenets of traditional French cuisine. (France is an essentially conservative nation, and it is unlikely that patrons would have embraced a truly radical menu.)

To Julia's mind, the entire nouvelle narrative smacked of "that Paris PR game." On the other hand, it got people talking about food and encouraged chefs to try new techniques, which was all to the good. "Well, if they can get away with it—why not?" she said. "They've made it a lot of fun."

III. An Elegant Hustle

In November 1973, Julia received a query from a fan in New Jersey, a Mr. Philip W. Nash, about the "young Turks" who were stirring up French cooking and getting a lot of press for it. She replied:

> One thing to remember is that these articles are all written by publicity people, not by cooks . . . It gives them something exciting to write about. Fish baked in seaweed, truffled this and that, amazing sauces with sorrel in them, and so forth and so on . . . However, you have to thicken a sauce with something—mustard at times, but then it tastes like mustard. You can't use egg yolks all the time. You can't reduce a brown meat juice to nothing and not come up with a meat glaze, and that would be too strong. Peeking over the shoulder of the chefs you would probably see a bit of cornstarch, or a spoonful of velouté, or demi-glace.

She pointed to an article that had appeared in *Time*, in April 1973, in which the correspondent Steven Englund reported on a lunch chez Bocuse, with parenthetical asides from the chef: "It began with sausage in a brioche ('You really have to eat sausage when you come to Lyon') and continued with *pâté de foie gras* that had been made the same morning. Next came the shrimp soup ('Escoffier would have been horrified at how simple it is. Just some shrimp, white wine, heavy cream, butter, a few shallots'). The fourth course was wild duck in green pepper sauce ('If you come in December, you can eat duck that I shoot myself') . . . the goat cheese—Collonges goats, of course—but a sense of self-preservation made [me] turn down the pastry and the seven varieties of fruit in wine."

In her copy of the story, Julia circled the above paragraph in thick blue ink and scrawled "awful menu!" Writing to Mr. Nash, she added: "What kind of healthy menu is that? Somebody is pulling the hanky-panky, is what . . . Don't take any wooden nickels or foie gras."

Indeed, there was an element of enterprising showmanship to the nouveller's shtick that occasionally lurched into farce.

In September 1971, Chef Pierre Laporte of the Café de Paris in Biarritz invited six other renowned nouvelle cuisine chefs to join him in cooking the "Dinner of the Century." One hundred and forty diners paid significant sums to eat the meal. As the food writer John L. Hess reported in *The New York Times*, the meal began with a consommé that melted, unforgivably; moved on to a respectable sea bass in red wine that was paired with an awful pink 1959 Dom Pérignon Champagne (quickly replaced by a different wine, an excellent Château Haut-Brion, 1962); a bland crayfish dish; and a novelty corn purée whipped with foie gras; a dessert of pear sherbet was "without interest." The dinner was, Hess concluded, "a pretentious fiasco." Robert Courtine, a leading French food writer, considered the affair "quite simply . . . a commercial venture, some kind of 'biznesse.'"

The problem, noted the chef Charles Barrier, was that inviting seven superstars to cook together was "like putting seven artists to work on the same painting." He believed that each meal should be built around a single spectacular dish. But there was no central focus to the dinner of the century, no crescendo or decrescendo. The chefs admitted they would never have served such foods in their own restaurants.

Nevertheless, the idea of treating chefs as stars and promoting marquee culinary events as theater had arrived. In January 1973, Paul Bocuse flew to New York to cook another dinner of the century, this time at The Four Seasons Restaurant. Bocuse's real agenda was to promote his private-label wine. This dinner of the century began with crayfish soup, proceeded to foie gras and a salad of sliced truffles, a poached chicken stuffed with truffles, a gamy woodcock, green bean threads, and nubbins of goat cheese. It was hardly a simple meal. "The dinner is *énormément trop*" ("enormously over-the-top"), Bocuse conceded. "It is a dinner for Louis XIV. Simplicity is for Lyon. This is New York."

In the fall of 1973, Gael Greene, *New York* magazine's vivid restaurant critic, accompanied a pack of celebrities on a three-star *Grande Bouffe* (or "Great Nosh," in her translation) to sample nouvelle cuisine in Paris and Biarritz at harvesttime. Greene; the actor Danny Kaye; the editor of *Screw* magazine, Al Goldstein; the writer Nora Ephron; and others were flown to France aboard a corporate jet. There, they indulged in Champagne and caviar breakfasts, then gorged on a spinach and almond milk soup at Roger Vergé's Moulin de Mougins, the Troisgros brothers' famous salmon in sorrel butter, Bocuse's sturgeon eggs, and—best of all—fish steamed on seaweed followed by pigeon brains at Michel Guérard's Le Pot-au-Feu in Paris.

"Never was there a more elegant hustle," Greene reported. "I have been seduced and I have seduced. But this, dear friends, and gentle mouths . . . this was a Seduction."

The boondoggle had been arranged by Yanou Collart, whom Julia characterized as "the very clever French publicity agent for the 3-star chefs, and also, I am sure, for Gault and Millau." Julia suspected that many of the nouvellers were motivated by a hunger for revenue and publicity as much as, if not more than, by a sincere quest for gastronomic invention.

The following year, Julia's views hardened against this vogue after she attended a gala Dinner for Women in New York, an event orchestrated by Bocuse and his nouvelle brothers Jean Troisgros and Gaston Lenôtre.

Gael Greene had been the only woman invited to the 1973 Dinner of the Century, a predicament that she loved and hated in equal measure, causing her "feminist spirit [to become] schizophrenic." This time she was in charge of the guest list and advised on the menu. Greene and Julia were seated with ten other ladies who were ready to eat. They included the playwright Lillian Hellman, "*une femme d'un certain âge*, wonderfully raddled face (no *sacquépage! [sic]*)," Julia wrote; Marya Mannes, "a colorful journalist, novelist and personality"; Charlotte Curtis of *The New York Times*, "a very smart girl"; and *Gourmet* magazine's Naomi Barry, "just back from neck surgery, looking very pretty." There was also Louise Nevelson, "an elderly, long, eccentric and renowned sculptress"; Pauline Trigère, the French clothing designer; and Sally Quinn, from CBS television. Rounding out the group was Margaret Tynes, a black opera singer; Bess Myerson, a former Miss America and former head of New York's Department of Consumer Affairs; and Dena Kaye, the daughter of Danny Kaye. There were no men present, other than the chefs and waiters.

When Bocuse landed at Kennedy Airport, U.S. Customs seized his bags filled with a prized rump of veal, a haunch of venison, fresh foie gras, a brace of chickens, strings of Lyonnaise sausages, vats of French cream, and strands of garlic—though the chef did manage to smuggle in two hundred dollars' worth of black truffles, which he passed off as "chocolates." Bocuse knew how to play the PR game: he posed for photographs at a McDonald's and clowned for network TV. Stopping at a butcher shop, Greene reported, he "fondled" a rump of veal and declared, "It's lovely, but nothing like the ass I lost."

In place of the veal, Bocuse baked a *loup* in seaweed and topped it with scallops and a beurre blanc. He filled a ramekin with truffle ragout, foie gras, and spinach. And he prepared crayfish tails and a salad of dandelion greens.

The *loup* was overcooked, and the scallops and dandelions were past their prime, but the truffle ragout and Lenôtre's citrus sorbets were "exquisite," Greene wrote. The Bocuse and Troisgros house wines were "simply pleasant country wines, no more . . . neither complex nor memorable," she added. "Imagine an evening cuddling with a confirmed virgin. It just wouldn't give. It's not ready to be loved."

"The revolution just didn't work," she wrote of the Dinner for Women. "The dinner itself must go down as a bizarre hiccup in the annals of serious gastronomy. There is no question that Bocuse and Troisgros are wizards. But I can't believe they would have dared serve the same menu to male muck-a-mucks." As for the all-women conceit, Greene added: "Forgive me Gloria [Steinem] . . . No one was outrageous or bitchy. No one was noisily brilliant. Men might have provoked us, stirred our unreformed competitive instinct, upped the decibels of wit and the ultrasonic intimations of erotic possibilities. Yes, I know these notions are dangerously revisionist."

Julia judged the meal fine, if unmemorable, and agreed with Greene about the lack of dynamism at the table. "Dinner with 12 women is not very exciting!" she wrote. "One so clearly sees that the spark is missing . . . It's rather like a class reunion at Smith." She had enjoyed the meal as spectacle, but left feeling more dubious than ever about the self-important hype of the nouvellers. "Heaven knows what all of this proved, but I wouldn't have missed it for the world," Julia wrote. "It certainly had nothing whatsoever to do with serious gastronomy, and everything with publicity and promotion, which, of course, all of us were quite well aware of."

IV. "Is Escoffier Dead? Really Dead?"

In an article for *New York* magazine titled "'La Nouvelle Cuisine': A Skeptic's View," Julia mocked the exhortations of Gault and Millau:

" 'Down with Escoffier and his dreadful heavy cooking,' was the universal cry . . . It all made very good copy—something revolutionary, at last, to talk about." But, Julia wondered, "Is it a hoax, a public relations snow job . . . Does a new cuisine really exist in France? . . . Is Escoffier dead? Really dead?"

She didn't buy it. "It is obvious . . . that the Gault-Millau publications have had a profound influence in France, since without their continual pushing of the nouvelle cuisine, I do not see how it could have been launched," she wrote. "Now almost any restaurant of any pretensions has its little salad of green beans more or less lavishly garnished, or has copied the greats with artichoke hearts and *écrivisse* tails, or a mousse of sea scallops and salmon." The drawback, as Julia saw it, was "a certain sameness of menu . . . that is probably inevitable since not every chef is a creator, and those who cannot create will copy those who can."

While the *Guide Miche* granted L'Auberge du Père Bise, at Talloires, three stars, GM accused the same restaurant of oversauced food and a tired menu. "Dieu! How can one refuse to experiment, to perfect, and to share with one's clients the creative adventure?" *Le Nouveau Guide* sputtered. The magazine cautioned readers not to patronize Le Père Bise until the chef "understood" the nouvelle revolution. Julia considered such admonishments "browbeating" and accused GM of "threaten[ing] restaurants that they'd better conform."

The chefs who "understood" nouvelle cuisine, she noted, were rewarded by GM with favorable reviews. The light puff pastry with sweetbreads and wild mushrooms served by the Troisgros brothers in Roanne was lauded with red toques in *Le Nouveau Guide*. And so were dishes by Chef Henri Faugeron of Les Belles Gourmandes, and Michel Oliver of Le Bistrot de Paris. Describing in loving detail Chef Frédy Girardet's salad of crayfish tails and slivers of duck liver at the Hôtel de Ville, in Crissier, Switzerland, GM awarded him four red toques and raved, "You will have one of the great meals of your life!"

While Bocuse liked to pillory the *grande cuisine* for its soporific sauces, not all nouvelle chefs agreed with the Lion of Lyon. Indeed, some agreed with Paul Child's observation that nouvelle was more an evolution rather than a revolution in French cooking. Nouvelle cuisine certainly didn't mean "down with Escoffier," a French chef told Julia. "Where would any of us be without him?"

V. Cuisine Minceur

At least one chef managed to please everyone with his inventive cooking. In April 1977, the *Guide Michelin* bestowed a third star on Michel Guérard, while *Le Nouveau Guide* applauded him with a bouquet of red toques.

It had been a long time coming. When Le Pot-au-Feu, his two-star restaurant in a Paris suburb, was razed to make way for a new superhighway, the five-foot three-inch Guérard sank into despair and put on twenty-six pounds. In 1974, he retreated south, to the Pyrenees mountains, where he restarted his career. At a spa owned by his wife's family, Les Prés et les Sources d'Eugénie, Guérard banished butter, oil, cream, starches, and sugar from the kitchen. He developed new methods to cook food quickly, using its own moisture, and seasoned his dishes with wild herbs, like heather or pine needles. Cooking wines were heated to burn off the alcohol. Saltwater fish were steamed under fresh seaweed, while freshwater fish were cooked in a light vegetable sauce, and accompanied by a julienne or purée of vegetables. He called this approach *cuisine minceur*—the "diet of slimness," or "slimming cooking"—and promptly shed seventeen pounds. And by all accounts the results were delicious.

"I don't want to make dieting a punishment," said Guérard. *Cuisine minceur* "will never replace" the refined, traditional cuisine of Escoffier, Guérard vowed. "That would be awful."

Simca was impressed. While she "scorned" most of the "debased" nouvelle cuisiniers, she applauded "the inventive, creative spirit of our great chefs . . . After all, who wants to eat a *coq au vin* that always tastes the same?" After dining chez Guérard, she wrote: "He is the only one who really did invent a whole new way of cooking . . . All of his sauces are miraculously light and harmonious, even the ones made with zero-percent fat, low-cal fresh cheese. I growl at foolish women who try to diet for no special health reasons but just want to look like fashion models. But Guérard's diet ideas convert to truly acceptable, well-balanced, and delicious food."

Julia initially expressed doubts about his approach: "I don't think people are really going to want to go out to an expensive French restaurant to eat puréed carrots," she told *The New York Times*. But she later revised her opinion, writing that Guérard's *cuisine minceur* was "obviously . . . a really original style of cookery, a calorie-counting haute cuisine [that was] his alone."

Notably, Guérard served two different menus at his spa: a classical, Escoffier-style *cuisine gourmande*, and his own, groundbreaking *cuisine minceur*. It was his "continual inventiveness in every realm" that really impressed Julia. In Guérard's kitchen, at least, the two cuisines were not mutually exclusive, but coexisted harmoniously, commenting on and playing off of each other.

VI. "A Refreshment of Traditional French Cooking"

Julia made and revised her position on nouvelle cuisine several times. When the trend first arrived in America, she vociferously rejected nouvelle's "bouillon-cube"–thin sauces in favor of what she considered properly cooked green beans (with butter), perfectly cooked fish (with cream), and rich brown sauces (with plenty of flour, wine, and butter) à l'Escoffier. Yet, even as she pleaded for authenticity in French kitchens, Julia was moving away from the classics in her own cooking, as evinced by the transnational recipes she included in *From Julia Child's Kitchen* in 1975.

This contradictory message was no doubt perplexing to her fans (at least those paying close attention), though in typical fashion Julia didn't dwell on it. She seemed to draw a distinction between what the French were, or "should be," doing, and what was happening on her own stove and in kitchens across America. It took some time for Julia to reconcile this disconnect.

By 1977, it was clear that nouvelle was no mere flash in the pan, and that for Julia to understand its appeal, and adapt to it, she would have to go to the source. She had occasionally sampled new-style dishes, but had yet to undertake a serious tasting tour of nouvelle restaurants in France. In June, Paul and Julia did just that. They spent a week in Paris, followed by a long weekend at Guérard's spa in the Pyrenees, and ended with a tour through nouvelle restaurants in Provence. At the end of the trip, Julia asked herself: "What is this nouvelle cuisine, really?"

Her answer was equivocal. While she remained unconvinced that the new cooking was truly new or especially healthful she decided that the movement itself was promising. She liked the young cooks' sociability, creativity, and public appeal. She enjoyed their use of gelatinous stocks, or stocks thickened with cornstarch or rice, their focus on fresh ingredients, and their inventive compositions. Best of all to her mind, the nouvellers had excited the public about food, enticed them into restaurants, and inspired people to shop and eat.

Yet the Childs had also witnessed the dark side of the revolution. One day Julia lunched at an (unnamed) restaurant that had recently lost one of its two Michelin stars. The owner had suffered a nervous breakdown and had just emerged from the clinic. He was heartbroken and had no idea why his food had been demoted by "them," the anonymous inspectors from the *Guide Miche*. In desperation, he had turned away from classical cuisine and attempted a nouvelle menu. Julia ordered his *magret de canard*, a braised duck napped in brown sauce. But the sauce tasted "for all the world like liquefied bouillon cubes," she judged, "utterly drowning the flavor of that *magret*."

After tasting the hits of nouvelle cuisine—dainty salads, fish poached with a julienne of vegetables and truffles in a white wine sauce, duck with green peppercorns—Julia found herself hungry for "the sanity" of old-fashioned, Escoffier-style brown sauces. She dreamed of a satisfyingly classic bistro meal—*oeufs en gelée* flanked by thick slices of *pâté maison*, a *blanquette de veau à l'ancienne* with new peas; a fresh green salad with a *chapon* of garlic toast; a cheese course featuring a thick, blue-veined wedge of Roquefort and a rich Camembert; for dessert, a fresh strawberry tart with a crisp, buttery crust and a sturdy dollop of cream, followed by a dense *café filtre* and a tot of Calvados. That, as far as she was concerned, was a real meal.

"It's not that I don't appreciate the nouvelle cuisine. I love it! We need it!" she wrote in *New York* in 1977. "It's a shot in the arm to good cookery. But please, let's not throw out the comfortable old glories."

In a 1984 interview with *Stars and Stripes*, Julia modulated her criticism further: "When we were [in France] a long time ago you couldn't change anything at all. It was just absolutely rigid, too traditional. But I also think that more natural food is going to come back again . . . People are much more conscious of calories now . . . Nouvelle cuisine has been needed."

To her mind, then, nouvelle was a necessary development and diversification: an approach to cooking that would not supplant classical *grande cuisine*, but one that would complement and push it in new directions. Nouvelle, Julia concluded, was "a refreshment of traditional French cooking."

VII. "Organic, Chaotic, and Unstoppable"

Nouvelle cooking landed in New York in 1971 and quickly spread across the country, mutating in wonderfully unpredictable ways. With its year-round bounty and a sunny emphasis on wellness, California was a natural place for nouvelle to take root and flourish.

At Chez Panisse, which opened in Berkeley in 1971, Alice Waters—inspired by rustic country restaurants in the South of France—and colleagues such as Jeremiah Tower and Mark Miller embraced food that was fresh, light, beautiful to look at, and composed of new ingredients or combinations of flavors. Waters's acolytes helped to spread the gospel across the country. Miller left Chez Panisse to open Coyote Café in Santa Fe, where he became a star of southwestern cooking. Jonathan Waxman worked at "Chez" and, with Michael McCarty—who had trained in France in the 1970s—applied the fresh-and-light ethos to Michael's, the famed in spot in Santa Monica. In New York, Waxman cooked California cuisine at Jams.

In Los Angeles, Wolfgang Puck, the Austrian-born, French-trained chef, brought "modern French cooking for the American kitchen" (the title of his 1981 cookbook) to Ma Maison. In the 1990s, he popularized California-style pizzas—topped with nontraditional ingredients, such as goat cheese, sun-dried tomatoes, or smoked salmon—at Spago. Today, Puck is a ubiquitous celebrity chef and TV actor, and his Wolfgang Puck Companies run more than twenty restaurants, and catering and merchandise businesses across the country.

When Michel Guérard helped to open Regine's nightclub in New York, in 1976, the American chefs Larry Forgione and Michael Romano worked under him, and later opened their own restaurants—Forgione's An American Place, and Romano's Union Square Cafe—in the city. Charlie Trotter trained in the United States and Europe, and opened his eponymous restaurant in Chicago in 1987, won two Michelin stars, and promoted a healthier menu.

These chefs and legions of others were inspired to make "edible art" that promoted their American roots. Their kitchens filled with plastic squeeze bottles used to paint slashes, smears, and squiggles of multicolored sauces. They made culinary puns, layering grilled vegetables into savory "napoleons," or adapting the classic *navarin* of mutton into lobster *navarin*. They served their creations on large white plates, as the Troisgros brothers did. And they created a new kind of menu with long, evocative explanations of their food. As the New American chefs pushed gustatory boundaries, magazines ran colorful, stylized photographs of gorgeous plates and wrote about traditional recipes "with a twist"— substituting cilantro for tarragon in béarnaise sauce, for instance, a simple trick that had never been used before the arrival of nouvelle. Inspired, home cooks demanded the ingredients used by their culinary heroes—arugula, flavored olive oils, Cajun spices, Mexican chiles, Japanese wasabi—from specialty food stores.

Today nouvelle cuisine and its American cousins have been so thoroughly subsumed into our daily eating habits that they have become invisible. But this is not surprising, and has been the fate of most immigrant traditions in the New World. Much as English, Dutch, and German recipes were adapted to American ingredients by the colonists of "Thirteen Feasts," nouvelle cuisine techniques were adapted by the Californian and New American chefs in the seventies and eighties. With a premium on creativity, freshness, and healthfulness, the new cooking enlarged people's idea of what great food can be. For chefs, it was liberating; for investors, it was remunerative; for food purveyors and home cooks, it was inspiring; for diners, it was satisfying.

"What that movement left was a feeling to pursue our goals without the pressure of conforming," said the chef Larry Forgione. "A sense of freedom was felt by every culinary artist throughout the world. That is why nouvelle cuisine should be recognized as one of the most powerful culinary movements of our time."

In 2013, Christopher Kimball, then host of *America's Test Kitchen* and editor of *Cook's Illustrated*, appraised the gastronomic uprising of the 1970s: "A by-the-book American revolution, the culinary shift to come bubbled up without guidance or permission from established authorities. It was, and still is, organic, chaotic, and unstoppable."

10

A Go-To Cultural Figure

1. Jacques and the Clam Strips

It's not very *tender*," Julia says reprovingly, as she munches a bit of the spinach that Jacques Pépin is sautéing in a pan.

"It's *not*?" Pépin replies with amused Gallic incredulity.

"It tastes *okay*," she continues. "I like that old-fashioned way of *boiling* it and *squeezing* it. You get it tender, and you don't get that slight *bitterness* to it . . . But, you can do it either way."

"I mean, *I* tend to do it this way," Pépin replies, with a hint of defensiveness, as he briskly mounds the cooked spinach into cleaned artichoke hearts. "With less loss of nutrients—"

"We don't care about *nutrients!*" Julia interrupts.

"We don't care about nutrients, okay . . . ," he mumbles.

"We care about *taste!*"

"*Yes,*" Pépin says with infinite patience. "But when we can have both, *together*—you know?"

"It's still a little . . . it's not very *tender*," Julia says. "It still has a slight *bitterness* to it."

Pépin tastes the spinach for himself, gives the camera an imploring glance, and defends his technique. "It is *very* tender!"

"Ha-ha." Julia laughs, and slips in the last word. "Well, maybe you have sharper *teeth* than I do!"

This scene was typical of *Julia & Jacques Cooking at Home*, the popular PBS series that debuted in 1999. By then, Child and Pépin had been honing their he-said, she-said act for years in live performances across the country. Their genial sparring was as educational as it was amusing, and it made for great television.

Jacques first met Julia in New York in 1961 when they were both unknowns. He was fresh off the boat after cooking for President Charles de Gaulle. She was in Manhattan with Simca and Judith Jones, promoting the just-published *Mastering the Art of French Cooking.* They spoke about food in French that night, and began a conversation that would last until the end of her life. "It always felt completely natural between us," Pépin recalled, whether "at home, in front of a live audience, or on television."

He was born in a small town near Lyon, and learned to cook at his mother's restaurant, Le Pélican, before moving to the Plaza Athénée in Paris, cooking for the French secretary of the treasury, and then for President de Gaulle at the Élysée Palace. In August 1959, when Pépin was twenty-four years old, he sailed from France to Quebec City aboard the converted troopship *Ascania*, and took a train to New York City in search of a new life. Arriving in Manhattan with just a few words of English and hardly any money, Pépin discovered that a promised job had disappeared. Within days, he found his way to Le Pavillon, Henri Soulé's shrine to gastronomy on Fifth Avenue at Fifty-fifth Street. There, he met Chef Pierre Franey, who hired Pépin "on the spot," Pépin recalled. "Number one, because I was French; and number two, because I was a chef." Franey had arrived in New York in 1939 to cook at the French pavilion at the World's Fair, and stayed. Pépin and Franey hit it off and began to cook up a storm.

So successful were they that in 1960 the two Frenchmen were poached from Soulé's haute cuisine restaurant by one of his regular customers, Howard D. Johnson, who ran the eponymous restaurant and motel chain. "HoJo's" was the largest such chain in the country; its orange roofs appeared along most American highways, and catered to the motorized masses. So why would two noted French chefs care to join such an establishment?

Johnson had started the business in 1925 with a $2,000 loan, which he used to buy a corner pharmacy with a soda fountain in Wollaston, Massachusetts. By 1961, the company had gone public and had expanded to include 605 restaurants (265 company owned and 340 franchised) and 88 Howard Johnson motor lodges, ten Red Coach Grill restaurants, and manufacturing plants across thirty-three states and the Bahamas. Known for serving quality fried clams and twenty-eight flavors of ice cream, HoJos were distinguished by iconic turquoise cupolas topped by weather vanes in the shape of the company's Simple Simon and the Pieman logo. By the mid-seventies, Howard Johnson's included nearly 1,000 restaurants and more than 500 motor lodges across the United States and Canada, and had become synonymous with the American car and turnpike culture. (In 1959, Howard D. Johnson handed daily operations over to his son, Howard B. Johnson, though he kept a hand in the business until his death in 1972.)

The HoJo's business model relied on serving prepared food made with high-quality ingredients at countertops or in traditional dining rooms. Johnson hired Pépin and Franey to keep standards high and innovation constant. But first, he believed that his new recruits needed to learn the business of serving mass-produced food to Americans. He subjected the three-star chefs to a crash course in flipping burgers, grilling hot dogs, frying hash browns, scooping ice-cream sundaes, and baking apple pies at his restaurants around New York City.

Pépin didn't view his new job as a step down in culinary stature, but rather as "my most valuable apprenticeship." He worked as a line cook at the HoJo's on Queens Boulevard, in Rego Park, and did an even longer stint at the company's outpost in Times Square. Franey would later gain fame as co-author with Craig Claiborne of the *New York Times* column "60-Minute Gourmet," and spin-off books. He and Pépin spent a decade working for the Johnsons, pushing standards at the roadside restaurants higher and higher.

Like crazed inventors sequestered in a remote laboratory, the chefs worked until all hours of the night at the company's Queens Village commissary. They grew accustomed to making 250 pounds of mayonnaise in gigantic mixing machines, and cooking 3,000-gallon batches of clam chowder. They experimented with dozens of versions of beef stew and tweaked elaborate dishes, like scallops in a subtle mushroom sauce, for the HoJo's in Des Moines, Kalamazoo, and Oklahoma City. "After working on a standard Howard Johnson's recipe in the test kitchen, Pierre and I would prepare it in progressively larger quantities, improving its taste by cutting down on margarine and replacing it with butter, using fresh onions instead of dehydrated onions, real potatoes instead of frozen ones," Pépin recalled. "We made fresh stock in a quantity requiring three thousand pounds of veal bones for each batch, and we daily boned a thousand turkeys and made ten tons of frankfurters."

Pépin and Franey were given carte blanche by Howard Johnson Sr., a connoisseur who often stopped by the test kitchen to debate the proper thickness of a stew, ask why they had changed the size of the chicken croquettes, or debate the merits of frozen versus fresh mushrooms in their beef Stroganoff.

On their off-hours Pépin and Franey would go undercover to HoJos along the New England Thruway or on the New Jersey Turnpike to see how their food stood up to the rigors of roadside dining. And they especially enjoyed slipping into the Times Square restaurant, to eat fried clams washed down with "the best Manhattan cocktail in town," which was served with a full pitcher for refills.

When the noted Swiss pastry chef Albert Kumin joined them, the trio began producing ten tons of Danish pastries a day, and thousands of apple, cherry, blueberry, and pumpkin pies for Mr. Johnson's empire. The three Europeans also influenced the menus at the Red Coach Grill, the Ground Round, and other restaurants owned by the company, as well as the supermarkets and schools supplied by the HoJo's grocery operation.

Pépin loved the work, earned a BA from Columbia University on the side, and turned native. During the sixties, he and Franey immersed themselves in American eating habits and witnessed firsthand the nation's culinary revolution. "We were foot soldiers, not chefs working in an elitist restaurant, serving food to only a few privileged people," Pépin wrote. "The most important thing I [learned] at HoJo's was that Americans had extremely open palates compared to French diners. They were willing to try items that lay outside their normal range of tastes. If they liked the food, that was all that mattered. I wasn't constantly battling ingrained prejudices as I would have been in France, where something as simple as adding carrots to *boeuf bourguignon* could have gotten me guillotined, not because carrots make the dish taste bad (they are great), but because it wouldn't be the way a boeuf was supposed to be made . . . In the States, if it tasted good, then fine, the customer was happy. A whole new world of culinary possibilities had opened up before me."

Hit by the gas crisis of the seventies, and a public preference for fast-food restaurants, HoJos' business slipped into decline. In 2005, upon the demise of his beloved Times Square HoJo's, Pépin wrote a eulogy: "For me, Howard Johnson's reliable, modestly priced food embodies the straightforwardness of the American spirit." The branch was a victim of real estate prices, changing tastes, and pressure from leaner, cheaper fast-food chains. (Ownership of the company has changed hands several times, and as of this writing there is only one Howard Johnson's restaurant extant.) "It saddens me that New Yorkers looking for this kind of gentleness and simplicity will soon have to find it elsewhere. It won't be easy."

While scooping ice cream and flipping burgers, Pépin had not forgotten haute cuisine, and in his off-hours, Helen McCully—the diminutive, fiery food editor of *House Beautiful*—introduced him to the small group of gastronomic aficionados in New York, including James Beard, Dione Lucas, and Craig Claiborne.

Pépin was raised in France during the chaotic years of the Second World War, and at age six his parents sent him to live temporarily with a farmer to keep him out of harm's way. Though he attended high school, he never earned a diploma. Arriving in New York in 1961, he was a phenomenal cook but rough around the edges. So McCully—Pépin's "friend, mentor, and surrogate 'American mother,'" as he described her—took it upon herself to instruct the young chef on how to dress, cut his hair, write thank-you notes, and comport himself in polite society. She also tried to fix him up with a succession of editorial assistants, without much success. In New York, Pépin enrolled in an English class at Columbia University "because it was the best school in New York." He later earned a BA, and nearly added a PhD from the university; he toyed with the idea of becoming an academic, before returning to his "first love," cooking.

One evening in 1960, McCully handed Pépin a cardboard box full of 750 typed pages: it was a cookbook written "by a woman up in Cambridge" and two French friends, she explained. Though it had been rejected by Houghton Mifflin, she thought it was "an amazing piece of work," and added, "I want to know what you think."

Pépin lugged the heavy box home and began to flip through the manuscript at the kitchen table. As he went, he passed the pages over to his roommate, Chef Jean-Claude Szurdak, whom Pépin had met while cooking at the Élysée Palace. They read the entire manuscript from start to finish. The authors "had taken the training and knowledge that Jean-Claude and I had acquired as apprentices and *commis* and codified it, broken it down into simple steps that someone who had never boiled a kettle of water could follow," Pépin recalled in his memoir, *The Apprentice*. "I was a little jealous. This was the type of book I should have written."

In late 1961, Pépin met two of the book's three authors—Julia Child and Simca Beck—at a dinner party at McCully's apartment on the Upper East Side. At that point, *Mastering* had just been published by Knopf, and Child and Beck had embarked on their self-financed cross-country publicity tour. "I wasn't in any way prepared for the woman I met that night." Pépin laughed. "With Julia, who could be?" She was about a foot taller than he was, loud and self-confident, but also sympathetic and accomplished. "She was larger than life in every way," said Pépin.

Julia and Jacques spoke mostly in French that evening, comparing notes about food, cooking, eating, drinking, and *la belle France*. And thus began a friendship that would last until Julia's death forty-three years later. Along the way, the two collaborated on hundreds of cooking demonstrations, culminating in *Julia & Jacques Cooking at Home*, which won an Emmy Award in 2001.

"Julia revolutionized cooking in America, but she was not a revolutionary cook," Pépin said. "Her idea was to do classical French cuisine well. And, believe me, that's not easy!" In the great restaurants of France, a young chef will apprentice for six or seven years, trying to emulate the head chef's dishes as closely as possible, and thereby gain his accumulated knowledge; only then can the young chef begin to experiment creatively on his own. "A head chef will never say to his sub-chefs, 'Do you agree with my approach?'" said Pépin. "It's immaterial if they agree. They are there to learn the classical approach. Julia agreed with that. She'd make a hamburger the way she learned from chef Bugnard in Paris: mix sautéed onion with the meat, press down on the patty in a skillet, make a little sauce for it, and serve it with a piece of good bread. I cook a burger the way I learned at Howard Johnson's—don't press it, salt the meat, serve it with iceberg lettuce, a slice of tomato, red onion, on a plain roll. In some ways, she was more French than I was."

Pépin teased Julia about her Frenchness, and Julia teased him right back: "Of course, you don't serve it that way in *Connecticut*, do you, *Jack*?"

she'd say, pronouncing his name in a cowboy drawl. (Pépin had settled in Madison, Connecticut.)

Like many French chefs, Julia kept a copy of *Le Répertoire de la Cuisine*, a reference guide to seventy-five hundred classical recipes originally complied by Louis Saulnier, a student of Escoffier's, in 1914. (It remains in print today.) *Le Répertoire* is an aide-mémoire, a shorthand list of ingredients and just a few basic steps for the experienced cook to use as a reference to make, say, salmon-in-brioche crust. "Julia's books were at the other end of the spectrum," laughed Pépin. "She liked to work *in depth*."

JULIA ENCOURAGED THOUSANDS of cooks but mentored only a few of them. For someone to be worthy of her undivided attention they had to prove themself, as Julia put it, *"sérieux"*: she liked people who were serious about cooking. "No flimsies!" she'd insist. Jacques Pépin was one of the chosen. There was not much Julia could teach him about cooking, but there was a lot she could teach him about performing—something that personal circumstances dictated he do more of, and better.

In 1974, Pépin was driving too fast in upstate New York when a deer tumbled off an embankment onto the road in front of him. He swerved and smashed into a telephone pole, knocking it down; the car was totaled, and he was left with fourteen fractures, including a broken back, two broken hips, and a broken pelvis. After the accident, Pépin found it difficult to stand for hours behind a restaurant stove. So he began to teach classes, do live cooking demonstrations, consult for restaurateurs—like Joe Baum, the impresario behind Windows on the World atop New York's World Trade Center—and teach cooking on television.

Julia was twenty-three years older than Jacques, and she was older than his mother and aunt. All three of them were powerful women and excellent cooks, Pépin recalled, "and none of them was too impressed with me."

Julia adored and respected Pépin, but was not cowed by his résumé. "She was a very good home cook, and never pretended to be anything else. But she didn't consider herself any less of a cook than I was," he said. "When we cooked together, sometimes I was right, sometimes I was wrong. But she didn't look at me like 'Wow, that guy can do things

I can't do.' She was very secure in her skin. If people asked her about the latest kind of ginger, she had no problem saying, 'I have no idea what you're talking about—I've never heard of it.' And if she made a mistake, she'd just say, 'Remember, you're alone in the kitchen.' Julia was confident but modest."

In 1978, Julia and Jacques began to do live cooking demonstrations before audiences for the IACP (International Association of Culinary Professionals, a food education group that Child and Pépin helped found with cooking teacher Anne Willan). They developed a freewheeling risk-taking approach, with no set recipes and a lot of mutual ribbing. When Julia explained to the audience the proper way to form an omelet, Jacques would sneak a piece of bread behind her back. While he demonstrated how to turn a mushroom, she'd sneak a little more butter into the pan on the stove. It was fun, but the high jinks were a tactic to keep the audience focused on the cooking lessons. Without saying so directly, their message was that making good food together can be challenging and playful; that mistakes are part of cooking, and fixable; and that creative tension can push you to extraordinary heights. The public lapped it up.

Jacques and Julia took their act on the road so often, and so successfully, that producers took note. "We were learning on the job, and having a good time," said Pépin. "So we were ready to do television together."

II. "THE CAMERA IS YOUR FRIEND"

Television is a medium with its own peculiar set of requirements and skills, and performing well on air does not come naturally to everyone. James Beard was a deeply knowledgeable chef who had trained as an opera singer and hosted cooking shows for years, yet he didn't have the knack for broadcasting. He spoke in rapid-fire bursts or lectured in a monotone, looked everywhere but at the camera, and wordlessly stared at the countertop for long stretches: in the audiovisual realm of TV, this was deadly. Even the charming and eloquent *New York Times* food writer Craig Claiborne "would get the shakes before going on set," Pépin recalled. "He needed to drink three scotches, and then he'd forget to add the olive oil."

Julia, on the other hand, would wink at the lens, address her potatoes as "neuOrotic vegetables," snort at limp cookies and toss them into a garbage can. Then she'd veer off-script to pontificate on why, say, homemade English muffins are so much better than store-bought: "They taste better, they cost less, and they are such fun to make"—plus, "they are butter mops!"

Pépin noticed that Julia would taste and correct the seasoning of a dish a half dozen times in thirty minutes. "She was always tasting-tasting-tasting," he said. "She was very concerned about correct seasoning, and she was good at it." Although viewers couldn't actually taste the difference a dash of salt made to Julia's cake, she made them feel as if they could, and they emulated her.

Julia was not afraid to ask Jacques for advice, or to offer it right back:

Julia "tasting-tasting-tasting"

"You're pretty good on TV, but you're too tight and serious," she advised Pépin when he started to do TV spots in the 1970s. "This is *television*. Loosen up. Have some fun."

"The camera," Julia coached him, "is your friend."

While humor was crucial to her appeal, so was her underlying seriousness. Julia considered herself "a teacher of cookery," and at the end of a shooting day she always wanted to know: "What did the audience *learn*?"

She drilled these lessons hard, and Pépin was a quick study. He taught himself to smile, look into the camera, pause a beat now and then, to *show* and not just *tell* the audience about technique. He worked and worked on these skills in the same dogged way he had learned to speak English or teach and write about food in America: by doing a lot of it.

In the seventies, Pépin began contributing recipe articles to Helen McCully's *House Beautiful*, and in the fall of 1976 he published an influential book, *La Technique*, a step-by-step demonstration of more than 150 basic cooking techniques. (It remains in print.) On his first book tour, he'd typically pull into a town, do a live cooking demonstration, sign copies of his book at a bookstore, and end with a few radio shows and a cooking class on the local television station.

"This was the age of guerrilla TV," he chuckled. "Not sophisticated *at all*." At a tiny TV station in Eureka, California, where the general manager was also the mayor of the town, the show was taped by a single unmoving camera, and the "teleprompter" was a man lying on the floor unspooling notes scrawled onto a roll of paper towels. "It was hard to do my recipe and not laugh," Pépin fondly recalled. "But I survived. I learned a few tricks out there."

He and Julia first cooked on TV together in 1993, for a PBS series called *Cooking in Concert*. Pépin quickly learned that Julia's humor could be as naughty as Paul Bocuse's, and sometimes tilted toward the bawdy or obnoxious. Making a lobster soufflé, she'd say, "Now, Jacques, there's a nice piece of tail for you." When a turkey needed to be deboned, she'd say, "Jacques is a great boner." If he objected to one of her jokes—"No, Julia, stop!"—she'd say it again and again, with a widening grin. "You didn't ever tell Julia what to do," he said. "If you did, she will only do it more."

It was a lesson that he, Julia's sponsors, and her putative bosses learned many times over. Julia was relentlessly courted by advertisers, yet she remained adamantly independent and noncommercial for most of her career. Even in the gray area where private money met public television she pushed the envelope of acceptability, and was not beyond subverting her show's underwriters.

On a TV show sponsored by the Kendall-Jackson winery, for instance, Julia suddenly announced, "I am in the mood for a beer," and pulled a bottle of Samuel Adams beer from the prop refrigerator. (Samuel Adams was not a sponsor. The brewery was in Boston, and Julia knew some of the people involved; she pulled this prank entirely on her own.)

On a show sponsored by Land O'Lakes Butter, Julia and Jacques were preparing to make dough for chicken potpie and an apple galette, when she suddenly announced that she wanted to use Crisco instead of butter. Jacques was taken aback. "But Julia, we have plenty of butter and no Crisco," he protested. "Oh yes we do," Julia replied with a gleam in her eye, whipping a tin of Crisco out from beneath the counter. "I happen to have some right here!"

Telling this story, Pépin gave the weary smile of a straight man, and muttered, "She did that many, many times to me . . ."

He wasn't alone. Now that Julia was a celebrity, people and organizations frequently wanted her to conform to their idea of who she was, or tried to use her fame to promote their own agendas. But Julia had a deep aversion to being coerced, and usually found a humorous way to confound those who tried to co-opt her. Julia was infinitely patient with her public and put up with the usual questions about how much wine she drank on TV ("None," she said. "I couldn't cook if I did") or the time she dropped a chicken on the floor ("I never did that"); but when interviewers pressed Julia to name her "favorite" restaurant or food processor or chef, she'd wag a finger and say, "Oh, those are media-type questions, and we don't answer those."

"It was like she said 'Don't Tread on Me,'" said Pépin. "People respected that . . . Well, most of them, anyway."

III. Speaking Out

Julia was comfortable with her stature and understood its power (though she rarely talked about it), and in the mid-seventies—when she was in her mid- to late sixties—she was increasingly willing to "speak out on any subject I feel strongly about."

By that point, the choices people made about what foods to buy, cook, and eat had become political statements that divided America into opposing camps. On one side were those who relied on conventional supermarket fare, largely produced by "agribusiness." On the other side were converts to local, natural, organic, macrobiotic, or other "health foods." Underlying these two fiercely defended positions were strata of educational, class, and racial divisions. Somewhere in the middle stood Julia Child, outspoken, and not always politic.

When food activists began to ask pointed questions about the pesticides, fertilizers, antibiotics, and growth hormones used by the food industry, Julia—who was suspicious of orthodoxies in general, and food fads in particular—was vehement. "I just hate health food," she said, because it seemed to be a diet of "nuts and berries," akin to "bird food," that tasted bad and left her hungry. She worried that nutritionists—especially "that dreadful woman" Adelle Davis—were cold-blooded scolds who considered food merely as fuel, or worse, medicine. "I have never met a healthy, normal nutritionist who loves to eat," Julia declared.

At a moment when Americans began to worry about cholesterol and cancer, and embraced vegetarianism, bottled water, and distance running as prophylactics against those diseases, Julia denounced "the food police" and "the fear of fat mania." She lamented that "the dinner table is becoming a trap rather than a pleasure," and predicted that "if fear of food continues it will be the death of gastronomy."

At times, Julia could be downright provocative, as when she declared, "The only time to eat diet food is while you're waiting for the steak to cook."

Looking back on the vegetarian movement, she said in 1999:

Personally, I don't think pure vegetarianism is a healthy lifestyle. It's more fear of food—that whole thing that red meat is bad for you. And then there are people who don't eat meat because it's against their morals. Well, there's nothing you can do with people like that. I've often wondered to myself: Does a vegetarian look forward to dinner, ever?

   I don't think we were as afraid of food in the early days, except for pesticides. I do take some steps—I wash everything I eat in hot water . . .

Now there's worry about irradiation and bio-engineering, but I think
the critics are often short on facts.

Such pronouncements upset and confused many of her followers,
who wanted to believe that Julia Child was always perfect, according
to their worldview. When she declined to criticize irradiated food, for
instance, one fan felt betrayed: "*You*, of all my favorite people!"

Julia's stridency was rooted in her determination to popularize excellent cooking and "hearty eating" in America. She believed that good
food took "time, and care, and a little extra effort to do things right," as
her mentor, Chef Max Bugnard, had taught in Paris. Julia wanted Americans to think of their meals as fun, exciting, and delicious; a sensory
adventure that nourished and inspired. Unless something was actually
dangerous, such as tainted shellfish, she wanted to increase rather than
restrict people's culinary options.

Julia may have distrusted organic food even more than health food.
In 1981, she declared that the organic movement was built on "balderdash." And she opined, "Most people don't really know what they mean
by organic. What they really mean is that they don't want to get poi-
soned. Most of what they're feeling is fear . . . The public is swamped
with misinformation. It's just emotion, not science." Julia liked to quote
from "The 'Organic Food' Kick," an essay by R. A. Seelig published by
the United Fresh Fruit and Vegetable Association, a trade group: "There
is no room for the cult that regards 'natural methods' as good, and all
improvements on nature as bad. Many of the organic food cultists . . .
appear to have a semi-religious conviction that what is natural is a mani-
festation of God's purpose, while what is scientific is a denial of God's
plan."

Such language, equating organic farmers with religious extremists,
seemed calibrated to push the buttons of the Childs. Neither of them
trusted blind faith—or, at least, blind faith as they interpreted it—and
Julia reacted strongly against any perceived zealotry. When the group
CHEFS (Chefs Helping to Enhance Food Safety) asked her to advocate
for organic produce, Julia responded, "I just do not want to be allied to
any cultist type of operation, which this could well turn out to be. I am
for hard scientific facts."

The latter sentence was a favorite Julia trope. She prided herself on having a logical mind that valued rigorously tested "science" and "fact" over hope and gut intuition. But where did Julia's facts come from? In researching her books, TV shows, and articles, she had long relied on trade groups, such as the National Livestock and Meat Board or the Poultry and Egg National Board, or government offices, such as the Agricultural Research Service of the U.S. Department of Agriculture (USDA) or the California Department of Fish and Wildlife, to supply her with technical information. Yet she credulously quoted them without taking into account their potential for obfuscation or self-interest.

Julia spoke out in favor of MSG (monosodium glutamate) and the "ongoing need to excite our taste buds." She considered GMOs (genetically modified organisms), which have been controversial, "one of the greatest discoveries" of the twentieth century, which fed millions of poor people around the world. And she dismissed the Food and Drug Administration as "insane" for regulating the sodium nitrate used to preserve hot dogs, bacon, and other cured meats. Most famously, Julia defended her love of butter and cream on the grounds that they tasted better than the alternatives, and she was skeptical of claims that they were unhealthy.

Julia's mantra on eating rich foods was drawn straight from her years in France: "Food is joy," Chef Bugnard taught at the Cordon Bleu. "But everything in moderation."

Julia sometimes changed her mind, and there were instances when her opinion on food trends grew nuanced, or convoluted and self-contradictory. Consider the question of supermarkets and fast-food restaurants. One of her motivations for making "The French Chef in France" documentaries was to preserve traditional cuisine from mechanized, American-style food production. Yet in 1977, she unfavorably contrasted a French village market to her local American supermarket. Shopping in San Peyre, she found "Asparagus . . . just laying there for who knows how many days, no refrigeration, sometimes right in the sun, and the stems . . . all withered. Rotten apples, limp carrots, very limp lettuce." She missed the clean Star Market on Beacon Street, and she concluded, "All this romance about French products written by people who don't do the shopping, and read by people who want to read lovely prose. People don't want to hear what they don't want to hear, and furthermore, they don't hear it."

Later that year, Julia invited *cuisine minceur* star Michel Guérard and his wife, Christine, to dinner at 103 Irving Street. Julia served them lobster mayonnaise, saddle of lamb, broccoli, and a tarte tatin. The Guérards raved about the dinner, including the tarte—for which Julia had used Golden Delicious apples, a variety that critics of U.S. agribusiness derided as tasteless. "All this good food came from plain old markets," Julia crowed to Simca. "I was interested that Guérard had no complaints about shopping, about butter, or cream, or vegetables, meat or fish."

There were exceptions, of course: Julia still loved the traditional markets in Cannes and Grasse, and disliked the giant, homogeneous, fluorescently lit American supermarkets that sold days-old fish, flavorless melons, and rock-hard tomatoes wrapped in plastic. Moreover, the French weren't passive consumers of American efficiency: they tailored the speed and convenience of supermarkets to their own proclivities—selling wines, cheeses, breads, and locally grown vegetables in *supermarchés.*

Then there was the subject of fast food. Initially, she worried that quick, cheap burger chains were serving junk to Americans—"We don't believe good food is to be found at McDonald's," Julia stated in 1972—and would destroy the traditional social fabric of France. Yet Julia was not a snob. She enjoyed hot dogs, hamburgers, and French fries as much as the next person—especially if the fries were cooked in beef tallow, as McDonald's did. (When the company discontinued the practice, Julia publicly complained.) But her feelings about McBurgers evolved. Just a year later, she told *Time* magazine: "The Big Mac I like least because it's all bread. But the French fries are surprisingly good. It's remarkable that you can get that much food for under a dollar. It's not what you would call a balanced meal; it's nothing but calories. But it would keep you alive." And by 1979, she handed the chain a backhanded compliment in an article for *New York* magazine: "Would you rather have an airline lunch with mystery meat, frozen, tasteless vegetables, and lettuce with sugar, or would you rather have a nice Quarter Pounder and an apple turnover and French fries? What's the choice there? . . . I'd certainly rather eat that." Her only suggestion was that McDonald's serve a decent glass of red wine in America, as it did in France.

The first French McDonald's opened in a Paris suburb in 1972. It was greeted with derision as yet another example of American cultural imperialism, and the chain was lampooned as "McDo" (pronounced "Mac dough"). In 1999, the sheep farmer José Bové scrawled *"McDo Dehors, Gardons le Roquefort!"* ("McDonald's Get Out, Let's Keep the Roquefort!") on a McDonald's in the town of Millau. He famously "dismantled" the restaurant by using his tractor to tear off the roof. The stunt landed him in jail and turned him into a hero to the antiglobalization movement. But over time, the fear of "McDomination" abated, and the French grew as fond of the burger maker as billions of other global citizens had. The company ingratiated itself good-naturedly, even referring to itself as "McDo," and serving cafés au lait, beer, and specialty items, such as the McBaguette (two hamburgers, Emmentaler cheese, lettuce, and mustard on a baguette). By 2014, there were more than twelve hundred McDos across France, including branches in the Louvre and the Sorbonne, and the company employed 69,000 people. Meanwhile, native fast-food restaurants, such as the Franco-Belgian chain Quick, sprang up to serve "Le Double Mix," "Dark Vador," and "Jedi Burgers."

Julia liked food that was well made and tasted good. While she detested Jell-O, salty canned soups, and limp cookies, she did not reject all convenience foods. In contrast to Simca, she felt that a box of potato flakes—when mixed with plenty of butter, cream, salt, and pepper— could produce delicious mashed potatoes. She didn't mind canned carrots or frozen beans, as long as they were cooked with care, and she even developed a refined recipe for tuna casserole fortified with butter, Swiss cheese, and hard-boiled eggs.

She exhorted Americans to get over their squeamishness, and learn to steward limited resources by eating cheaper fish, such as skate, in order to preserve overfished cod stocks. Or by substituting high-protein, low-cholesterol rabbit meat for expensive, fatty steak. "We've been terribly spoiled in America. Meat has always been cheap here," she declared. "Now we're beginning to live the way the rest of the world always has."

Julia wanted Americans to love food, not fear it. "It was supposed to be about *pleasure*," Judith Jones observed. "The French use a word, *soignée*, to describe their approach to cooking. It means you *care*. You make a little extra effort, even for something as mundane as green beans. Julia always emphasized that. People heard her, and they walked away thinking, 'You know what? She's right.'"

When it came to other cultural issues Julia could be equally outspoken or confounding. In 1970, Julia was a budding feminist. "What do you think of women's lib?" she asked a reporter from *TV Guide*. "It wasn't until I began thinking about it that I realized my field is closed to women! It's absolutely restricted! You can't get into the Culinary Institute of America in New Haven! The big hotels, the fancy New York restaurants, don't want women chefs . . . You know, people with skills are becoming scarce. If they need people who are earnest, intelligent, and dedicated, they're going to have to allow women in. Fewer men are interested in devoting these qualities to this type of work." And later she said, "We who are pro women's rights must do a great deal to get our views across."

Yet Julia resisted attempts to label her a feminist and pointedly extolled the virtues of marriage and homemaking. "Women should stop squawking and start cooking!" she proclaimed in 1973. "Julia and I felt the same way about that," Judith Jones said of feminism. "We were from a different generation." Child and Jones didn't like the stridency of the bra burners, even as they were paragons of strong womanhood.

Julia identified herself as a liberal Democrat, and a proud supporter of Planned Parenthood. Some on the right criticized her, such as the disenchanted fan who wrote, "I wish Mrs. Child would stick to her cooking and keep her personal views to herself." Julia was unapologetic, and defended her position on the grounds that a woman should be able to decide what is best for herself and her potential child. "What are your plans for these children once they are born?" she wanted to ask the right-to-lifers who picketed her in Memphis. "You run into so many situations where the child is not wanted and miserable," she told *Boston* magazine. "What's so sacred about a life when you think of all the people who are getting killed and murdered and slaughtered all over the world?"

Over the course of the 1970s, Julia refashioned her public persona from the chic, multicultural French Chef into something akin to "Julia Child, Down-Home American." This transition seemed perfectly natural to many, but confusing and even vexing to others. Was Julia Child more French than American, or the other way around, or was she some kind of ersatz invention? Was she a real cook, or a fraud? As Julia expressed her opinions more forcefully, some lost interest in her, while others became openly hostile; a few attacked her to gain attention for themselves.

Madeleine Kamman, a noted American cooking teacher born in France, snubbed Julia as "neither French, nor a chef." And the food writers John and Karen Hess sneered that Julia was "not a cook, but she plays one on TV."

Kamman—who ran a cooking school, Modern Gourmet, and a restaurant, Chez La Mere Madeleine, in Newton, Massachusetts, not far from Cambridge—was an early adopter of nouvelle cuisine who grew infuriated by the success of *The French Chef.* "Why Julia? Why not me?" wondered the famously opinionated Kamman. "I am French! Why would they want an American 'French Chef'?" Kamman banned her students from reading Julia's books or from watching her TV show.

Julia was taken aback by the ad hominem attacks, but knew better than to respond publicly. She would say only that Kamman was "very controversial," though "some people think the ground she walks on is holy." Kamman, Julia deduced, "doesn't like anyone in her bailiwick . . . I follow the footsteps of James Beard and welcome everyone in the business. It is her problem, not mine." In private, however, Julia grew weary of the "loathsome" Kamman, and referred to her as "she who will not be named," once writing to a friend: "I shall grab her by the short hairs (wearing gloves of course) and I will grind her alive, piece by piece, in my food processor."

By the 1990s, Kamman suffered from heart disease and high cholesterol, and had turned to Buddhism. "I was a good fighter, sister," she told the food writer Molly O'Neill. "My own intensity has been a lifelong battle . . . Now, I cultivate peace and forgiveness." And, she added, "I may disagree with Mrs. Child's technique and what she does, but that doesn't mean the person is obnoxious. I recognize what she has done has been very useful for the country, and I have been the beneficiary."

Others were less forgiving. In their 1977 philippic *The Taste of America,* the American food writers John and Karen Hess wrote, "How shall we tell our fellow Americans that our palates have been ravaged, that our food is awful, and that our most respected authorities on cookery are poseurs?" Aggravated that *Time* had put Julia on its cover in 1966, the Hesses declared that twentieth-century American food was industrially produced "crud" and "glop," and that Julia Child was largely responsible. Julia, they charged, promoted inferior supermarket produce, used shortcuts, did not really know culinary history, had a sweet tooth, and employed a phony Frenchness to pass off mediocre dishes. Once again Julia declined to respond in public. But when it came to their acid comments about the quality of American food, she wrote, "What are these people talking about? You can get disgusting things anywhere."

The Hesses didn't spare the lash on any of the contemporary food stars, save James Beard. They deemed Pierre Franey "a hack," Craig Claiborne "disgusting," Mimi Sheraton "stupid," and Alice Waters "so stupid."

The food establishment was horrified by the assault from within their own ranks. "Those of us who were new recruits to America's food revolution of the 1960s and '70s were shocked when our leaders got hit by friendly fire," Betty Fussell said of the Hesses. "We felt betrayed . . . it sabotaged what should have been our shared message that good food was a good thing." In Fussell's estimation, the Hesses were misguided: American cuisine is based on foreign precedents, after all, and Julia simply translated exotic-sounding French dishes into everyday American.

Julia herself didn't spend much time dwelling on her critics. She simply did the kind of cooking she enjoyed, and trusted that her audience would follow her, whether to France or elsewhere.

In her book *Masters of American Cookery*, Fussell pointed to Julia—along with M. F. K. Fisher, Craig Claiborne, and James Beard—as one of four "masters" responsible for the culinary revolution of the sixties and seventies. In Fussell's view, the masters shared a pioneering spirit, an egalitarian outlook, tremendous energy, and a pragmatic streak. In other words, they were quintessential Americans. If the United States were to become "the food capital of the world," Fussell wrote, then "Julia will be more responsible than anybody because through the newest mass media she has brought home-cooking back into the American home. That she snuck it in with a French accent is tribute to the cunning of this master showman."

Julia's outspokenness had raised her profile in a new way, and turned her into a cultural icon. The attention paid wasn't always controversial, or food related. She made headlines by reading *Tubby the Tuba* with the Boston Pops. She was a tireless fund-raiser for WGBH, and used a large cleaver to "edit" film in a promotional short for the station. She even made a humorous educational film about primordial soup—the stuff that makes up the Universe—in her kitchen, with a contraption provided by

Julia cooks up a primordial soup in her Cambridge kitchen.

the Smithsonian. In 1978, Julia was paid what is perhaps the ultimate American compliment, when she was satirized on *Saturday Night Live*.

IV. From Julia Grownup to "Save the Liver!"

Julia understood that when she appeared on a TV show—virtually *any* TV show—book sales would spike, no matter how silly or serious it was. If imitation and satire are the sincerest forms of flattery, then she was doing very well by the mid-seventies. Spoofs of her patrician bearing and singsong warble cropped up as soon as she reached celebrity status, most of which played on the misperception that Julia performed drunk.

As early as 1965, in a variety act called "Cooking While Gassed," a San Franciscan named Charles Huse donned a toque and zealously stuffed a turkey as he chugged a bottle of wine. In the early seventies, the actress Judy Graubart played the character Julia Grownup on The Electric Company's skit "Here's Cooking at You." Dressed in a pink shirt, with a red bow tie and floppy white toque, her character lectured kids on locution while making zany recipes, such as Grilled Dill Pickles with Chilled Vanilla Filling. Using an enormous drill to bore holes through a dill pickle, she filled the holes with dollops of whipped cream while yodeling, "Use lots of napkins, otherwise your guests might find themselves in a pickle!" The skit was funny, and stealthily encouraged ten-year-olds to use big words and enunciate them clearly; adults enjoyed it, too. "I adored Julia, and she was a natural model for us," said Graubart, who was a faithful *French Chef* viewer and sometime cook. "I got a lot feedback from kids—they'd send me pictures of their wacky sandwiches."

Julia's esprit may have also influenced the Muppet character the Swedish Chef—an overenthusiastic, mustachioed puppet who waved forks, saws, and hockey sticks around the kitchen, while explaining "recipes" in a Swedish gibberish: *"Yur puuurt thuur chiir-ken airn der bewl—bork, bork, bork!"* And in 1989, Julia inspired the musical monologue "Bon Appétit," in which actress Jean Stapleton trilled about "rich buttery brown batter for *le gâteau au chocolat—l'éminence brune.*" Julia was flattered, and noted that she had performed a musical about bouillabaisse at a Smith reunion, which included the line: "If you don't have any fish, you can put in some tennis balls!"

But without question Julia's most revered parodist was Dan Aykroyd, the veteran *Saturday Night Live* (*SNL*) star, who was raised near Toronto in a food-loving family.

"JULIA CHILD WAS directly responsible for the Bass-O-Matic," Aykroyd told me. He was referring to one of his most famous *SNL* sketches, which aired in April 1976 (and reprised, word for word, on the show's fortieth-anniversary show in 2015). In it, Aykroyd appears as an intense, motormouthed salesman with manicured hair and mustache, dressed in a loud checked jacket and wide maroon tie.

"How many times has this happened to you? You have a bass. You're trying to find an exciting new way to prepare it for dinner. You could scale the bass, remove the bass's tail, head and bones, and serve the fish as you would any other fish dinner," he exhorts at maximum speed. "But why bother—now that you can use Ronco's amazing new kitchen tool, the Super Bass-O-Matic '76!"

The skit was inspired by the real infomercial pitchman Ron Popeil,

Julia's antics inspired Dan Aykroyd's famous skits.

who hawked items such as the Veg-O-Matic ("It slices! It dices!"), GLH (Great Looking Hair) spray-on hair, the Pocket Fisherman, Smokeless Ashtray, and the tagline "But wait, there's more!"

Aykroyd channeled Popeil's manic energy and ratcheted it into the absurd: "The days of troublesome scaling, cutting, and gutting are over. Because the Super Bass-O-Matic '76 is the tool that lets you use the *whole* bass, with no fish waste, without scaling, cutting, or gutting. Here's how it works: catch a bass, remove the hook, and drop the bass—that's the *whole* bass—into the Super Bass-O-Matic '76. Now adjust the control dial so that that bass is blended just the way you like it."

With that, he drops a "bass" (the fish looks more like a porgy) into a standard blender, turns it on high, and liquefies it into pale brown goop. "Yes, it's just that simple!" he exhorts. "The Bass-O-Matic '76 works great on sunfish, perch, sole, and other small aquatic creatures . . . it's clean, simple, and after five or ten fish it gets to be quite a rush!"

Although Julia's name is never uttered, Aykroyd credits her with inspiring the skit, via a semitraumatic piscatorial experience of his own.

Both his mother and aunt were excellent cooks, and devotees of *Mastering the Art of French Cooking*. In fact, his aunt, Helen Gougeon, was "a Canadian clone of Julia Child, if you will," said Aykroyd. She was a French Canadian who ran a cookware store in Montreal, wrote books like *Cooking . . . with an Accent*, and hosted a radio and TV show on the CBC called *Bon Appétit*.

Julia befriended Helen Gougeon and gave her an early version of the Cuisinart food processor before it had arrived in North American stores. Gougeon immediately took to the machine. When Aykroyd was visiting Gougeon at her lake house, she decided to make bouillabaisse, the famed fish stew of Marseille. Instead of chopping her freshly caught trout into chunks and stewing them first, Gougeon simply dropped the entire uncooked fish—head, tail, fins, gills, and all—into her new Cuisinart and blended it to a pulp.

"My eyes went wide, and I was stammering, 'Wh-wha-what just happened to the *fish*?!'" Aykroyd recalled. "Years later, I remembered that for the Bass-O-Matic."

In the seventies, Aykroyd was fascinated by Julia as "a go-to cultural figure," and would rush home from *SNL* rehearsals to watch her on PBS. It was this devotion to Julia that inspired one of the most iconic skits in *SNL*'s history, one that defined his career and cemented Julia's celebrity status.

It was Thanksgiving 1978 when Julia and Jacques Pépin appeared on *The Tomorrow Show* with Tom Snyder. The show aired at 1:00 a.m., and was billed as a "conversational chat show" with Snyder, an idiosyncratic, six-foot four-inch, cigarette-smoking host. Moments before airtime, Child and Pépin were backstage, rushing through their preparations for *volaille demi-désossée*—a chicken that has had the backbone removed, is stuffed, and then sewn back together again.

Julia borrowed Jacques's razor-sharp knife, and as she surgically sliced the chicken, she lopped off a fingertip. Blood gushed, and her finger clearly needed stitches. But the producer was already counting down the final seconds before they were to go on air. Julia was a seasoned performer and, in "the show must go on" spirit, pushed the flap of skin back onto her fingertip, stanched the blood with a clean kitchen towel, and bound her finger with a bandage.

"Don't worry, Jacques will cook, I will explain, and it will all work out *fine*," Julia told a worried Snyder. She asked him not to mention the accident on air because she wanted to focus on the chicken.

They walked onstage, and within minutes Snyder blurted out, "Julia, do you mind if I tell people you just cut your finger?" As the camera zoomed in for a close-up of her bandaged hand, there was little she could do but smile. After the show, Julia, Paul, and Jacques went to a hospital, where she was given eight stitches. (Julia then led a late-night charge to L'Ermitage, a French restaurant in Los Angeles.)

Julia considered the finger cut a minor incident, but thanks to Snyder, news of her julienned digit quickly spread. When she appeared on *The Tonight Show* a week later, Johnny Carson asked about the injury; and when she made an omelet on *The Kathryn Crosby Show* in San Francisco, she was mostly asked about her mishap.

Dan Aykroyd, meanwhile, had parodied Tom Snyder on *SNL* for years: the host's honking laugh, occasionally brusque manner, awkward questions, and contrasting gray hair and jet-black eyebrows made him an easy target. "We saw Julia cut herself on Snyder," Aykroyd explained, "and thought it could be something funny."

Within days, *SNL* writers Al Franken and Tom Davis cobbled together a sketch based on the incident. Although *SNL* had women such as Gilda Radner, Jane Curtin, and Laraine Newman in the cast, "for some reason they asked *me* to read the part," Aykroyd recalled.

In the skit, Aykroyd's "Julia Child" was dressed in a curly brown wig, pearls, earrings, a pink shirt, and a blue apron. ("I look like a busty version of my mother," he said to me with a laugh.) As he demonstrated how to make a holiday *poularde* with a *demi-désossée*—"a fine, fat roasting chicken" that has been partly deboned—he narrated in a high-pitched warble: "You can save the liver and fry it up with some onions for a little *snack*. Or, if you have a number of livers, you can make a lovely liver pâté. Or a delicious liver*wurst*, which you can spread on a cracker—a Ritz cracker, a sa-a-hhaa-ltiiine—or on a bread, a rye bread . . . Or, if you have a pet cat or a dog, they love liver. *Save the liver.* Don't throw it away. I hope I've made my point: don't throw the liver away!"

As he prepares to bone the chicken, Aykroyd's Julia says, "For this you need a very sharp knife—you can't do nothin' without a sharp knife!" Operating on the chicken, he adds, "You cut along the backbone to the pope's nose, like so—rrrrrraaAHHH! Oh! Oho! *Now* I've done it. I've cut the *dickens* out of my finger!"

Blood begins to squirt vigorously from his hand onto the chicken, and pools on the countertop.

"Well, I'm glad, in a way, this has happened. We have never really discussed what to do. First, we must stop the bleeding." As blood spurts across his chest and runs down his arms, "Julia" attempts to stanch the flow with his apron while attempting to smile and keep things upbeat. "You want to raise your hand over your head . . ."

As blood arcs through the air, the audience's squeals and nervous laughter grow louder and louder. Aykroyd carries on: "I recommend natural coagulants, such as chicken liver. Another reason not to throw away the liver . . . Oh, God, it's throbbing!" he wheezes.

Pink blood sprays across the counter in great jets.

He suggests making a tourniquet from cheesecloth and a chicken bone. When that doesn't stop the torrent, "Julia" grows woozier and says, "I'm remembering a time when I was a little girl and I had a dog named Amber . . . I used to give him liver. And my mother gave me a doll . . . Why are you all spinning? Uhhh, I think I'm going to go to sleep now . . . *Bon appétit.*"

He falls face-first across the bloody counter. With a final twitch, he raises his head to cry, "Save the liver!"

The audience laughed hysterically, unaware that the skit had almost failed.

In order to pump the fake blood through Aykroyd's hand, the *SNL* prop department had filled an old, brass fire extinguisher with stage blood, and rigged a long black rubber hose down Aykroyd's arm. "We had to get the rhythm of the blood perfectly timed, but it wasn't working at dress [rehearsal]," he remembered. When it came time to perform the show live, the script's writer, Al Franken (now the Democratic junior U.S. senator from Minnesota), was determined to make it work: he hid under the counter and enthusiastically pumped the blood himself.

The skit was a silly "blood joke, a fluid joke," Aykroyd admits, and he had "no idea it would become a classic." But then he makes sure to add, "It came from a place of total respect for Julia Child. I was a huge fan of hers, *of course*. It was a tribute."

The *SNL* sketch aired on December 9, 1978. It happened that

Julia and Paul had been out to dinner in Cambridge that night. They returned home to 103 Irving Street, switched on the little television in the kitchen—"just so that it would make a noise," she'd recall—and there was Aykroyd's Julia, spraying blood and warbling about livers.

The Childs settled in to watch. While Julia loved a good laugh, she didn't like mean-spirited comedy. As the skit ended, the phone began to ring: it was friends and family members from across the country calling to ask if Julia had seen the send-up and what she thought of it. "We thought it was *terribly* funny," she replied.

The Childs kept a videotaped copy of the *SNL* skit by their TV, and would occasionally break it out for friends. Dorie Greenspan, who co-authored *Baking with Julia* in 1996, recalled one high-spirited evening when Julia acted out the Aykroyd skit, crying, "Save the liver!" at the top of her lungs.

11

Bursting Out of the Straitjacket

1. The American Way of Doing Things

By January 1978, Julia had sold more than 1.2 million copies of the four books she had written or co-written: volumes I and II of *Mastering* had sold more than 800,000 copies (Volume I accounted for more than 560,000), *The French Chef Cookbook* had sold more than 250,000 copies, and *From Julia Child's Kitchen* had sold nearly 140,000 copies. They would continue to sell, as they do today, providing the Childs with a comfortable annuity. Yet, she had not published a new book in three years or produced a new TV series in five years.

As Paul's health gradually improved, Julia had more time to think about her next project. The demise of "Thirteen Feasts for Thirteen Colonies" in 1975, and the mixed success of the White House bicentennial show in 1976, left her dissatisfied. She could have comfortably retired, but that was never a prospect she relished. In September 1978, at age sixty-six, Julia Child was ready to launch a new kind of book and TV series. This project would be a step further away from French cooking, and would expand on the polyglot approach she used in *From Julia Child's Kitchen*.

While that book had included both French recipes and dishes from Italy, Belgium, and India, they were similar to what Julia had done on *The French Chef.* In the new project, she fully embraced her roots and a forward-looking, American-style approach to food. "In French cooking . . . you only have such and such [ingredient] that you can serve with such and such, or they say you are an ignoramus. So I've decided I've had enough of that," Julia declared. "I'm not tired of it. I just feel like I'd like to burst out of that straitjacket into something else."

The something else she was bursting into was a TV show and companion book called *Julia Child & Company*, a project with an unapologetically American flavor. "We felt it was time to . . . go in for general cooking where we could draw from anywhere and everywhere," she wrote in the book's introduction, "since that really is the American way of doing things."

As she was wont, Julia ratcheted up the ambition, risk, and difficulty of the new project. She decided to tape the *Company* TV series at the same time that she wrote the *Company* book, in order to release them to the public contemporaneously. It seemed crazy. But there was a method to Julia's madness: in combining the action and visual flair of a TV show with the printed recipes, detailed instructions, and still photographs of a book, Julia was providing her audience with the most comprehensive, in-depth, mutually reinforcing cooking instructions possible in those pre-Internet days. A secondary function of the TV/book project was, in essence, to relaunch Julia's "brand" as a cook in tune with her nation and time, using the latest multimedia tools.

The title for *Company* was a fitting nod to several definitions of the word. The book and TV episodes were built on a series of complete menus for guests (or company) rather than on individual recipes. With a significant budget from Knopf and WGBH, Julia was able to build two teams: one to write and photograph the *Company* book and the other to cook, stage, and videotape the *Company* TV series; the teams worked side by side, and occasionally together (like a repertory theater company). To keep the enterprise rolling forward, Julia played impresario and ringmaster, juggling dozens of people and elements while keeping an eye on the bottom line (as a CEO manages a company). This high-energy, sometimes raucous collaboration was the opposite of the enforced calm and quiet of the last few years, and for Julia it came as a welcome relief.

II. COMPANY

Other than the fact that *Julia Child & Company* was a cookbook by Julia Child published by Knopf and edited by Judith Jones, nearly everything about the project was a departure from her previous work. Most fundamental, it was a book built around a TV show, rather than the other way around. Julia's first words in the book are: "It didn't take too much persuasion to induce me to do another television cooking series . . ." This was a statement of fact, a tacit acknowledgment that print had taken a backseat to television in American media by that point.

While Julia's previous books were collections of recipes organized by food group (bread, meat, vegetables, dessert), *Company* was a "menu book" designed to teach people how to cook entire meals, from planning and shopping to preparing appetizers, entrées, and desserts, to tips on cleaning up. The book was structured around thirteen "special occasions"—such as a breakfast party, a VIP lunch, a birthday dinner, and a backyard barbecue. The recipes were supplemented by a welter of shopping lists, advice on timing, hints for using leftovers, and other addenda and arcana.

"Whatever the occasion, Julia Child takes all the stage fright out of cooking for company," the book flap promised. Inside, Julia wrote, "What do you feed to 19 people when you're the cook and butler combined? . . . Or, the big boss is coming to dinner; you don't know him (or her!) very well . . . What do you plan for them? Or you are to have a comfortable family-style Sunday night supper, with both grown-ups and children. What would be fun for all?"

(Simca had taken a similar, menu-driven approach in *Simca's Cuisine*, published in 1972 and co-written by Patricia Simon, which included chapters with titles such as "A hunt breakfast," "A carefree luncheon," "A high tea," "A spectacular dinner with Champagne," and "An earthy dinner for high-spirited friends.")

Julia focused on developing, testing, and perfecting recipes for *Company*, and left much of the book writing to E. S. "Peggy" Yntema, an editor at Atlantic Monthly Press. Each menu in the book was introduced with a short preamble, or what Julia referred to as "the blah-blah." Yntema would write a draft and then Julia would rewrite it in her own voice—deleting a too-literary reference to Henry V here ("not my style at all"), or adding a Julia-ism there, such as "Like the 'Blue Danube,' [roast beef] may be square, but it's wonderful and everybody loves it."

When Houghton Mifflin rejected *Mastering the Art of French Cooking* in the 1950s, the editors had said it was too long and complicated: "Americans don't want an encyclopedia, they want to cook something quick, with a mix." Julia was despondent at the time, but vindicated by *Mastering*'s eventual success. Yet, one could argue that by 1978 the Houghton Mifflin/"quick, with a mix" mind-set had triumphed. Julia would not succumb to baking mixes, but in explaining her approach to *Company* she told reporters: "You've got to make it as easy as possible so that you can encourage people to cook. It's like the difference between using a pocket calculator and adding up a huge column of figures yourself. If you give someone a calculator, suddenly mathematics becomes fun."

Company was roughly a third of the length of *Mastering*—which clocked in at 684 pages—and *From Julia Child's Kitchen*. It was also physically larger: *Company* measured eight and a half inches wide by eleven inches long, compared with the six-and-a-half by nine-inch dimensions of *From Julia Child's Kitchen*. And the new book was graphically bolder and brighter than Julia's previous efforts.

These changes were a reflection of the times. Not only were books competing with the visual jazz of television, but in the sixties and seventies magazine design had become a celebrated art form, a graphic analogue to New Journalism; they grew bigger and bolder, and art directors such as *Esquire*'s George Lois or *New York*'s Milton Glaser were stars. *Company* was designed by Knopf to approximate the look of food magazines. The pages had eye-catching headlines and amusing subtitles set in large type. There were blocs of type surrounded by lots of white space on the page. Sidonie Coryn's line drawings in *Mastering* and Paul's photographs in *From Julia Child's Kitchen* had been supplanted by color photographs of Julia and her crew in action, or seductive portraits of their food, taken by Jim Scherer.

The *Company* menus strove to be up-to-date. The Lo-Cal Banquet— "Light food for sharp appetites"—for instance, tipped its hat to nouvelle cuisine by including a shrimp, green bean, and raw mushroom appetizer; chicken bouillabaisse; rice; and a steamed apple dessert. "This meal is so delicious, they'll take big helpings and return for seconds," Julia promised. "But a moderate portion of each dish, though you'd hardly believe it, adds up to a sensible 678 calories. There's no trick to it, and no secret—only a well-considered application of the simplest principles of sound gastronomy: contrast, balance, beauty, savor, and style."

Here, Julia admitted that she was forced to diet from time to time, and kept notes on her caloric intake, though she insisted on allotting one hundred calories for a glass of wine, "to keep up morale." In truth, she hated to diet, and didn't care much for lo-cal food: "'Diet food' . . . is dismal food: no fun to plan, no fun to fix. Pure labor in vain," she lamented. "It is fake food . . . unnatural, almost immoral, a bane to good eating and good cooking. Dieters are the best audience a cook ever has, for they savor and remember every morsel."

In her Cocktail Party menu, Julia strikes a different tone: "We like to give our guests a *spread*. I hate it when people get hungry after a couple of drinks and charge out somewhere to supper before I even get to see them. So . . . I serve a great big puffy something I baked specially, and something fishy and fresh, and lots of good hearty treats on the side: chicken wings and oysters and clams and stuffed eggs, and meatballs and rabbit food [carrots and celery] . . . and peanuts, of course. Without peanuts it isn't a cocktail party."

In the case of her New England Potluck Supper, Julia recycled some of her "Thirteen Feasts" research for a menu of fresh fish chowder, coleslaw, and Indian pudding—chosen, Julia writes, because "I wanted to make a point of the earthy, primal simplicity of these great American dishes." She associated chowder with August lunches at the Child family house on the coast of Maine, "with salty sunbaked granite around me and the sea crinkling below—and with the knowledge that a pail of wild berries is waiting in a cool purple cranny in the rocks." As she had discovered about bouillabaisse recipes in Marseille, "there are loads of recipes around for fish chowder . . . and many cooks insist their particular recipes are the only authentic versions." After much testing, Julia found a version that used croutons instead of pilot biscuits and sour cream and parsley instead of a final blob of butter. "For me [this is] the best, the most genuine, indeed the only recipe worth cooking," she wrote.

Julia added a Postscript about "a friend of ours" who won eternal familial fame by cooking "Bean Hole Beans." This friend was my paternal grandfather, Hector C. Prud'homme. He was born in Peking to Belgian parents, went to school in America, and had worked as a diplomat, banker, and teacher; he fancied himself a frontiersman. Perhaps inspired by something he read in a Louis L'Amour cowboy novel, he decided to cook beans "the old-fashioned way." He instructed us grandchildren to dig a deep hole in his backyard, line it with rocks, and allow a fire to smolder on its bottom for several hours. He filled a cast-iron pot with beans, onion, molasses, and thick hunks of pork, and lowered it into the pit; he raked the coals over the pot, piled seaweed on top, and covered it with a canvas tarp. The beans simmered for hours, emitting mouthwatering smells that made our stomachs gurgle in anticipation. That evening, he pulled the bean pot up to the surface and unveiled his creation. Julia described the moment: "We sat out on the grass, in a circle, while he lifted the lid to release the aroma of those slow-cooked beans with the flavor . . . baked right into them. They were almost crusty although surrounded by thick juices, and we ate them with great helpings of coleslaw and homemade rye bread." The beans were sweet, smoky, and deeply satisfying. It was a meal I will never forget, and it inspired Julia to include a Crock-Pot version in *Company*.

She also, at long last, managed to work the recipe for "fish in a crust" into print—an Americanized version of the *Loup de Mer en Croûte* that Julia and Simca discovered at L'Oasis in 1969. (Simca included her own version of the dish in *Simca's Cuisine*.)

Studded throughout *Company* were mini essays on some of Julia's favorite subjects, like rice, fish, and tomatoes. And sidebars on a few of Paul's famous homemade cocktail recipes, including the Buddha's Eye (a gin, lime juice, and crème de menthe concoction inspired by the J. Milton Hayes doggerel poem "The Green Eye of the Little Yellow God"); Ivan's Aperitif (a drink made of vermouth, gin, and orange zest, and named after Julia's brother-in-law, Ivan Cousins); or a drink called *À la Recherche de l'Orange Perdue*, a dark rum, orange, and marmalade homage to Marcel Proust. For the lo-cal meal, Julia included a nonalcoholic Angosoda Cocktail, made of Angostura bitters, a slice of lime, and sparkling water ("It tastes like a real drink," she insisted).

Company was designed to be user-friendly and included a profusion of suggestions: notes on Preparations, including what kinds of knives and pans the cook will need; a Marketing and Storage shopping list; a graphic of a clock to indicate how much of a recipe could be done ahead; suggestions on Timing, to help the home cook produce every element of a meal in sync; Menu Variations, which suggested, say, replacing clams with crab, broccoli with zucchini, or potato salad with bread; recommendations for how to use the Leftovers; and the occasional Postscript—and Post-Postscript—in which Julia mused about cooking with children, suggested books about beef, or exhorted her audience to cook with gusto. "In private or public cooking, broad, firm gestures are the most efficient. Wallop your steaks! Whoosh up your egg whites! And, behind your chafing dish and before your guests, act with assurance and decisiveness," she wrote. "Let every move accomplish something, and don't twiddle."

And, as she had done before, Julia could not resist adding a plea for the metric system. *Company* included heating directions in both Fahrenheit and Centigrade, and both imperial and metric measurements—noting that meatballs, say, should be rolled in "gobs of 1 inch or 2½ cms." A die-hard enthusiast, Julia editorialized: "Some day we shall convert from our illogical system of pounds, ounces, feet, and inches to metrics, where all will be easy divisions of 10 rather than a mishmash of 2's, 4's, 12's, 16's."

III. Harmony Inc.

The *Julia Child & Company* television series stood out with a distinctive new aesthetic. *The French Chef* had used a temporary structure in a WGBH studio; it took two hours to set up, and another two hours to break down, a rigmarole that had been a sore spot. "We wouldn't do the new series unless we had a kitchen that was ours—that we could just walk into and work in and leave," Julia explained. For *Company*, WGBH built a new set in a factory loft, featuring an open kitchen with white walls and blue countertops, a central island with butcher block around a six-burner stove, two wall ovens, a fridge, pans and copper lids on the wall, and a collection of cookbooks, oils, spoons, and spatulas, and bottles of wine arranged on a countertop. Julia, the self-professed "gadget freak" was likely to whip out one of her contraptions—a mechanical pea sheller, industrial blender, pasta maker, a scale and calculator—at the slightest provocation.

To the right of the kitchen stood a small "dining room" with gray wallpaper, a mantelpiece with a candelabra, and a table where Julia could slurp fresh oysters from the half shell. Behind the scenes was a ready room, equipped with an extra stove and sink, where the *Company* team could prep items for the day's menu.

Julia thrived on pressure, and with only a half hour to get through each *Company* program, many dishes were prepared in advance. When she placed a meringue in the oven, another prebaked meringue was ready for her to take out, and a third was on standby, in case of complications.

To bring her new creation to life, Julia relied on a familiar, tested crew. Russ Morash was the show's producer. Willie Morton, who worked on Julia's 1962 pilot and on 1970's "The French Chef in France" documentaries, was in charge of sound. Ruthie Lockwood and Avis DeVoto researched recipes, wrote scripts, and choreographed the staging of meals. Julia's kitchen team included Liz Bishop and Rosemary "Rosie" Manell. Rosie, a painter, cook, food stylist, and Northern California earth mother, moved into the 103 Irving Street guest room, and was, Julia judged, a "marvel of cookery, workery, [and] good humor." The only drawback was that Rosie was a "compulsive eater . . . as am I," Julia said. "If there is anything in sight anywhere I'll eat it unless I most sternly and with supreme willpower and reasoning turn from it."

The musical theme for *Company* was developed by Robert J. Lurtsema, the molasses-voiced host of WGBH-Radio's *Morning Pro Musica:* it was a sprightly tune played by bassoons, with a sound that Julia described as "an elephant walk."

Julia loved nothing better than to be shoulder to shoulder with fellow cooks, elbow-deep in barbecue sauce or a scrambled eggs and mushroom gratiné. Though she came up with most of the menus for *Company*, she did not pose as a grand master speaking down to her disciples, but pushed everyone to speak up and pitch in. "The show is fun to do because it's real team work," enthused Julia, who had dubbed the collaboration Harmony Inc. Complete Food Production.

Occasionally, the Harmony train went off the rails. When she demonstrated the making of choulibiac—sole with mushrooms and fish mousse wrapped in a pastry crust—Julia suffered a half dozen mishaps. On the first take, she sneezed and the scene had to be reshot; on the second, the plate slipped and a thick slice of choulibiac fell to the counter; and so it went for the star-crossed dish. The clock was ticking, but every time something went wrong the Harmony Inc. team descended on the choulibiac like a pit crew servicing a race car. They scraped off the top layer of pasty, replaced it with a new one, rebaked it, and reshot the sequence, lickety-split. In the photograph she used in the book, Julia notes that the choulibiac's top layer "is a bit thick . . . and not quite cooked!"

To accomplish her many tasks Julia kept a rigorous schedule. On Mondays, she and Ruthie Lockwood scheduled upcoming episodes, and reviewed them with Paul. Tuesdays they did a "cook-through," in which they blocked out shots, cooked dishes to judge how much time they took, and discussed how to explain the food. Wednesdays were devoted to fine-tuning the week's menu and rehearsing the show with producer-director Russ Morash. Once those details were ironed out, they held a dress rehearsal. On Thursday, Harmony Inc. taped the show for TV.

In the days of *The French Chef,* the crew would have devoured the food Julia had cooked "like a pack of wolves" after the episode was shot. But for *Company,* the food had to be preserved for Jim Scherer to photograph for the book. "There it was, beautifully displayed at the end of the program, hot, tempting, and ready to eat—and there it sat, and sat, and was moved around, and lit this way and that, and moved again, and reheated and fussed with, and finally most carefully photographed," Julia recounted. Her team would spend an hour changing lights and camera angles to clearly show how to, say, devein a shrimp. But once they were done, they used laughter as a pressure release. It was "hard to believe five grown people could spend more than an hour most earnestly bent over something like a shrimp's intestine," Julia marveled.

The *Julia Child & Company* book ends in a thicket of "Menu Alternatives": entirely different dishes for the Lo-Cal Banquet (with recipes from *The French Chef*) or A Dinner for the Boss (with dishes from *Mastering,* Volume II), and added new suggestions, such as A Pizza Party (last seen in *From Julia Child's Kitchen*). In those final pages, Julia displayed her vaulting culinary imagination and hinted at what could have been a whole other book. It was as if she couldn't let go, and just wanted to jam a few more ideas into that slim volume. So it was not surprising that she began a follow-up to *Company* shortly after the TV *Company* wrapped.

IV. More Company

Called *Julia Child & More Company,* the second book and TV series appeared just a year later, in 1979. The crew remained largely the same, a team of about fifteen people, with a few new players. While Julia liked to keep the mood loose and eschewed titles, she was learning how to man-

Julia with Sara Moulton (*third on the right*), Marian Morash (*second on the right*), and others from the *Julia Child & More Company* crew

age on the job. Deadline pressure and human nature led to friction in the kitchen, and team members took Julia aside to ask her to clearly define the roles they were expected to play. So Julia bestowed official-sounding titles, naming Marian Morash—the wife of Russ Morash, and chef at Nantucket's Straight Wharf Restaurant—executive chef; Sara Moulton, a rising young cook in Boston, executive associate chef; Liz Bishop as the executive associate; Rosie Manell as food stylist; and Ruthie Lockwood as the talent coordinator. Julia's friend Pat Pratt was in charge of fresh flowers and folding napkins into fleur-de-lis shapes. Her husband, Herbert, a wine maven, was a beverage adviser. Paul was deemed "husband and officially unofficial photographer." Once the hierarchy was clarified, Harmony Inc. operated a lot more harmoniously.

"Whether we were devising a quick ice-cream glorifier or judiciously comparing versions of a new lobster soufflé, the whole team pondered, cooked, and tasted together," Julia wrote. "Serious artist or weekend amateur, it's more fun cooking *for* company *in* company."

As with its predecessor, the recipes in *Julia Child & More Company* were written, photographed, and taped for television in one fell swoop. Unlike *Company*, however, the new book focused on components of meals—what to do with rabbit ("It's nice to see city people raising their own for home consumption"), how to prepare monkfish (*en pipérade*, Julia recommended, demonstrating with a twenty-five-pound "Sydney Greenstreet of the ocean . . . a tadpole almost the size and shape of a baby grand piano"), a then newly trendy vegetarian meal ("In America we eat needless, indeed preposterous, quantities of animal protein")—rather than on special events.

One of the benefits of working with Julia was that the crew always stopped for lunch. Not for them soggy sandwiches on wilted paper plates. Rather, a long table was dressed with a tablecloth, and set with real china and decent flatware. The meal began with a vermouth aperitif and was accompanied by wine. The team ate what they had cooked, either the outtakes of the recipe they were working on or composed salads made from leftovers in the fridge. Julia thoroughly enjoyed the camaraderie, and would exclaim, "Isn't this fun!" (Work in the afternoon tended to go more slowly, and Julia reluctantly gave up wine with lunch.)

At times Julia's high spirits caught her *Company* mates off guard. One day, she announced that a store-bought baguette was not up to snuff, and blithely flung it over her shoulder. As the offending loaf spiraled over tureens of French onion soup and platters of carefully prepared food, Sara Moulton and Marian Morash held their breaths in dumbstruck terror. The doughy projectile could have destroyed an entire day's work in an instant. Instead, it whistled over the trays of food and wrapped itself harmlessly around a wine bottle in the corner.

"No question, it was great TV," Moulton recalled. "And we never did tell her about the near disaster."

v. Laying an Egg

When *Company* was published in 1978, Knopf printed 190,000 copies, and the book was named as a Book-of-the-Month Club alternate. Yet, both the *Company* and *More Company* books received mixed reviews.

In *The New York Times*, Mimi Sheraton praised Julia's recipe for puff pastry as "worth the price of the book," but criticized *Company* for promoting frozen fish and "some unnecessarily gimmicky recipes." Even some of Julia's friends were underwhelmed. Of *Company*, Jacques Pépin observed: "Julia did not write that one with her *guts*, you know?" As for *More Company*, he said, "That one was too slick."

Yet Julia's appeal remained intact, and a Knopf executive claimed that *More Company*, published in 1979, was "selling as if it were free." While that was a stretch, sales were healthy, and some 240,000 copies had flown out of bookstores by the fall of 1980. The TV shows, however, did less well, especially *Julia Child & More Company*, which did not become the breakout hit the team had labored so hard to create.

Julia had high standards and a competitive streak, and she felt stung by the public's collective shrug. To make things especially galling, she did not believe her herculean efforts were destined to fail. She suspected that she had been overlooked, let down, or even sabotaged.

IN 1978, most PBS stations across the country decided to air *Julia Child & Company* at 6:00 p.m., a time when much of the show's potential audience was in transit or otherwise busy. The ratings were decent but not great, and Julia's frustration was palpable. In a 1978 interview with *The New York Times*, she worried that the *Company* programs were "awfully expensive—all that personnel and studio time. There's very little payment on our side, but everything else is so expensive that we can't spend all the time on taping that we'd like." In commercial terms, the shows were primarily vehicles to advertise her cookbooks, she said: "We really make very little from the series. We get a one-time payment from public television, and no residuals, even if it runs for twenty years. I make money out of selling books. I don't do anything commercial except selling books of mine. I endorse nothing, and I won't appear on anything that implies endorsement."

When it came to *Julia Child & More Company* in 1979, WNET—the big New York public TV station, to which many other public stations looked for guidance—decided not to air *Julia Child & Company* at all, for reasons of its own. Julia was disheartened by the lack of support over *Company* and *More Company*. In a 1981 interview with *Dial*, an in-house PBS magazine, she uncharacteristically pointed a finger of blame: "We just KILLED ourselves. We had the best team we've ever had. But PBS—I don't know whether they forgot we taped it or what, but it never got on in New York, and if you're not on in New York, you ain't nowhere."

Julia had suffered setbacks before, but rarely vented her anger in public. *Company*, she fumed, was "paid for by Knopf, our publishers. They gave the advance for the book, and it never got off the ground, and I just thought to hell with that."

Years later, Judith Jones remained mystified by the programming snafu. "The *Company* books sold, but not extremely well, especially in comparison to Julia's previous books," she said. "I'm not sure we'd have published them if we'd known" that PBS would not promote the television shows with much enthusiasm. (Unwilling to let her hard work fade into obscurity, Julia combined the texts of *Company* and *More Company*, and Wings Press republished them as *Julia Child's Menu Cookbook*, which Knopf distributed in 1991.)

There was no single explanation for the lackluster performance of *Company* and *More Company*, but the quirks of public television likely contributed. First, PBS is a "network" in name only. Unlike at a commercial TV network—which dictates that its affiliates broadcast certain programs at certain times across the country, in order to assure continuity for viewers and advertisers—local public TV stations are run as independent fiefdoms. Their programmers air whichever shows they like at whatever time they like. Lacking the ability to promote a single airtime for a national audience, it is an arrangement that practically guarantees internecine rivalry and a certain amount of public confusion.

"It's the Balkanization of the system, like a bunch of independent countries fighting with one another," explained Russ Morash. "There's no discipline. *This* guy in San Francisco decides to run *Nova* at four a.m. on a Wednesday, and *that* guy in Philadelphia runs the same program at six p.m. on a Friday. It makes it very difficult to know what you're going to get when you turn on the TV. That lack of universal coverage is the weakness that almost killed PBS. It wasn't a secret. We deplored it. But there wasn't anything we could do about it."

Second, local programmers would sometimes promote their own, in-house shows over those produced by rival stations. "They would do their mischief," said Morash. "There was bad blood—I don't think there was any question about it." He pointed to WNET, the New York station behind *Nature*, among other shows, as an example: "New York was a bunch of arrogant bastards. It seemed they would deliberately not run our [WGBH] programs in prime time. I don't think they were particularly impressed with Julia, or any of our offerings, despite their good ratings in other markets." As petty as it sounds, he said, "it goes back to the Yankees versus the Red Sox. Large or small, that old rivalry had a role."

Third, while WGBH was producing some of the nation's best educational programs—including performances by the Boston Pops, documentaries about the Vietnam War, *Nova*, and Morash's hit shows *Victory Garden* and *This Old House*—there were only so many hours of "prime time," between 8:00 and 11:00 p.m., when the audience was largest. The competition for those precious hours was fierce, and the station was rife with internal politics. In the meantime, public tastes were shifting.

"After a while, the whole how-to genre wasn't a top priority," recalled Henry Becton, who ran WGBH's cultural programming in the late seventies. "Julia may have been feeling she wasn't getting as much audience reaction as she had hoped for, compared to some of the other shows."

Lastly, the *Company* series—and Julia herself—may have been taken for granted by WGBH. Despite the fact that she was the station's first breakout star, her programs were considered "quirky," a mere afterthought, "some little cooking show" next to the "truly" Important Programming the station was known for, Morash said. "You have to remember the context of the time. No matter what the revisionists would have you believe, Julia's shows were never, ever *that* important to GBH. Ever."

By 1980 Julia had confronted these realities and made a previously unthinkable decision: she would quit public television and take her talents elsewhere.

"It's a twelve-hour day and seven-day week, and I'm not going to go into that kind of thing and have it just lay an egg," she told *Dial*. "That's a damn good book, and there were damn good shows and very original recipes. A lot of places didn't get [*More Company*] because [PBS] never announced that it was going out there and they made their fall schedules without it. So I'm through, frankly. It was so good, that's what annoys me."

In the seventeen years she had been at WGBH, Julia had produced 250 television shows that were broadcast on 104 PBS stations, had written or co-written five books, and was a major fund-raiser for public TV. But after the bungling of the *Company* series she was disenchanted.

"As soon as you're off the television for a year nobody will know who you are, which is fine," Julia said philosophically. "That makes fame quite bearable."

She had enjoyed an enviable career and could have slipped into a quiet retirement with Paul, perhaps at La Pitchoune. But that prospect did not interest Julia Child. "I love working," she would tell the *Los Angeles Times* when she was ninety years old. "You don't have to retire nowadays, do you? I don't even know what it would mean."

Part III

Following the Gleam

★ ★ ★

12

Prime Time

1. GMA

In 1980, Julia was approached by producers from ABC-TV, who wondered if she might be interested in a regular cooking segment on *Good Morning America* (*GMA*), the network's popular variety show. By then, the American food revolution was well under way, and they were searching for a marquee cook to add to their talent roster. They may have caught wind that Julia was available.

Julia had appeared on network shows with Johnny Carson, Dick Cavett, Tom Snyder, and the like, and was keenly aware of the reach and power of commercial television. But she had concerns. Paul was ailing in Cambridge, and she did not want to commit to a heavy TV schedule in New York. Anticipating this, the ABC executives offered an elegant solution: Julia could fly to New York once a month, perform one live show and tape several others, which would be shown in ensuing weeks. To entice her, *GMA* offered to pay her $605 per appearance, fly her to and from Boston, put her up in a top hotel, and hire a team of trusted cooks to help prep the food she would use on air. It was a generous and well-timed offer, and Julia gladly accepted it.

Her segments on *GMA* ran for about two and a half minutes each, which seemed like hardly any time at all for someone accustomed to doing half-hour shows, each of which took a week to prepare for. In typical fashion, Julia carefully researched and rehearsed each show, but struggled to adapt to the velocity of commercial production. "I feel things are still a bit rough, but are improving," she confided to Simca. Each short

GMA segment "must be made to appear like plenty of time" to demonstrate a recipe, she wrote. But with practice she got into the rhythm of performatory cooking and found her stride. "Actually, now we are into it, one can do a surprisingly rather large amount in that time," she noted.

In a typical week in October 1980, Julia and Paul rose early Monday morning in Boston, caught an 8:00 a.m. flight to New York, and checked into a midtown hotel. That afternoon, they wandered through SoHo, poking their noses into food emporia like Dean & DeLuca, Raffetto's, SoHo Charcuterie, and the venerable Vesuvio Bakery. That evening, they had an early dinner at The River Café, on a barge under the Brooklyn Bridge with sweeping views of the East River and lower Manhattan.

At 5:15 Tuesday morning, the Childs were picked up by a limousine and whisked to ABC's studio, where Julia taped six cooking segments— one aired live and five were broadcast later. That afternoon, the Childs ate lunch with Judith Jones and took a walk before an early dinner. On Wednesday, Julia and Paul flew to Providence, Rhode Island, where she patiently submitted to a string of radio and TV interviews, and appeared at a benefit for Planned Parenthood.

Returning to Cambridge, the Childs socialized with friends, or at the private St. Botolph Club, visited a bird sanctuary, and had a bit of fun—judging a pie contest and going to a hair salon. Then it was back to the daily routine of researching recipes and writing articles. "Julia cleans her closet!" she wrote in her date book.

Under the watchful eye of the English producer Sonya Selby-Wright, Julia's cooking spots appeared at 8:40 every Tuesday morning, and she soon became a popular fixture at *GMA*. The key to making her segments work in the allotted 150 seconds was a reliable crew of behind-the-scenes cooks, such as Nancy Verde Barr—a cooking teacher in Providence, Rhode Island, whom Julia had met at a Planned Parenthood fund-raiser—and some TV sleight of hand. In a show about rice pilaf, Barr recalled in a memoir, Julia would briefly demonstrate chopping and sautéing vegetables, and would then employ a carefully choreographed "swap"—in which the camera switched to a second, identical pan filled with already-cooked vegetables. Julia would add rice, stock, and seasoning to the second pan, and the camera would switch again. Julia would uncover a third pan to show the audience a fully cooked pilaf. As the seconds counted down, she'd ladle the finished pilaf into a serving dish, proudly display it, and sign off with a hearty *"Bon appétit!"*

To help prep her early *GMA* cooking segments, Julia hired a trusted protégée from Boston: Sara Moulton, who had been part of the *Julia Child & More Company* crew. Though Moulton was pulled away by other commitments, she returned to *GMA* in 1987 as food editor, and eventually had a stellar career in New York as a cookbook author, chef of *Gourmet*'s executive dining room, and the host of popular cooking shows. But first she had to get past Chef Cazalis.

11. Getting Over It

Sara Moulton was destined to become a cook on the day in 1952 when her mother, Elizabeth, an editor at *Mademoiselle* who was nine months pregnant, interviewed Henri Soulé at Le Pavillon. Soulé, the restaurant's charming and autocratic *patron*, made sure she ate every delicious morsel to benefit the baby.

"Years later, my mother decided that *that lunch* was the reason I became a chef." Moulton laughed.

A diminutive blonde, Moulton had a passion for chopping carrots and baking brownies in the modest kitchen of her parents' Manhattan apartment. Unlike most French chefs, who come from blue-collar backgrounds without much education, she attended a private all-girls school on New York's Upper East Side, and graduated in 1974 from the University of Michigan with a major in the history of ideas. Feeling aimless after college, Moulton slung hash at an Ann Arbor bar. Concerned, her mother wrote to Julia Child and Craig Claiborne, asking, "If my daughter wants to become a chef, what should she do?" Julia did not respond, but Claiborne did: "She should go to cooking school," he wrote.

It didn't occur to Moulton that she could make a career out of her love of food until her mother urged her to apply to the Culinary Institute of America (CIA) in Hyde Park, New York. Sara was accepted. After some trepidation about leaving her boyfriend, Bill, in Michigan, she packed for cooking school. There, she learned many valuable lessons, and not only about the art and science of cooking food.

"Housed in an old monastery and run like a military academy,"

Moulton recalls, the CIA would deduct points from your grade if you were not dressed in clean whites, with your hair completely tucked under a hat, all jewelry removed, and nails trimmed. If you missed a class because you were running a fever of 102 degrees, too bad: more points off. Most of the faculty and students were men, and they did not welcome women. More than one chef told her point-blank: "Women do not belong in the kitchen!" This remark was breathtakingly offensive, but Moulton did her best to ignore it and eventually thrived at the school.

Like most aspiring chefs in the 1970s, Moulton watched Julia Child on television and stayed up late reading her cookbooks. In 1976, Moulton took an externship to cook at Harvest, in Cambridge. She got to know the restaurant's owners, Jane and Ben Thompson, and kept tabs on their interesting customers, including Paul and Julia Child, through the window of the kitchen door.

Upon graduating from the CIA the following year, Moulton worked as the chef-manager of a catering operation in Cambridge. One of her co-workers was Berit Pratt, a daughter of the Childs' good friends Pat and Herbert Pratt. Sara and Berit made thousands of hard-boiled eggs together, and discussed Julia's famous "no boil" method (start the eggs in cold water, bring them almost to the boil, pull them off the stove and let them sit, then plunge them into ice water). Berit mentioned that she volunteered on *Julia Child & Company*, and Sara asked if she could join the fun. The next day, Berit said to her, "I told Julia all about you. She wants to hire you."

Moulton was stunned. The next thing she knew, she—who is short, slim, with a blond pageboy, a wide smile, and the face of a youthful teenager—was staring up at her hero and shaking her large hand. "Julia was like Big Bird. She couldn't go anywhere without people recognizing her. She was endlessly curious, and just so lovely to so many people, including me."

It was 1979, and Julia was about to start taping *Julia Child & More Company*. But her trusty assistant cook, Rosie Manell, was delayed in California. "Do you style food, dearie?" Julia asked casually, not betraying her predicament.

"Oh yes, I'm very good at it," Moulton lied.

She was hired on the spot.

"I think anyone else would have lied," Moulton said unapologetically. "Why be honest when you have an opportunity like that?"

There were only two problems: Moulton had no experience as a food stylist (one who prepares and arranges food to look attractive for photos and television); and she had just started a job as the chef at Cybele's, a French restaurant in Faneuil Hall. She solved the first problem by learning on the job, and the second by rearranging her schedule so that she cooked five days a week at the restaurant and two days a week with Julia at *More Company*.

Julia noticed that Moulton was a hard worker and accomplished cook with a sunny personality, and took a special interest in her development. Once *More Company* wrapped, Julia arranged a three-month summer "*stage*," an apprenticeship, at a respected restaurant in France. It was a tremendous honor for the grateful, if slightly terrified Moulton. "Oh, I worried so much about everything!" she recalled. "Will I be able to cook well? Will I be able to speak good enough French? Will I get everything done? I was *so* nervous."

Julia had recommended Moulton to the Henri IV, a one-star establishment in Chartres, a small city southwest of Paris and home to the famed Gothic cathedral. The restaurant's chef-proprietor, Maurice Cazalis, was a restaurateur of some note.

In person, Cazalis was short, plump, and egocentric. He welcomed Moulton to Chartres warmly, explained that he would cover her room and board but would not pay her for her restaurant work (this is standard). His son had died in an accident, he explained, so he, his wife, and their daughter had devoted themselves to the Henri IV. Moulton couldn't wait to get behind the stove.

Every day, she would walk through Chartres Cathedral and pause to listen to the voices of the choir drift high up to the arched stone ceiling and slip into the ether. This became her ritual, a moment of subdued privacy in the shadowy church before diving into the hot, bright cacophony of the restaurant kitchen.

Moulton was twenty-seven, well trained and experienced, if slightly too American and female for the chef's taste. She was not allowed to work "the line" as a cook behind the main stove, but the honor and experience of working at such an establishment would suffice. Or so everyone told her. "It was, uhm, *rigorous*," Moulton recalled. "I was stressed all the time." Her duties were to make salads, pizzas, lunch for the crew, chicken stock from scratch, and anything else the chef wanted. "There was a lot of scrambling," she said. "It made me crazy to not be cooking on the line." She felt isolated, and missed Bill.

During her *stage* at the Henri IV, Moulton befriended two affable fifteen-year-old apprentices, was dogged by a mean-spirited Japanese sous-chef, and was hazed by a gang of hyperaggressive French line cooks. Worst of all, Chef Cazalis revealed himself as a screaming bully who used humiliation and the occasional slap or punch to keep his crew in line. One day, a cook placed a bubbling-hot cassoulet in a beautiful copper casserole in the dumbwaiter to send it from the first-floor kitchen up to the second-floor dining room. But the pan's handle stuck out, and as the dumbwaiter's door slammed shut, the cassoulet exploded and seeped onto the kitchen floor.

"Who did that?" shouted a red-faced Cazalis. "Who did it?"

"She did!" the Japanese cuisinier said, pointing an accusing finger at Moulton. (It was clear that the mistake had been his, but "he knew Chef wouldn't hit a woman," said Moulton.) Enraged, she stormed out of the kitchen without a word. Jean, the friendly *chef de cuisine*, comforted her, and then she began to cry. "I just uncorked," she said, grimly. "Then Jean began to cry. He said, 'I'm so, so sorry.' It was a mess."

Moulton was the only woman in the kitchen, and she resented the staff's casual chauvinism. Cazalis was no help, and tried to woo Moulton, telling her that "This is how it's done in France." The seventy-two-year-old chef once cornered her in the wine cellar, and another time in the walk-in refrigerator. She managed to fend him off, but did not enjoy his overtures.

When Cazalis invited Moulton to visit the Élysée Palace, where a former apprentice was the sous-chef for President Valéry Giscard d'Estaing, she happily agreed. He booked them into the same room at a hotel near the Champs-Élysées. That evening, Cazalis took Moulton to dinner at the Folies Bergère, a topless burlesque in Montmartre, where he attempted to ply her with drinks. Back at the hotel the chef announced he usually slept *très nu* (very naked), but out of chivalrous deference to her tender sensibilities he would wear pajamas. Moulton retreated to the bathroom, slipped on her pajamas and raincoat "with the belt tied tight," and slept on top of the covers at the far edge of her bed. "I was no more to this old goat than a tender young lamb," she said. "I vowed to never go anywhere alone with him again."

Back at the Henri IV, Moulton was tempted to quit. She and Bill debated the question on long, expensive transatlantic calls. "In the end, I decided to grit my teeth and stick it out," she said. "I mean, [Chef Cazalis] was a dear friend of my old mentor. *Julia* had sent me there, and I couldn't just leave. What would I tell her?"

In fact, she never called or wrote to Julia to complain about her treatment. Besides, life in Chartres wasn't all bad. The cathedral was her solace, and the cooking was phenomenal. She learned wonderful sauces and to cook specialties like a dreamy prune soufflé. She also learned practical lessons, such as how to limit food costs. Cazalis insisted his crew use every last scrap in the kitchen. "We'd collect leftovers, sweetbreads, whatever, combine them and put them on pizza for *amuses*," Moulton recalls. "I still do that to this day."

Once her *stage* ended, Bill joined Moulton and they ate their way through Burgundy. (They are now married.) When she returned to Boston, it took Moulton six months to summon the courage to tell Julia about her harrowing experience at the Henri IV.

Julia didn't bat an eyelash. "Oh dearie, what did you expect?" she said. "They're *all* like that. Get over it."

Moulton was stunned: *Get over it?* It struck her as a shocking and unsisterly thing to say. Then, collecting her wits, she understood the message: *If you really want something, don't let anything—even sexual harassment—get in your way.*

"I don't think it was feminism," said Moulton. "Julia would have given the same message to a man. She was willing to go into a man's world and cook this food that women weren't cooking. She was a role model."

From Julia's perspective, Cazalis's boorish groping "was not a real problem," Moulton said. "He was like a mosquito—ignore it, move on. 'You've had the privilege of cooking in a one-star kitchen in France, and in the long run that's what matters.' Now, I think she was right on the money."

Looking back, Sara Moulton considered the episode, and Julia's reaction, a defining experience. It is a lesson that she has passed on to her own followers: "There are *always* going to be roadblocks. Get over it.

Learn what you can, and move on. It was the greatest lesson Julia ever taught me."

iii. "FCiF" Redux

In the summer of 1983, Julia rounded a circle by bringing *Good Morning America* to Provence, to reprise "The French Chef in France" documentaries. Before leaving Cambridge, Julia wrote a tender note to Simca in Paris: "How time indeed flies, and now it is almost 35 years since we have known each other, and how much I have treasured our deep and intimate friendship. *Tu es ma soeur, vraiment* [You are my sister, truly]. How lucky to have such a good relationship, and a working relationship, and deep affection. It is too bad we cannot see each other daily, but we are close by thought and by letter."

Thirteen years after shooting the original documentaries in France for WGBH, Julia had convinced ABC to revisit the idea. She taped five segments about shopping, cooking, and eating along the Mediterranean for *GMA*. Now seventy-one, with a slightly puffy face (she had undergone two of her three *"sacquepages,"* or face-lifts, by then), she took to the project with her usual vigor and vim, in spite of her stiff and painful knees.

The miniseries was shot in September 1983. In contrast to the wide-ranging "FCiF" documentaries of 1970, Julia did not venture far from La Pitchoune this time, and focused largely on the cookery of Nice. In keeping with her American persona, she eschewed the stylish outfits she wore in the 1970 documentaries in favor of plain green shirts and blue skirts. (Simca did not appear in the *GMA* segments.)

In the first installment, the camera panned from on high across Old Nice, looking much as it did in the seventeenth century, with yellow-walled buildings, red roofs, a gray stone beach, and the blue Mediterranean Sea. Plunging into those streets, Julia took her audience to the outdoor food stalls and the Marché aux Fleurs (flower market) to shop for wild mushrooms, cured olives, and a bouquet of brightly colored zinnias. From there, she invited viewers into her little kitchen at La Pitchoune, where she prepared ratatouille, the region's signature combination of tomatoes, eggplants, peppers, onions, and zucchini.

"It can be perfectly delicious when it's carefully made," Julia cooed, as she patted a purple eggplant affectionately. While this would not be the legendary "ratatouille done right" that Julia and her friend Jane Thompson had made on Cape Cod (they picked the vegetables from Thompson's garden, prepared and cooked each ingredient separately, then layered the elements together and baked them in a casserole, a process that took nearly a day), the *GMA* version was a simplified dish that baked for an hour, by which point, Julia said, "everything bubbles up" aromatically.

As the segment ended, Julia sat on the simple stone terrace at La Pitchoune, backed by a wall of bright pink bougainvillea. Raising a glass of white wine over the steaming ratatouille, she toasted America from France once again: *"Bon appétit!"*

In the next segment, "Behind the Making of Candied Fruit," Julia toured Maison Auer in Nice—"a culinary delight, and a dentist's nightmare"—where candied fruits had been handmade since 1820. (In the 1970 series, she had focused on a similar store, Maiffret, in Cannes.) The Auer family had originated in Switzerland, and the experience of stepping inside their store, run by the family's fifth generation, was like entering a time machine. It was decorated in a swirling, somewhat overwrought Florentine style, with crystal chandeliers, a stained-glass skylight, marble-topped display cases, and pale green floor tiles. In the ornate salesroom, platters of candied oranges, pineapples, pears, and cherries lined glass shelves: "Picture-perfect candied fruits," Julia narrated. "They take seconds to devour, but long months to make."

In the workrooms, the candy makers hand peeled cantaloupes, scooped them out, and pricked them with sharp tines to allow their juices to be released. Following tradition, they were soaked in water and boiled in sugar syrup in large copper pots, up to fifteen times, to raise the sugar content manyfold. Then the melons were transferred to large, glazed terra-cotta terrines for eight weeks of steeping in the syrup. The fruit was then canned, packaged, and displayed.

Thence to the harbor, where fishermen left well before dawn and returned to Nice as the sun rose to sell their silvery catch of the day: anchovies, sardines, jellyfish, squid, and the famous *rouget barbet*, a small red fish with a "beard" (*barbet*) on its chin. Back at La Pitchoune, Julia demonstrated the making of a *soupe de poisson*—a fisherman's soup made with a plateful of mixed fish, onions, tomatoes, garlic, and fish stock; it is traditionally served with a *rouille*—a red garlic sauce, pounded up in a large olive wood mortar with a pestle—and toasted rounds of bread.

For the next episode, Julia realized a dream by taking her audience into a sanctum sanctorum that most would never have the chance to visit: through the hallowed doors of Le Moulin de Mougins, one of only eighteen three-star restaurants in France. "Eating is one of the French national sports," she explained. "You plan your trip according to the [*Guide Michelin*] map." Dressed in a pink shirt and a beige skirt, Julia led Paul through the big wooden doors of the restaurant, which stood just up the road from La Pitchoune. "What makes it so good, why is it a three-star restaurant?" she wondered to the camera. "So, c'mon, let's take a look at it.

"Good food is always enhanced by its ambience," Julia said in a reverential tone, as if entering a sacred space. As waiters set up the dining room in a precise, unhurried way, she noted that "silver and porcelain are polished daily. The fresh flowers are *never* yesterday's leftovers. Everything is *spotless* in the quest for perfection."

In the kitchen, seventeen chefs—"each with his own specialty"—began work at dawn to prepare for lunch. The camera glided by rooms devoted solely to fish, fruits, and butter. "Don't forget the *butter*—the French never do!"

Eating lunch at a corner table adjacent to the restaurant's crowded terrace, Julia bent to a platter of *rouget* presented by Chef Serge. "Of course, the true taste of any restaurant is your *own* taste," Julia said. She cut the fish, placed it in her mouth, chewed, and thought about it for a moment. "*Hmmmm*, this is just a *lovely* dish, Serge," Julia said with real feeling. "*Merci beaucoup.*"

Paul was dressed in a blue shirt and looked thin. He didn't say a word, but decades of experience kicked in as he raised his wineglass and gamely toasted the camera.

After lunch, Julia wandered into the Moulin's busy kitchen and discovered a smiling woman in a pink shirt and a white apron rapidly peeling asparagus spears. "I'd like to introduce you to Kathie Allen, from Long Beach, California," Julia shouts to the camera over the clatter and din. "She came here for a week, and has been here for two months, and has one month longer."

The woman's name was actually Kathie Alex (not Allen), and she was in the midst of a rare *stage* at the Moulin. Blushing and smiling, while continuing to strip asparagus, Alex said that she appreciated the professionalism required in a three-star kitchen, and loved cooking the cuisine of Provence. "I plan to take [the experience] back with me and expand my catering business. And maybe open a small restaurant in Long Beach," she said hopefully.

Kathie Alex did not open a restaurant in California: instead, she stayed in France, studied cooking with Simca at Bramafam, and worked as a private chef aboard yachts in the Mediterranean. In the mid-nineties, she purchased La Pitchoune from the Fischbacher family, and ran it as a cooking school called Cooking with Friends in France, before she retired in 2016.

The final *GMA* documentary was called "Snack Foods of Nice." In it, Julia strolled through the familiar narrow stone lanes of the Old City, chatting with shopkeepers, sampling Niçoise delicacies like the onion-anchovy tarts known as *pissaladières*, sardines and Swiss chard, onions stuffed with cheese, and *soccas*, the chickpea crepes. Holding up a large round sandwich overflowing with tuna, tomatoes, cucumber, lettuce, hard-boiled egg, and dribbling vinaigrette, she said, "Here's the Niçoise answer to the American hamburger, called the *pan bagnat* . . . You can tell if it's properly made if [the olive oil] really drips down and falls off your elbow."

Wrapping up the segment, Julia declared, "The fast foods in France are certainly wonderful, but when you get tired of all this foreign stuff you can always ask for . . . *le 'ot dog!*" Pulling a large pink hot dog from behind her back, she poked it toward the camera, took a hearty bite, then tilted her head back and roared with laughter.

13

The Celebrity Chef

I. A Revolutionary in Pearls

Julia Child was the nation's first "celebrity chef." Though there were other chefs on television, and Julia's fame was just one aspect of the nation's growing interest in food, she played a pivotal role in revolutionizing the way Americans shopped, cooked, and ate. Julia, it turned out, had brought the right message to the right place at the right time, and she was the right messenger. She appealed to a broad swath of the public, helped to popularize fine dining, and changed the grocery and cookware businesses. Inventing her career as she went, Julia inspired many people to pursue jobs in the culinary arts, education, advocacy, and journalism.

Henry Becton, WGBH's head of cultural programming in the seventies, praised "the Julia model" of how-to television. Until *The French Chef*, such shows were hosted by slick if inexpert "presenters." But "Julia was a real *authority* on her subject matter, and she had a distinctive, uninhibited personality," said Becton. "To the people at home, that combination was *key*." The other key was her continuing refusal to endorse products. While her stance cost Julia untold income, it reinforced the audience's faith in her: if Julia recommended an ingredient, you could trust her judgment because she was not being paid to say it. "I really respected her for taking that stand," said Becton. "It influenced our editorial guidelines for that kind of program."

The traditional chef—particularly a chef from France—was an uneducated man from the provinces who learned a set of mechanical skills and formulaic recipes under the tutelage of a master. Even if he went on to earn three Michelin stars, the chef was essentially a trades-man, akin to a highly skilled plumber. He rarely left his kitchen, almost never spoke to other chefs or his own patrons, and worked such grueling hours that he was a virtual slave to his restaurant. The more sensitive chefs were high-strung, with a temper that could explode into verbal and physical abuse of underlings. In the hoary cliché, the chef was a miser-able, misanthropic drunk.

Regardless of the accuracy of that profile, Julia was the opposite sort of person. She was a quintessentially American personality: a confident, outgoing Californian educated at Smith College; a worldly diplomatic wife who had lived in Paris and trained at the Cordon Bleu, wore pearls with her apron, and loved to cook with others. I think of her as "a revo-lutionary in pearls." As such, she was a tremendously appealing ambas-sador from the Land of Food to the American public.

While Julia enjoyed her success, she felt ambivalent about it. She saw herself as "a teacher of cookery" and "an eternal pupil," rather than as a celebrity to be fawned over. She preferred to carry her own luggage through airports, and to wait in line "like regular people," rather than to get special treatment (although she occasionally used her name to secure restaurant reservations). Julia was more interested in trying new foods,

Julia with the photographer Jim Scherer and her editor, Judith Jones

meeting new people, learning new skills, exploring herself by exploring cookery, than in looking back in self-congratulation. Her philosophy was that few dishes were too complicated for the average cook; all people needed was a little "gumption" and "elbow grease," and they could make anything their hearts desired. "If I can do it, anyone else ought to be able to do it too" was her mantra.

Perhaps that is true of her recipes, but it is not true of her career. When I asked if she understood what a huge impact she had had on America, Julia shrugged and demurred: "Well, if it wasn't me, it would have been someone else."

But it *was* her. And it is unlikely that anyone else could have done what she did, when she did, and how she did it. Julia Child changed the nation, even if she didn't like to admit it.

"The more you do, the more you learn," she told *Boston* magazine. "We always say there aren't any set rules. If you're persistent and enthusiastic, you'll find a way. We just tell [people] to follow that gleam."

11. A Totally Different World

One day in 1979, Julia, Paul, and four friends arrived for lunch at the Parker House Hotel, in Boston, and said to the eager young assistant sous-chef, "Why don't you create something different for our table?"

The young man's name was Emeril Lagasse. He viewed Julia's offer as a friendly challenge. "I went back into the kitchen and I was psyched, but I was as nervous as crap!" he recalled. "I took the idea of snails, which were popular in French restaurants, and Julia liked them. So I did a thing with periwinkles—steamed them in parsley, oil, garlic, and Portuguese chiles—and she loved it. And Julia, she didn't forget much, so after that we became friends. Out of the blue she'd call me and say, 'I need you to help me with this or that event.' We broke a lot of bread together, all over the place. Julia was really my influence, from books to television."

Raised in gritty Fall River, Massachusetts, Emeril was a devotee of *The French Chef* as a teenager in the seventies. He was inspired by Julia's stories about learning to shop in Paris and cook seafood in Marseille. "That was a big reason why I went to study in Paris and Lyon," Lagasse said. "No one had more passion for the art of culinary than Julia. She was so intellectual about it, and she wanted to share. She cared more about teaching than celebrity."

In 1982, Lagasse was named the executive chef of Commander's Palace, in New Orleans, where he mastered Cajun and Creole cooking; in 1990, he opened his own restaurant, Emeril's. In 1993, Julia invited Lagasse to appear in the TV series and book *Cooking with Master Chefs.* Filming in New Orleans, Lagasse taught Julia how to make a traditional crawfish boil and how to cook étouffée (crab, shrimp, or crawfish in a spicy roux over rice).

"Julia's advice was: Be who you are. Be true to what you are, and to your craft," Lagasse said. "It was never about coming up with some persona."

Today, Lagasse is considered the prototypical celebrity chef—a manager of television shows, restaurants, and cookbooks, and purveyor of products like knives, steaks, and spice blends. He is the most direct link between Julia's television cookery in the 1960s and '70s and the twenty-first-century breed of celebrity chef CEOs.

With his Julia-esque performing style—she called for "more butter," he called for "more pork fat"—Emeril became one of the original stars of the Food Network. It debuted in 1993, and shone a bright light on chefs, their work, their rivalries, and their personal struggles. It was a different kind of television from what Julia had done.

While *The French Chef* was documentary in nature, the Food Network focused on the drama and competition in kitchens, and turned cooking into entertainment and spectacle. "The Food Network made being a chef cool and sexy," said the cookbook author Dorie Greenspan.

Suddenly, high-school kids aspired to have their own food shows on TV or the Web, even before they had learned to cook properly. And established chefs were not simply food providers; they became entrepreneurs, CEOs of global multimedia corporations worth millions of dollars, and were seemingly ubiquitous on the page, airwaves, and screens, not to mention the stock market.

"Food is the new tech!" hollered investors. A new cadre of entrepreneurial chefs, whose primary focus was the boardroom rather than the kitchen, sprang up. "Plating food and running a corporation are completely different skill sets," said Russ Parsons, the former food editor of the *Los Angeles Times*. For the super chefs, "it's become a CEO culture rather than a chef culture."

The chefs Jean-Georges Vongerichten and Daniel Boulud arrived in New York from France in the mid-eighties as country boys who had been trained in the guildlike system of France. They dreamed of nothing more than owning their own restaurants. Vongerichten's trip to the United States was sponsored by Louis Outhier, the chef at L'Oasis. Outhier would fax his protégé menus, allowing Vongerichten to experiment with one (and only one) daily special. Vongerichten quickly took to the Big Apple, and at age twenty-nine won four stars from *The New York Times* for his cooking at Lafayette. In 1991, he opened JoJo, which was named best new restaurant of the year. Now he oversees a food empire that extends from New York to Las Vegas, London, and Shanghai. Boulud, meanwhile, operates restaurants from Palm Beach to Washington, D.C., New York, and Montreal; has authored books and is a frequent presence on television. Today, the two country boys are known around the world simply by their first names, Jean-Georges and Daniel.

"It's become a totally different world" for chefs like them, said Greenspan. In 1985, Vongerichten and Boulud "couldn't have conceived of where they'd be today. Paul Bocuse was probably the first 'flying chef,' but he didn't have an empire. No one did. It would have been impossible for Jean-Georges and Daniel to even *dream* of an empire."

JULIA CHILD WAS NOT solely responsible for the extraordinary growth of the American food business, of course. But by single-mindedly following the gleam in her eye, she played a significant role in establishing the right conditions for it. Julia created a new model for what cooks and food could be, and thus changed public perceptions. She encouraged people to have large appetites, both literally and figuratively.

"If you don't eat with gusto, the gastric juices are not going to work properly," she advised. "You just won't digest your food properly. So don't eat meekly!" This was vintage Julia, both in its humor and its underlying seriousness. She loved food, and she wanted others to love it as much as she did. Yet, I suspect Julia would have reservations about some of what has been wrought in her name—the glitz, the melodrama, the nonsensical competitions that make up much of today's 24/7/365 televised culinary circus. Julia loved cooking for the camaraderie and creative satisfaction, not for cutthroat competition and soap opera storylines.

She could sense the coming change, even as early as 1979, when she wrote to Simca: "I'm really getting tired of all the cuisine brouhaha, jockeying for place and prestige. I think we were lucky, you and I, to be in at the beginning. OUF."

14

"Bon Appétit, America!"

1. Holy Fire

I'll never, never, never retire," Julia said. "I'll go on cooking and writing and experimenting . . . That's the best part about having your own thing: you can keep right at it 'til you drop."

She regarded the techniques and attitudes that she learned in France, and the knowledge she had honed at the stove and typewriter and in front of a camera, as "a sacred trust" to be "handed down" from generation to generation. "You have to show people that learning about food is a continuing thing, that as you progress through the years, you find different ways of doing things," she told *Boston* magazine. "An old chef wrote . . . 'I've been cooking more than fifty years, and almost every day I find something new.' I never talk to one of the great chefs who doesn't say that. It's just a continuously creative process."

Julia would continue to create through the eighties, the nineties, and into the aughts, almost until the day she died. Through it all she maintained her "passion for the métier," and "the holy fire" she believed is required for fine cooking.

"If you want to be a chef, you have to like *work*," she said. "Oh, my God, how you have to work."

In the eighties, Julia continued to branch out in new directions. Concerned that the public was ill-informed about wine and food, Julia and the California winemakers Robert Mondavi and Richard Graff established the American Institute of Wine & Food (AIWF): a nonprofit whose mission is "to advance the understanding, appreciation and quality of wine and food through fun educational experiences."

In 1982, Julia dropped her *McCall's* column to become the first food editor at *Parade*, a magazine supplement to Sunday newspapers. Calling itself the world's largest-circulation magazine, *Parade* had a circulation of 21.5 million, and a readership of 43.5 million. *Parade* was "a perfect fit for Julia because it wasn't elitist," said Judith Jones. "She was able to reach all kinds of people all over the country." (Julia wrote for *Parade* through 1986.) For her inaugural column, a smiling Julia appeared on the cover under a headline that neatly summed up her ethos: "Bon Appétit, America!"

And there was always television. In 1983, Julia returned to PBS—while continuing to appear on *Good Morning America*—with a new series, *Dinner at Julia's*. A thirteen-episode program underwritten by Polaroid and taped in Santa Barbara, California, the show synthesized many of her previous ideas but presented them with a new look and tone. Each program followed Julia as she roamed fields, forests, and vineyards in search of ingredients; Julia appeared in short stints behind the stove, but much of the cooking was done by a rotating cast of celebrity chefs, including James Beard, the former Kennedy White House chef René Verdon, and a young Wolfgang Puck. The episodes concluded with Julia hosting an elegant dinner party at the Hope Ranch, attended by well-dressed guests who arrived in a chauffeured Rolls-Royce.

"It was meant to be upscale, high-level entertainment," explained executive producer Russ Morash. Determined not to be tripped up by the scheduling gaffes that hobbled *Julia Child & Company*, Morash inserted the word "dinner" into the title to not so subtly nudge PBS programmers to air the show in the evening.

Morash had been doing pioneering single-camera work on *Victory Garden* and *This Old House*, and applied the same techniques to *Dinner at Julia's*. A video magazine that looked at food production broadly, and ingredients from the American West in particular, *Dinner* showed Julia foraging for wild mushrooms, learning how goat cheese is made, fishing for salmon in Puget Sound, gathering fresh artichokes or peaches, and interviewing California winemakers. Now seventy-one years old, she gamely dressed in a pith helmet and slogged through mud to hunt for chanterelles, donned sparkling earrings and a high-necked blouse for swanky dinner parties, and smiled broadly. In private, however, Julia's knees had grown stiff and painful, and required anti-inflammatory drugs.

While it was all glamorous fun on camera, behind the scenes tensions were boiling. Bob Johnson, Julia's lawyer, had inserted himself into the production—claiming final say on Julia's hair and makeup, and casting himself as the head butler on the show. Julia liked Johnson's gruff, "macho" manner, considered him an effective negotiator of her contracts, and loyally stood by him. Others—friends, family members, colleagues—had a less benign view of Johnson. "He was an odious character," said Morash. "The result was that her hair [a short, dark, frizzy 'do] and makeup [heavily applied] looked ridiculous and cost a fortune." When Johnson and a friend demanded to be lodged in the same house as Morash and his wife, it was nearly the last straw. Julia refused to take sides, and Morash threatened to walk off the production. "It's amazing we got through it," he said. "But once we started shooting we had a wonderful time."

Dinner at Julia's debuted in the fall of 1983 and ran into 1984. The show featured a few vintage moments—Julia spilling flour on the counter, dancing and shouting, "Yippeee!" and being lassoed by a cowboy at a barbecue. But it was panned as unfocused and overproduced. *The New York Times* complained that *Dinner*'s elegant mise-en-scène was "silly and distracting," that the recipes were "not-uncomplicated," and that Julia took a "cavalier" approach to expense. The first episode demonstrated a beef tenderloin and salmon dinner for ten people. Food, transportation, and paper towels for each episode cost a thousand dollars a week, *The Washington Post* reported, which was seen as excessive; and "the cost would be higher but the lamb, shrimp, wines, and such are donated by the producers." Used to seeing her in casual dress and unpretentious surroundings, some of Julia's confidants felt uneasy about this luxe vision, grumbling that had Paul been well enough he would have intervened.

"To gather a sufficient audience, we had no choice," Morash explained. "We couldn't continue doing the same show over and over—another 'Julia in the kitchen' series." Mindful of the tepid response to Season Two of *The French Chef*, Julia had pushed for something new and different. "A handful of people didn't like [*Dinner*] because it wasn't the way they were *used* to seeing Julia. It made them uneasy," said Morash. The new approach "was the only way we were going to get the show done," and was worth the risk. Besides, "Julia had a ball."

She brushed off the criticism and moved on.

II. *La Dégringolade du Corps*

In January 1983, Paul and Charlie Child turned eighty-one. In quiet moments Paul was lucid and thoughtful, and he was able to write or paint. But he tired easily, and in large crowds he grew confused and would sometimes growl intemperately. "What a bore, *la dégringolade du corps!*" (the tumbling down of the body), Julia confided to Simca.

His twin was in better health. After the death of his wife, Freddie, in 1977, and trouble with high blood pressure, Charlie sank into a dark despond. He sold their large stone house in Bucks County, Pennsylvania, and moved to a nearby retirement community. There, he began to socialize, paint, write, and travel again; his mood slowly improved. He visited Paul and Julia in California, realized a long-held dream by traveling to China, and was planning a trip to England. On February 8, 1983, Paul was on the *Dinner* set with Julia when the news arrived: Charlie—known as Cha—had suffered a heart attack while writing letters, and died.

Paul was devastated. He crossed out all of the appointments in his date book that day, and scribbled, "I suffer because of Cha's death." A few days later, a letter from Charlie arrived in the mail, full of news and good cheer.

The "twinnies," as they called each other, had shared a complex, loving, competitive, mutually dependent relationship that was never fully resolved. Paul had recovered enough to start painting again, but Charlie's death stopped him cold. In ensuing years, Paul had a series of small strokes, and suffered prostate, dental, eye, and other health problems. To ease the strain, the Childs stayed at an apartment in Santa Barbara during the icy months. Julia wrote to Simca: "Mon pauvre Paul is in a bad state . . . He has deteriorated a great deal . . . and is suddenly now un vieillard [an old man]. He is very unsteady on his feet and the other day . . . he lurched forward and plunged down a flight of wooden steps onto the cement below. Fortunately a neighbor's little dog . . . alerted his master, who rushed to help us. Result, a cracked rib, cracked bone in one wrist, and broken tooth. He's in a lot of pain."

Julia and Paul, 1989

Julia kept herself busy. In 1985, *Good Morning America* dispatched her for a five-part series called "Julia Child in Italy," which proved wildly popular. ABC received letters from more than a hundred thousand fans, and re-aired the series.

In 1988, while "plunging around" her office in Santa Barbara, she tripped and broke her hip. She was hobbled and frustrated, but managed to finish writing her latest book, *The Way to Cook*, which was published the following year. This gorgeously produced tome took its title from six one-hour videocassettes Julia had made, though it incorporated recipes she had developed over forty years for *Dinner at Julia's*, *Parade*, and *Good Morning America*. *The Way to Cook* took her five years to complete, and was dedicated to her attorney Bob Johnson (who had succumbed to AIDS in 1986).

Published in a large, colorful format, it was a calorie-conscious primer for cooks of all skill levels that emphasized Julia's tried-and-true formula of theme and variation. *The Way to Cook* sold three hundred thousand copies in its first year, though the videocassettes fared poorly and a TV series never materialized.

Nevertheless, Julia kept up a full schedule of appearances on both *Good Morning America* and public TV, columns for *Parade*, and emceeing fund-raisers for the AIWF, IACP, Planned Parenthood, Smith College, and other organizations she was willing to lend her name to.

BY 1989, leaving the house had become impossible for Paul, the man who had once roamed the world. One afternoon, he wandered out of 103 Irving Street and got lost in the streets of Boston. He was rescued and returned safely home, but Julia was horrified by the incident. Paul had two prostate operations, suffered a series of strokes, and began to drift in and out of reality. He could no longer be left alone.

"It was extremely painful for Julia," recalled Judith Jones.

But Julia was pragmatic: "Let the living live!" she said.

That September, she moved Paul into an assisted-living facility outside of Boston. She visited him daily or, when traveling, set an alarm so that she could call him at the same time every day. In France (where local time is six hours ahead of Boston) she would wake at 2:00 a.m. to call Paul in Massachusetts.

Julia kept her spirits up in the way she always had: she appeared on David Letterman's show, encouraged Peter Kump to establish the James Beard Foundation, and teamed with Jacques Pépin and Rebecca Alssid to create the nation's first master of liberal arts degree in gastronomy at Boston University.

Julia and Simca continued to write back and forth, and *La Super Française* teamed with Suzy Patterson, an Associated Press reporter based in Paris, to write a new book called *Food & Friends: Recipes and Memories from Simca's Cuisine*. Impatient as ever, Simca badgered Patterson to work more quickly, and sent photocopies of half-completed chapters to friends and family for feedback. Patterson complained to Julia, who admonished Simca by mail: "You must be patient . . . Writing is not something you grind out like hamburger. It takes time, thought, calm, inspiration . . . CALM DOWN! RELAX! Let Suzy be at peace with her work. She'll do a good job," Julia wrote. "And don't keep sending sample chapters around on dirty Xerox paper. It gives a bad impression . . . People shouldn't see unfinished unedited bits anyway."

In July 1991, Simca turned eighty-seven years old and published *Food & Friends*. It would be her last book, and she dedicated it to her husband, Jean, who had died in 1986, leaving Simca inconsolable. In her introduction to *Food & Friends*, Julia wrote: "Both Simca and Louisette . . . took their craft with utter seriousness, as a beautiful, marvelous, and creative art form—but an art form with rules. It was that attitude, really, that drew me irresistibly to the profession."

Simca's health was failing. Her heart was wearing out, her eyesight and hearing were spotty, and she frequently stumbled. One day she fell and lay on her bedroom floor for two hours before a relative found her; she had gotten a chill in the meantime and contracted double pneumonia. Julia worried about her, and suggested she sign up for an assisted-living community. Predictably, *La Super Française* would have none of it, and insisted on finishing out her days at Bramafam, virtually alone. In December, Simca stopped eating, and expired.

"We were like sisters," Julia lamented. "We were a pair of cooking nuts. She was a wonderful and generous friend."

On May 12, 1994, Paul Child died at age ninety-two.

JULIA WAS a people person, and unsentimental about possessions. Without Paul, Simca, or Jean for company, or friends like Jim Beard or M. F. K. Fisher to visit, La Pitchoune had lost its allure. Moreover, she noted, Provence was becoming "hideously expensive" and "flooded with people, new little houses, streams of cars, great trucks plowing down winding country roads." By June 1992, Julia had decided it was time to turn the beloved house built on friendship over to its owners. She cooked a final *boeuf en daube à la Provençale* while a small group of family and friends toasted the house with Champagne. Then, as she had promised, Julia handed the house keys to France Thibault, Simca's sister-in-law, and bumped down the driveway for the last time.

"I must admit that I left France this time with no regrets whatsoever," she wrote to a friend.

Not one to mope, Julia returned to the States and proceeded to celebrate her eightieth birthday with a string of parties in Boston, Los Angeles, New York, and Cambridge. "It's such fun!" she declared after each one. *"Bon appétit!"* Some of these fêtes raised money for the AIWF, and others were used to promote the glories of *la cuisine française* at a time when French cooking was losing popularity in the States. The "Merci, Julia" party—the thirtieth celebration of her eightieth birthday—was "an intimate dinner for 500" people in Los Angeles. Julia was toasted by leading French chefs, including Paul Bocuse, Roger Vergé, Daniel Boulud, Michel Richard, and Jean-Louis Palladin. As they wrung their hands over declining revenues and Americans' fear of "rich, stuffy" French food, Julia stood firm. Railing against trendy, half-raw and half-burned "kiddie food," she declared, "If we ate the way nutritionists want us to eat, our hair would be falling out, our teeth would be falling out, and our skin would be drying up!" French food, Julia reminded the world, "can be rich, but it can be simple too."

The crowd ate it up.

III. In Julia's Kitchen

Back in 1972, Julia had pitched an idea for a show that would follow her as she cooked regional specialties with master chefs across the country. David Ives, the president of WGBH, had turned the idea down, telling Julia that he didn't believe other cooks "could come up to your standards" on television. Stubbornly, Julia held on to the idea for twenty years.

In 1993, she starred in the PBS series *Cooking with Master Chefs*. Just as she had originally imagined, the show followed Julia as she cooked with Emeril Lagasse in New Orleans, Robert Del Grande in Houston, Alice Waters in Berkeley, and Amy Ferguson-Ota on Mauna Lani, Hawaii, among others. The episode featuring Lidia Bastianich cooking orecchiette pasta and mushroom risotto in Manhattan was nominated for an Emmy and helped to launch Lidia's TV career five years later.

Master Chefs proved so popular that the following summer Julia taped *In Julia's Kitchen with Master Chefs*. In this iteration, Julia flipped the conceit by inviting twenty-six multicultural chefs with diverse specialties—from Madhur Jaffrey's Roasted Curry Powder to Jacques Torres's Chocolate Soup, Dean Fearing's Pico de Gallo, and Mark Militello's Pork with Jamaican Spices—to cook in her Irving Street kitchen. The show aired in 1995, and led to Julia's second Emmy. (Knopf published companion books to both Master Chef series.)

In the nineties, Julia was in near constant motion. She cohosted *Cooking in Concert* PBS specials with Jacques Pépin and Graham Kerr, the "Galloping Gourmet." She launched an eponymous foundation to support the gastronomic and culinary arts. She co-wrote *Baking with Julia* (1996) with Dorie Greenspan, and starred in a companion show. In 1999, she and Jacques Pépin created the buddy-comedy TV show and book, *Julia and Jacques Cooking at Home*, in which each presented his and her own version of a given recipe—for such dishes as roasted leg of lamb, Provençal tomatoes, and profiteroles. While they agreed to disagree about ingredients or approach, their rivalry was good-natured, and Julia and Jacques's marvelous chemistry won the show an Emmy in 2001. In 2000, she produced *Julia's Kitchen Wisdom* as a slim book and two-hour TV retrospective.

In August 2002, Julia turned ninety years old. Her shoulders were stooped, her knees were weak and aching; she used a walker and eventually a wheelchair. The cold, blustery New England winters without Paul were not much fun, so she donated the house in Cambridge to Smith

Julia, the self-described "kitchen gadget freak," and Paul in Cambridge

College, and moved to Santa Barbara, where she had summered as a child.

Before she left 103 Irving Street, though, the National Museum of American History at the Smithsonian asked if she'd be willing to donate her kitchen to the museum. "Why would they want my kitchen?" Julia wondered. The answer was obvious to everyone but her, and Julia gave her blessing.

On the morning of September 11, 2001—at the very moment that terrorists commandeered four airliners in a national tragedy—a team of Smithsonian curators arrived at 103 Irving Street, in Cambridge. They meticulously noted, deconstructed, and packed every piece of the kitchen, from the black Garland range to the gleaming copper pots hanging from Paul's Peg-Board on the walls, to the prints of fish on the walls. Even the bric-a-brac in kitchen drawers—pencil nibs, bits of string, egg timers, and the signal mirror she helped devise for downed airmen in World War II—was carefully catalogued, wrapped, and transported to Washington, D.C. There, the entire kitchen (save the asbestos tiles beneath its linoleum floor) was faithfully restored. Today, the underside of the Norwegian table in the middle of the room remains speckled with banana stickers from Paul, and a few bits of chewing gum, courtesy of Persons Unknown, who may or may not have been my sisters and me. "Julia's Kitchen" was unveiled in 2002. It was designed as a temporary exhibit, but proved so popular that it remains in place today.

A Civilized Art

1. Slipping Off the Raft

Julia was undaunted by age: "I have no fear of dying," she said. "It's something that happens."

To live a long life, she advised, you should "eat in moderation, exercise daily, and pick your grandparents." Her father had lived to eighty-one, and her grandfather to ninety-seven. Her mother, Caro, died young, at just sixty, but like many of the Westons, she had suffered from high blood pressure, which Julia did not. "I think I will go on for another ten years," she predicted in 2003.

Over the following spring and summer, Julia and I collaborated on her memoir, *My Life in France.* She was ninety-one years old, and lived in a small, neat apartment filled with Paul's paintings and her extensive cookbook collection in a retirement community in Montecito, California. It is a seaside town built on a green slope adjacent to Santa Barbara. The climate there is sunny, dry, and, Julia said, "reminds me of Provence." Most days, she ate breakfast with a group of friends she had known as girls in Pasadena.

Julia suffered from various ailments, and her energy waxed and waned. But she still had that gleam in her eye. She was learning to brine olives, loved to sample fresh strawberries, gnaw on lamb chops at a favorite restaurant, or visit friends at a nearby rose farm—where she picked out a hearty yellow flower now sold as the Julia Child Rose. I struggled to convince her to talk about herself, but in her modesty she usually turned the conversation around to me, or someone else. I finally cracked the code by reading aloud from the letters Paul wrote from France to his twin, Charlie, in Pennsylvania, in the fifties. His words took Julia back in time, and allowed her to talk about her loves—Paul, France, food—and, eventually, about herself. At times, she would reminisce in the present tense, as if she was reliving the moment: "I walk along the Seine while Paul takes photographs of the bridges and fishermen. Then we stroll up the hill to Montmartre. I have always loved Sacré Coeur, don't you? We walk down a little side street, and at the end is a bistro I've never seen before. Inside, there is an old doggie wearing a green sweater. Paul orders kidneys . . ."

The longer we worked together, the more her memories bubbled up, and the book gained momentum.

Food was a constant subject, and sometimes we played a game: "What would you eat for your last meal?" She usually chose a menu beginning with oysters or caviar with Champagne; followed by duck, or the *sole meunière* she had on her first day in France in 1948; a "lovely green salad," and a "perfectly aged" wedge of Camembert cheese, paired with a delicious wine; a dessert of poached pears or ice cream with chocolate sauce. To finish, she'd have a *café filtre* and a snifter of Calvados or cognac.

One day we bought take-out hamburgers, and she insisted that I drive up a small road past a large sign that said "Private" to an overlook with a dazzling view of the Pacific. When I asked if she realized we were trespassing, she grinned and assured me: "Oh, don't worry, dearie. If anyone bothers us, we'll just tell them we're looking for Mr. Smith!" (We ate in peace.) On another day she asked me to roll her in her wheelchair through a local cat show. She associated *"poussiquettes"* with France, and as she held cats of every size, shape, and hue, she became enrobed in cat fur and beamed at them with girlish delight.

On August 15, Julia would turn ninety-two. She had invited friends and family from across the country and around the world to celebrate with her in Montecito. Though she was suffering a kidney infection, and had declined treatment, she was determined to make it to her birthday. My wife, children, and I joined her for lunch a few days before the party, and found her sharp-minded and perceptive. "I viewed our recipes as a sacred trust, a set of rules about the right way and wrong way to approach food, and I felt a duty to pass this knowledge on," she said.

Alerted by her serious tone, I jotted those words down for her memoir. My wife, Sarah, snapped a photo of Julia and me, which appeared on the hardcover dust jacket of *My Life in France.*

The following day her assistant, Stephanie Hersh, made one of Julia's favorite comfort foods, French onion soup, for lunch. In retrospect, it seems that she must have reached a private decision by then.

In describing the death of others, Julia would say they "slipped off the raft." On the night of August 13, two days shy of her ninety-second birthday, Julia did just that: she died of kidney failure in her sleep.

In the meantime, guests were arriving for Julia's party. The birthday turned into a three-day Irish wake, filled with tears and laughter and songs and stories, and plenty of good food and wine. It was sad and joyous in equal measure, a celebration of Julia's remarkable life and esprit. She had done it again, attendees agreed: Julia had managed to exit her life as she had lived it, with a touch of drama and exquisite timing.

"My point is to make cooking easy for people, so that they can enjoy it, and do it, rather than make it a kind of art for the 'We Happy Few,'" she said. "It should be—and is—everybody's pleasure. And it's a civilized art, don't you agree?"

II. Child's Play

Throughout her career, journalists often liked to note how "childlike" Julia Child could be, and how she loved to "play with food." And it was true. Her audience laughed when she dropped a potato pancake on the stove, then scooped it back into the pan, saying "When you're *alone* in the kitchen, *who's* to know?" She flirted with David Letterman while blowtorching a raw hamburger, made winking double entendres on *Good Morning America*, and summoned Jacques Pépin to the stove with a honking duck call.

She encouraged this vision of childlike play, to a point, but it could be misleading. As Paul knowingly observed, "Practically every article on Julie . . . has concentrated on the clown instead of the woman, the cook, the expert, or the revolutionary." There was another Julia, one who saw something deeper, more profound, and mysterious in our ability to turn raw ingredients into something delicious to eat, and how life altering that experience can be.

I was reminded of this when I happened to glance at a postscript at the end of the "VIP Lunch" chapter in *Julia Child & Company*. It was a short, easily overlooked aside, titled "On playing with your food." I read it expecting to laugh. Yet something about it—the tone, the celebration of cooking as art, the encouragement and inclusiveness of its message—caught my attention. I read it again, and then again. I realized that Julia's lighthearted title masked a heartfelt cri de coeur. One that makes a fitting epitaph:

> Some children like to make castles out of their rice pudding, or faces with raisins for eyes. It is forbidden—so sternly that, when they grow up, they take a horrid revenge by dying meringues pale blue or baking birthday cakes in the form of horseshoes or lyres or whatnot. That is not playing with food, that is trifling.
>
> "Play" to me means freedom and delight, as in the phrase "play of imagination." If cooks did not enjoy speculating about new possibilities

in every method and each raw material, their art would stagnate and they would become rote performers, not creators. True cooks love to set one flavor against another in the imagination, to experiment with the great wealth of fresh produce in the supermarkets, to bake what previously they braised, to try new devices. We all have flops, of course, but we learn from them; and, when an invention or variation works out at last, it is an enormous pleasure to propose it to our fellows.

Let's all play with our food, I say, and, in so doing, let us advance the state of the art together.

ACKNOWLEDGMENTS

This book is dedicated to Judith Jones because without her dogged support Julia Child might not have had her career—or at least not the career that she did have—and I would not have had the fun of writing *My Life in France* and *The French Chef in America*. Judith has been an indispensable friend, editor, resource, sounding board, dining companion, and shining example of how to live a rich and meaningful life.

It is thanks to my editor at Knopf, Lexy Bloom, and her able assistant, Tom Pold; and my literary agent, Tina Bennett, and her assistant Svetlana Katz, of William Morris Endeavor, that *The French Chef in America* has come to pass. To all four I owe a great debt of gratitude.

This book grew out of my work on *My Life in France*, but unlike Julia's memoir, this is a journalistic project that required months of research and interviews with Julia's colleagues, friends, and family. It was a sometimes difficult but always rewarding process, and I am indebted to those who offered their time, resources, and the occasional meal or bed along the way.

Julia and Paul Child donated their papers to the Arthur and Elizabeth Schlesinger Library on the History of Women in America at the Radcliffe Institute, Harvard University, in Cambridge, Massachusetts. It is an unparalleled collection that is valued by scholars and accessible to the public, and it was essential to my work. Reading the Childs' letters and looking at their photographs brought them immediately to life. The Schlesinger's staff has been patient and helpful, and I salute Dean Lizabeth Cohen, Marilyn Dunn, Diana Carey, and their colleagues. Moreover, Dean Cohen's husband, Herrick Chapman, associate professor of history at the Institute of French Studies at New York University, provided welcome insights on modern France. The two of them went above and beyond the call of duty by welcoming me in Cambridge, Massachusetts, on numerous occasions.

Julia's home kitchen from 103 Irving Street has been preserved and displayed at the National Museum of American History (NMAH) at the Smithsonian Institution in Washington, D.C. It includes a popular video loop of Julia in action, and a trove of her cookbooks, furnishings, and kitchen gadgets—including TV props, such as her giant mortar and pestle, a "fright knife," a bottle of "Château Gravy Masteur," and the like. This display has helped to increase public awareness of Julia's teaching, inspired thousands of visitors, and furthered her legacy. At this writing, "Julia Child's Kitchen" serves as the anchor to the NMAH's first major exhibition about the history of food in America. The success of this presentation is thanks to a caring and dedicated team, including the curator emerita Rayna Green, the curator Paula Johnson, and the museum's charismatic director, John Gray.

For years, Julia's television "home" was WGBH, the public TV station in Boston. The staff there was welcoming and helpful, and I bow in gratitude to Russell and Marian Morash, Keith Luf, Henry Becton, and Alison Smith. I am especially grateful to the WGBH crew who shot "The French Chef in France" documentaries, and shared their stories and photographs with me: *merci*, David Atwood, Peter Hoving, Willie Morton, Nancy Troland, and Daniel Berger.

At The Julia Child Foundation for Gastronomy and Culinary Arts, I am grateful for the friendship and support of Eric Spivey, William Truslow, Philadelphia Cousins, Todd Schulkin, and Jennifer Krauss. A big thank-you to Julia's friends and colleagues on the Foundation's Advisory Council: Anne Willan and Jim Dodge. For their encouragement, thanks to Tanya Steel and Julia's longtime producer-director Geoffrey Drummond.

And here's a tip of the hat to Julia's treasured friend and colleague, Chef Jacques Pépin, who was the first recipient of the Julia Child Award in October 2015.

Julia influenced many cooks, and mentored a few of them: a *grand merci* to Sara Moulton, Emeril Lagasse, and Barbara Lynch. I would also like to thank the food writers Dorie Greenspan and Russ Parsons for sharing their memories of Julia and thoughts on celebrity chefdom.

For their patience and hilarious stories, I'd like to thank Dan Aykroyd and Judy Graubart. In wrangling those interviews, I appreciate the assistance of Fred Specktor, Susan Patricola, and Frank Oz.

For their insights on the relationship between Simca Beck and Julia, I sincerely appreciate the help of Jean-François Thibault and Jean-Max Guieu.

In Cambridge and Boston, the Childs' great friends—Pat and Herbert Pratt, Jane Thompson, Dorothy Zinberg, and Rebecca Alssid—were unstintingly generous. I'd like to acknowledge the help of Julia's friend Susan Davidson, Julia's former assistant Stephanie Hersh, the former owner of La Pitchoune Kathie Alex, and to everyone at Casa Dorinda.

Finally, I deeply appreciate the patience, support, and inspiring meals that sustained this project. To my family: Sarah, Hector, and Sophia; to my parents, Hector and Erica Prud'homme; Jon Child and Julie Winter; Merida, Olivia, Julia, and Emily Prud'homme; and to the memory of Rachel, Fredericka, and Charles Child. *Merci encore.*

And last, but foremost, to Julia and Paul Child: *toujours bon appétit!*

NOTES

ABBREVIATIONS OF NAMES IN THE NOTES

JC	Julia Child
PC	Paul Child
CJC	Charles Child
SB	Simone "Simca" Beck
LB	Louisette Bertholle
JBJ	Judith B. Jones
RJL	Ruth J. Lockwood
RM	Russell Morash
JP	Jacques Pépin
ADeV	Avis DeVoto

First, a note about my conversations with Julia Child and about her memoir. Over the course of eight months in 2004, I interviewed Julia while helping her write her memoir, *My Life in France;* she died that August, and the book was published in 2006. The notes below attributed as "JC to the author" are drawn from those conversations, and her memoir, which is referred to as *MLiF.*

Second, a note about Julia and Paul Child's papers, which include most of the letters, memos, TV scripts, articles, speeches, cookbooks, and Paul's photographs and paintings referenced herein. The collection was donated by Julia and is archived as The Julia Child Papers at the Arthur and Elizabeth Schlesinger Library on the History of Women in America, Radcliffe Institute for Advanced Study, Harvard University, Cambridge, Massachusetts (hereafter: Julia Child Papers). The collection is open to scholars and the public by appointment. A finding aid is available online at http://www.radcliffe.harvard.edu/search/site/Julia%20Child.

Finally, I have occasionally drawn details from a set of Julia and Paul's date books (referred to as JC or PC date books below), copyright the Julia Child Foundation for Gastronomy and the Culinary Arts. Used with permission.

INTRODUCTION: JULIA'S SECOND ACT

4   "a great bouillabaisse": JC date book, July 21, 1976. Copyright the Julia Child Foundation for Gastronomy and the Culinary Arts, used with permission.

5   (they had tried but it "didn't take"): JC to the author, 2004.

6   they "'sleep' late": PC date book, July 25, 1976. Copyright the Julia Child Foundation for Gastronomy and the Culinary Arts, used with permission.

6   The inn was established in 1920: James McAuley, "The Artful Lodgers," *The New York Times "T" Magazine*, May 10, 2015.

7   "the mental scrambles": JC to the author. And JC to SB, September 6, 1975.

1. DINNER AND DIPLOMACY

11   "Welcome to Washington. *I'm* Julia Child": JC voice-over, *White House Red Carpet*, WGBH, Boston, 1968.

12   "the kitchen magician": Percy Shain, "2d Helping Near for French Chef," *The Boston Globe*, April 12, 1968.

12   "the year that everyone seems to be cooking in the kitchen with Julia": Marshall Burchard, Ruth Mehrtens, et al., "Everyone's in the Kitchen," *Time*, November 25, 1966.

13   "a part of the iceberg that doesn't show": Mary Daniels, "A Supercook and Her Superman," *Chicago Tribune*, August 20, 1972.

13   "JP" or "Pulia": JC to the author. Also numerous JC and PC letters, Julia Child Papers.

13   Charles de Gaulle's decision to relocate the Les Halles food market: JC and PC, "Proposal" for documentary film, Julia Child Papers, n.d., 1967.

13   rejected it as too expensive: From Greg Harney to JC, re "Julia Child in Paris," July 21, 1967.

15   As Paul explained in: PC handwritten draft of a letter to Herb Caen, "Historique of White House Red Carpet," January 20, 1968, Julia Child Papers.

15   In a letter to Lady Bird Johnson: RJL to Mrs. Lyndon B. Johnson, October 18, 1967.

16   "essentially an 18th-century gentleman's mansion": PC to RM, August 25, 1967.

16   completely renovated the rickety building: Michael Beschloss, "Harry Truman's Extreme Home Makeover," *The New York Times*, May 9, 2015.

16   The cramped space: PC to RM, August 25, 1967.

17   "You do not serve barbecued spareribs at a banquet": Emma Brown, "Obituary: René Verdon, White House chef for the Kennedys, dies at 86," *The Washington Post*, February 3, 2011.

17   Henry Haller: Marian Burros, "White House Chef to Leave in Fall," *The New York Times*, June 7, 1987. Also, Richard Norton Smith, "Henry Haller," President Gerald R. Ford Oral History Project, The Gerald R. Ford Presidential Foundation, March 31, 2010.

17   "Many Americans who dislike President Johnson": PC, "*Cordon bleu* White House: From a Guest Who Went Behind the Scenes," *The Economist*, April 13, 1968.

19   Foreign ambassadors and deputy ministers led American governors: White House Press Release, November 14, 1967. Also, "A State Dinner for Queen Elizabeth II," PBS Program Information, July 7, 1976.

21   President Johnson quoted Abraham Lincoln: Betty Beale, "Johnson's Sato Toast Answers Criticism," *Evening Star*, November 15, 1967.

21   A story in the Washington, D.C., *Evening Star:* Ibid.

22   Paul Child struck a more bemused tone: PC, "*Cordon bleu* White House: From a Guest Who Went Behind the Scenes."

22   Even before it was televised, in-house reviews: PC to RJL, April 27, 1968.

23   "With world conditions as they are": RJL to JC, 1967, quoted in Dana Polan, *Julia Child's The French Chef*, 222.

23   "the house built on friendship": JC to the author.

24   "God, it was great!": JC to SB, December 1967.

24   "smelling all these breads": Noël Riley Fitch, *Appetite for Life*, 336.

25   "If the tumor is malignant": Susan Schindehette, Karen Schneider, and Anne-Marie O'Neill, "Victors Valiant," *People*, October 26, 1998.

25   "Left breast off": Marilyn Mellowes, "Julia Child," PBS *American Masters*, in reference to JC date book, February 18, 1968.

25   "They just sewed me up and I went home": Schindehette et al., *People*, October 26, 1998.

26   "No radium, no chemotherapy, no caterwauling": Fitch, *Appetite for Life*, 337.

26   "Death and degeneration sat on my chest": PC to CJC, April 22, 1968.

26   "didn't really bother me": Meg Whitcomb, "Life Started Cooking at 50," *50 PLUS*, February 1980.

26   "What You Don't Know Can Hurt You": From the series *Feeling Good*, hosted by Dick Cavett, a series for adults produced by the Children's Television Workshop (CTW). Press release: "Julia Child Speaks Frankly," August 25, 1975.

27   She flicked the butt out the window: Fitch, *Appetite for Life*, 337.

27   Judith Jones encouraged this idea: JBJ to author.

28   "Too bad, but it is a thing we can't hurry": JC to SB, July 10, 1967.

28   "Its courage, its perfection, and its imagination": PC to CJC, December 26, 1968.

28   "Tonight you are our guinea pigs!": Mary Roblee Henry, "The Wonder Child," *Vogue*, June 1969.

30   "The concentration of both Mary Henry and Marc": PC to CJC, December 26, 1968.

30   "Julia has so sedulously protected her": Ibid.

2. THE FRENCH CHEF

32   Avis DeVoto called to say: This is not a direct quote, but a composite, drawn from: the author's conversations with Julia; *MLiF*, 212; and JC, "*AD* Revisits Julia Child," *Architectural Digest*, July/Aug. 1976. To see the kitchen

itself, visit "Julia's Kitchen" at the National Museum of American History, the Smithsonian Institution, Washington, D.C., or online (http://amhistory .si.edu/juliachild/jck/html/textonly/visiting.asp).

35   "I want the dining table in the middle of the room": JC, "The Kitchen Julia Built," *The New York Times Magazine*, May 16, 1976. Also, JC, "A Cook's Tour of Her Kitchen," *Chicago Tribune*, July 18, 1976.

35   "a supremely comfortable house to cherish": JC, "*AD* Revisits: Julia Child," *Architectural Digest*, July/Aug. 1976.

36   *TV Guide* visited: Edith Efron, "Dinner with Julia Child," *TV Guide*, December 5, 1970.

37   "They walk about": JC, "A Cook's Tour of Her Kitchen."

37   "like living in the country": Dorothy Shore Zinberg to author, June 11, 2014.

39   Craig Claiborne launched *Mastering:* Craig Claiborne, "Cookbook Review: Glorious Recipes," *The New York Times*, October 18, 1961.

39   "With the Kennedys in the White House": JC to the author. Also, Sharon Hudgins, "A Conversation with Julia Child, Spring 1984," *Gastronomica: The Journal of Food and Culture*, summer 2005. (Originally published as "What's Cooking with Julia Child," *Stars and Stripes*, European Edition, September 27, 1984.)

39   "Get that tall, loud woman": JC to the author.

40   Julia typed a memo to WGBH: JC memo to WGBH, "A series of TV programs on French cooking," April 26, 1962.

40   "Because the French have treated cooking": Ibid.

42   "I careened around the stove": *MLiF*, 242.

42   "high-wire act": Ibid.

42   a viewer named Irene McHogue: Polan, *Julia Child's The French Chef*, 190.

42   Julia called it *The French Chef:* PC "diary concerned with the French Chef expedition in France," May–June 1970, Julia Child Papers, 34. (For an explanation of this diary, see notes below for Chapter 4, page 289).

43   "how to make cooking make sense": JC memo to WGBH, re "A series of TV programs on French cooking," April 26, 1962.

43   This reverence: Polan, *Julia Child's The French Chef*, 104.

43   between 1948 and 1955, nearly two-thirds: Originally in Lynn Spigel, *Make Room for TV* (Chicago: University of Chicago Press, 1992), referenced by Polan, *Julia Child's The French Chef*, 83.

44   The earliest TV cooking shows: Polan, *Julia Child's The French Chef*, 67–69.

45   "the people who cook better than any other": Ibid., 64.

45   the rubber-faced comedian: Ibid., 64.

45   Most of the hosts were women: Ibid., 50.

46   "It will taste even better this way": Quoted in Joan Barthel, "How to Avoid TV Dinners While Watching TV," *The New York Times Magazine*, August 7, 1966.

46   "That's beautiful!": Cited by Marc Muneal, "Julia Child's 'The French Chef' by Dana Polan," *Studies in Popular Culture* 34, no. 1 (fall 2011): 152–54.

47   "Through your efforts, our stores": Polan, *Julia Child's The French Chef*, 100.

47 "educational TV's answer": Barthel, "How to Avoid TV Dinners."

48 "To do *that* is not easy": JP to the author.

48 An important, if little-remarked-upon: Polan, *Julia Child's The French Chef*, 10–11.

48 "rubies on velvet": Barthel, "How to Avoid TV Dinners."

48 "Julia was revolutionary": JBJ to the author.

49 "It was the first time": RM to the author, May 28, 2015.

49 "It was absolutely beautiful": PC to CJC, April 17, 1965.

50 "I'm tired of gray food": Efron, "Dinner with Julia Child."

50 The first nationwide broadcast: From Ed Reitan, "The Day a Black and White World Changed into Living Color: January 1, 1954," Novia.net (http://novia .net/~ereitan/rose_parade.html).

50 If black and white denoted: Polan, *Julia Child's The French Chef*, 217.

50 wrote a heartfelt memo: Ibid., 214.

50 After reading the memo: Ibid, 215.

50 "Home economics [is] a person": Curtis Hartman and Steven Raichlen, "The Boston Magazine Interview: Julia Child," *Boston*, April 1981.

51 WGBH (which allegedly stood for "God Bless Harvard"): Polan, *Julia Child's The French Chef*, 202.

53 She tried to persuade appliance makers: Ibid., 135.

53 "Just last week I was offered": Whitcomb, "Life Started Cooking at 50."

54 "How many copies are you planning to print?": JBJ to the author.

54 "Crazy!": PC scribbled note, January 15, 1971. Julia Child Papers.

3. VOLUME II

56 One afternoon in 1969: Patricia Simon, "The Making of a Masterpiece," *McCall's*, October 1970.

57 "No one knows us here": Ibid.

57 "*Less talking*": Ibid.

61 baptized Simone Suzanne Renée Madeleine Beck: Simone Beck, *Food & Friends*, 8.

61 Zulma had a lifelong influence: Ibid., 4–5.

62 "What a big chassis": Ibid., 91.

63 George Artamonoff: JC, *MLiF*, 115.

63 "French cooking out of cuckoo land": Julia Child, Louisette Bertholle, and Simone Beck, *Mastering the Art of French Cooking*. Also, "Everyone's in the Kitchen," *Time*, November 25, 1966.

64 "This is certainly one of the great collaborations": ADeV, typed notes, "Some Scattered Notes on a Visit to Bramafam-Pitchoune," December 17, 1966, to January 3, 1967.

65 "I feel I was the prime mover": Beck, *Food & Friends*, 226.

65 "Writing does not come easily": Margaret Sheridan, "The Visionary Editor Behind Our Great Cookbooks," *Chicago Tribune*, April 23, 1981.

65   Mrs. Jones was born Judith Bailey: JBJ interviews with the author. Also, Andrew F. Smith, ed. *The Oxford Encyclopedia of Food and Drink in America*, vol. 2 (New York: Oxford University Press, 2004), 394.

69   "Ms. Jones may not be the mother of the revolution": Julia Moskin, "An Editing Life, a Book of Her Own," *The New York Times*, October 24, 2007.

70   "include a good honest recipe": JBJ to JC, May 12, 1967.

70   no one in France bakes bread: JC to JBJ, May 22, 1967.

70   "bread should lie directly": JC to JBJ, December 12, 1967.

71   "We used wet whisk brooms": PC to CJC, July 10, 1967. Also, JC to SB, July 10, 1967.

71   It took something like two years: *MLiF*, 254.

72   *Beard on Bread:* JBJ to author. Also, JBJ to JC, March 8, 1971.

72   Yet, Simca had developed: Beck, *Food & Friends*, 216–19.

72   "Knead that dough!": Ibid., 216.

74   "*Non!* We French—we never make": *MLiF*, 224.

76   "Disgusting!": JC to the author. Also, Whitcomb, "Life Started Cooking at 50."

76   "I am worried by your growing attitude": JC to JBJ, January 22, 1970.

77   "I am distressed that you think": JBJ to JC, January 29, 1970.

78   "I am sure there is nothing wrong": JC to JBJ, January 19, 1970.

79   An early point of tension: JC to SB, October 18, 1967.

80   "Julia and I work very well together": Jean Hewitt, "Simone Beck, the Cookbook Author Without Television Show," *The New York Times*, November 12, 1970.

81   "seven hundred and twenty-nine layers": JC interviewed by John Callaway, WTTW, Chicago, PBS, 1978.

81   Judith Jones attempted to make: JBJ to the author.

81   "I shall make several more": JC to SB, January 31, 1967.

82   Knopf had received a steady stream: JBJ to the author. Also, Nancy Nicholas of Knopf to JC, December 31, 1969; and JBJ to JC, March 8, 1971.

82   "You're only as good as your worst recipe": Julia to the author. And in Sheridan, "The Visionary Editor Behind Our Great Cookbooks."

82   "I have no desire to get into another big book": JC to SB, February 13, 1969.

82   "*Petites Remarques et Modifications, si possible*": SB to JC, January 1, 1970.

83   In the margin, Julia scribbled: Ibid.

83   "*Lettre avec Commentaires Indispensables*": JC to SB, February 1970 ("GATEAU LE SUCCESS; J. comments on Simca Comments of Feb. 18, 1970."), Julia Child Papers.

83   "This is entirely M*A*D": JC note to herself, n.d., 1970.

83   "I'm feeling terribly the pressure": JBJ to JC, January 16, 1970.

84   "it is like a sweat shop around here": JC to JBJ, February 3, 1970.

84   "Under no circumstances": JC to JBJ, February 1, 1970.

84   "It may not be the book": JC to SB, December 14, 1969.

4. THE FRENCH CHEF IN FRANCE

85 "This elaborate, expensive": From "To Press a Duck," *The French Chef*, Season Two, 1970.

85 La Couronne: *MLiF*, 16–19.

88 "I feel Nature is restoring": Laura Shapiro, *Julia Child*, 130.

88 "Never again am I going to get": JC to SB, April 17, 1970.

88 "I have felt that we needed something": JC to Robert Larsen, program manager, WGBH-TV, December 12, 1966.

88 Julia proposed a luxe: Ibid.

89 Julia's true agenda: *MLiF*, 273–74.

90 It was Shana Alexander: Much of the detail about "The French Chef in France" shoot comes from the meticulous "diary concerned with the French Chef expedition in France," kept by Paul Child in the spring and summer of 1970. It runs ninety-seven typed pages. The diary can be found in: "Paul Child to Charles Child and Freddie Child, May 1970: typescript re. filming in France," box 8, folder 86, Julia Child Papers, Schlesinger Library, Radcliffe. PC, May 5–June 17, 1970 (hereafter: PC, "FCiF" diary), 10.

90 For $40,000: JC to SB, April 17, 1970.

91 "Cooking with us is NOT": PC, "FCiF" diary, 12.

91 The Pan Am jet: Ibid., 33–34.

94 "Remember, France is halfway": Ibid., 31.

94 In a 2009 blog post: Daniel Berger, "Julia Child Joyeuse Revenante" ("Julia Child's Happy Ghost"), October 12, 2009 (http://www.mtonvin.net/2009/10/12/julia-child-en-revenante/). Berger's post was written in French, which has been translated by the author to the best of his limited ability.

99 "It comes over us again": PC, "FCiF" diary, 58.

99 "Julia and Paul were guided": Berger, "Julia Child Joyeuse Revenante." Written in French and translated by the author.

100 "Is that rigor mortis?": JC to fishmonger in Marseille, in "Bouillabaisse," *The French Chef*, Season Two, WGBH, 1970.

105 The Chablis was: Berger, "Julia Child Joyeuse Revenante."

107 Lyon enlisted Simca: PC, "FCiF" diary, 79–80.

108 "You are like Brigitte Bardot": Ibid., 81.

109 "We do feel that a lot of what we are filming": JC to ADeV, June 12 and June 20, 1970. Also, JC to JBJ, June 11, 1970.

110 "We have, like Pollyanna": PC, "FCiF" diary, 87–88.

112 "We will be off at once": Ibid., 96.

5. THAT'S IT

113 "I am not going to be put out": *MLiF*, 281.

114 "*Auggbhhhh!*": From JC to author. Also, JC to JBJ, June 28, 1970; JC to RJL, July 2, 1970.

116   "It is without rival": Raymond Sokolov, "Queen of Chefs," *Newsweek*, November 9, 1970.

116   "No serious scholar": Gael Greene, "Julia's Moon Walk with French Bread," *Life*, October 23, 1970.

116   "who learn to drive": Nika Hazelton, "Genghis Khan's Sauerkraut and Other Edibles," *The New York Times Book Review*, December 6, 1970.

117   "The French Chef Faces Life": From WGBH promotional material. Cited by the Julia Child Foundation, timeline: 1970 (http://www.juliachildfoundation .org/timeline.html).

117   "I really don't know how to explain": Terrence O'Flaherty, "What's More, She Can Cook," *San Francisco Chronicle*, October, 1970, Julia Child Papers.

118   Judith Jones met a doctor: *MLiF*, 282.

118   the entire piscatory chapter: JC to SB, March 5, 1970. Also, JBJ to the author.

119   "we may have a tetralogy": JBJ to JC, February 8, 1967.

119   "You must polish up": JC to SB, July 9, 1972.

119   Even those who adored: Beck, *Food & Friends*, 277–78.

120   "She wouldn't listen": *MLiF*, 287.

120   The tipping point: Ibid., 287–88. Also, JBJ to the author.

121   Jean-François Thibault: Phone interviews with the author, May 18, 2004; December 17, 2014; and e-mail of December 17, 2014. Also, Jean-Max Guieu, notes e-mailed to the author, "Just a few words concerning Simca. And Julia," December 17, 2014.

122   Simca declared: Beck, *Simca's Cuisine*, vii.

122   Judith Jones helped: JBJ to author. Also, JBJ to JC, November 16, 1970.

122   *Simca's Cuisine* "should be a very nice book": JC to ADeV, May 18, 1971.

123   "I was struck by how little emphasis": JBJ to SB, January 21, 1977.

123   On May 4, 1971: JC and PC, 1971 datebooks.

124   "Actually Paul and I are both": JC to RJL, June 6, 1971.

124   "I don't feel this year's shows": JC to JBJ, June 6, 1971. Also, June 29, 1971.

125   a den of Fellini-esque debauchery: *Stones in Exile*, a documentary film written and directed by Stephen Kijak; released July 12, 2010.

125   Mick Jagger called it: TimeisonOurSide.com: "Exile on Main Street" (http:// timeisonourside.com/lpExile.html). Robert Greenfield, "Making Exile on Main Street," *Rolling Stone*, September 8, 2006. Also, Robert Christgau, *Grown Up All Wrong: 75 Great Rock and Pop Artists from Vaudeville to Techno* (Cambridge, Mass.: Harvard University Press, 1998), 81.

125   "We can do it": RM memo to Michael Rice, WGBH, "RE: Julia's Cooking Demos," April 19, 1974.

126   "I have doubts": David Ives, WGBH, memo to PC, JC, RL, Michael Rice, Sylvia Davis, "RE: MORE PROGRAMS FOR JULIA IN 1974," August 20, 1973.

126   "10 Possibilities": PC handwritten list, n.d., Julia Child Papers.

127   "I personally will never do": "Close-Up: Julia Child, TV's Master Chef," *Life*, October 21, 1966.

127 "I'm tired of French cooking": Woodene Merriman, "When Christmas Comes, So Do the Cookbooks," *Pittsburgh Post-Gazette*, November 14, 1978.

127 "tangents, comments": Child, *From Julia Child's Kitchen*, ix.

127 "rather cavalierly": JC letter to David Ives, December 1973.

6. FROM JULIA CHILD'S KITCHEN

131 "For our next book": JC to JBJ, December 22, 1981.

131 She and her siblings: Philadelphia Cousins (Julia's niece), e-mail to the author, September 9, 2015.

132 Her struggle to find a comfortable: Sheridan, "The Visionary Editor Behind Our Great Cookbooks."

135 "a dreadful sight": Child, *From Julia Child's Kitchen*, 441.

135 When Julia's grocer: Ibid., 398.

135 Her most vociferous critics: Ibid., 349.

136 "I saw your show": Ibid., 173.

136 Caesar Cardini: Ibid., 431–32.

138 In April 1974, Julia wrote Simca: JC to SB, April 16, 1974.

139 "Your decision": Michael Rice to JC and PC, June 28, 1974.

139 "We wish to terminate": JC and PC to WGBH, June 7, 1974.

139 Season One of the show: WGBH memo to author, courtesy of WGBH, "Julia Child Series at WGBH," n.d.

140 Julia and Paul had privately: Numerous instances, such as JC to SB, March 5, 1970.

140 "real male men": JC to SB, December 10, 1974.

140 "Homosexuality. Haw Haw": JC to ADeV, 1955, quoted in Shapiro, *Julia Child*, 136.

141 "Thank God there are two sexes!": Laura Shapiro, "Just a Pinch of Prejudice," *Boston*, April 2007.

141 When William Rice: Shapiro, *Julia Child*, 139.

141 "Good food is also love": Shapiro, "Just a Pinch of Prejudice."

142 "It wasn't a roaring lion": *MLiF*, 296.

142 "Recovery is slow": JC to SB, December 10, 1974.

142 "like a snail": JC to SB, February 6, 1975.

143 "Not everybody realizes that Paul and I": Whitcomb, "Life Started Cooking at 50."

143 "We each need long, silent times": G. S. Bourdain, "Julia Child Is Stirring Up More Treats," *The New York Times*, December 24, 1978.

143 "I think the role of a woman": JC interviewed by John Callaway.

145 "I'm not driven": Christopher Lydon, "Julia Child and the Sex of Cooking," August 16, 2004 (http://blogs.law.harvard.edu/lydondev/2004/08/16/julia-child-and-the-sex-of-cooking/).

145 "Communication is the glue": PC notes for an undelivered speech, "COMMUNICATION," March 1973.

146   "He had a sophisticated eye": JC, typescript for article "About Paul Child," *Family Circle*, January 17, 1999. Courtesy of the Julia Child Foundation.

147   While Charlie "opted for chaos": PC to CJC, November 25, 1968.

148   "Charlie brings out": JC to ADeV, January 5, 1971. Julia Child Papers.

148   "Without Paul Child": JC to the author.

149   "DOING something": JC to SB, March 1, 1975.

149   "He is still having reception": JC to SB, April 7, 1975.

149   "He was even on radio": JC to SB, April 18, 1976.

149   "*L'âge, ma chérie*": JC to SB, March 30, 1976.

149   "And thank heavens": *MLiF*, 296.

150   "I have nothing more to say": JC to SB, January 19, 1975.

150   "1,000 cackling women": JC to SB, October 24, 1975.

150   "We are going to take": Ibid.

151   just a third: From Robert H. Johnson, Esq., to Michael Rice, WGBH, April 15, 1975 (courtesy of WGBH).

7. THE SPIRIT OF '76

152   Beard, whom *The New York Times* called: James Beard Foundation, "About James Beard," in reference to *The New York Times*, n.d., 1954.

152   "in the 200 years": JC and JB, from draft script for "American Cookery: Revolutionary Style," n.d., 1975.

154   "The persecuted Puritans": Ibid.

154   "As Massachusetts is the mother": José Wilson, memo to JC and JB, "Research Material from José Wilson," n.d., 1975, 1, Julia Child Papers.

154   "unlike the Southern states": Ibid.

154   "When young daughters": Quoted by Wilson, ibid., 2. Originally in Ann Seranne, ed., *America Cooks: The General Federation of Women's Clubs Cook Book* (New York: G. P. Putnam's Sons, 1967).

154   Julia's mother: JC and family members to the author.

156   "Bearded Child Manifesto": JC handwritten notes on yellow legal pad, Julia Child Papers.

156   Julia and Jim planned: PBS Program/Series Proposal, "Julia and Jim: Classical American Cooking," October 3, 1975.

158   "people feel very strongly": José Wilson to JC, February 5, 1975.

158   "The Great Indian Pudding Controversy": Craig Claiborne, "The Great Indian Pudding Controversy," *The New York Times*, February 17, 1975.

160   "Within a generation": JC and JB, script notes for "Thirteen Feasts," n.d., 1975.

160   "This is the colonial kitchen": JC narration of pilot, "Julia and Jim," 1975 (courtesy of WGBH).

163   "Our great week of TV trials": JC to SB, March 1, 1975.

163   "we're presenting great American cuisine": WGBH memo to JC, n.d.

163   Safeway: From Henry Becton, WGBH to Ronald Giglio, Safeway Inc., October 7, 1975 (courtesy of WGBH).

163 "Nothing at all has come": JC to SB, July 1, 1975.

164 "There is still some brain injury": JC to SB, n.d. (probably August 1975).

164 "Please give us a little more time": Rice to JC, October 24, 1975 (courtesy of WGBH).

164 "Oy!!!!!": Ibid.

164 Julia replied in a terse note: JC to Rice, October 26, 1975.

165 "We all (including Jim B.)": JC to SB, July 9, 1972.

166 "Day in and day out": Hugo Lindgren, "Another Reason You Might Not Want to Be President," *The New York Times Magazine*, October 12, 2012, quoting John Hersey, *The New York Times Magazine*, April 20, 1975.

166 In a speech to the Grocery Manufacturers: "People in the News: Gerald Ford," *Kentucky New Era*, June 18, 1974.

166 *a tête de lard:* JC to SB, December 10, 1974.

8. THE PRESIDENT, THE QUEEN, AND THE CAPTAIN

167 Inspired by a party. Betty Ford, *The Times of My Life*, 224–25 (excerpt available online: http://www.fordlibrarymuseum.gov).

168 "unavailable to the press": Marian Burros, "White House Chef to Leave in Fall," *The New York Times*, June 7, 1987.

168 "That's not much of a problem": Mimi Sheraton, "State Dinner for Queen Elizabeth: 224 Guests—and a Time Clock," *The New York Times*, July 6, 1976.

170 "I'm not at all nervous": Ibid.

171 "Washington is not a cookie town": Ibid.

171 "Nixon didn't eat many things": Ibid.

171 "one does not show the queen eating": Transcript of JC report to *McCall's*, on audiotape, Tape Two, July 1976. The magazine provided Julia with a portable tape recorder, on which she recounted her impressions of the bicentennial dinner at the White House for a *McCall's* column; the tape was then transcribed. Transcript of the tape, and a letter about Julia's assignment from *McCall's* editor Barbara Blakemore, in the Julia Child Papers.

172 "I hope that the viewers": Ibid.

173 "adding a soft impressionistic touch": Sheraton, "State Dinner for Queen Elizabeth."

173 Guests at the head table: White House guest list, July 7, 1976, and press accounts.

174 "That was not very well": JC to *McCall's*, on audiotape.

174 "an absolutely superb dinner": Ibid.

174 "For some reason, they thought": Ibid.

174 "I found her delivery quite a bit": Ibid.

174 "The Queen was easy to deal with": Ford, *The Times of My Life*, 224–25 (http://www.fordlibrarymuseum.gov).

175 "Only a person with a dirty mind": Robert Windeler, "Year of the Dragons," *People*, October 18, 1976.

175 "I don't know why they picked": JC to *McCall's*, on audiotape.

175 "I agree with Mrs. Child": Tracy Hummel, "Speaking of Muskrat Love," on Laura Ingraham Facebook Q&A: https://www.facebook.com/permalink .php?id=271042954725&story_fbid=10150928976689726.

175 "I laughed through": "Talk Today: The Captain and Tennille," USAToday .com, May 24, 2001.

175 United States Marine Band: Col. John R. Bourgeois (Ret.), "The President's Own": A History of the United States Marine Band: http://www.jrbourgeois .com/presidents-own-6.html.

176 "is the kind of thing that I love": JC to *McCall's*, on audiotape.

176 "Quaint Spectacle": Tom Shales, "Quaint Spectacle of a State Dinner," *The Washington Post*, July 8, 1976.

176 "Dear Channel 2": April Oray, letter to Channel 2, July 12, 1976 (courtesy of WGBH).

177 "Your coverage of the State Dinner": Archibald Murphy, letter to Channel 2, July 1976 (courtesy of WGBH).

177 "was the one bright spot": Mrs. Eugene Klein, letter to Channel 2, July 16, 1976 (courtesy of WGBH).

177 In a postmortem on July 8: Memorandum from Ron Nessen to Bob Mead, re "TV COVERAGE AT DINNER FOR THE QUEEN," July 8, 1976. From box 300, folder "Television Advisor Resignation," the Ron Nessen Papers at the Gerald R. Ford Presidential Library.

177 by the end of the day: Robert A. Mead, letter to President Gerald R. Ford, July 8, 1976. Ibid.

177 "one could not help wondering": Sheraton, "State Dinner for Queen Elizabeth."

178 By the time Julia's article: JC, "A White House Menu," *The New York Times Magazine*, January 16, 1977.

9. THE NEW FRENCH REVOLUTION

180 It's gotten much more expensive: Clifford A. Ridley, "La Cuisine? La Julia!," *National Observer*, May 1, 1976.

181 "adventures in eating": Linda Bird Francke, Scott Sullivan, and Seth Goldschlager, "Food: The New Wave," *Newsweek*, August 11, 1975.

181 "Americans": Ibid.

182 "There is a growing appreciation": Ibid.

182 "We really noticed the changes": Ibid.

182 They witnessed: Alex Kuczynski, "Public Lives: 30 Years of Love and Chronicling Cuisine," *The New York Times*, August 20, 1998.

182 "There are now so many": JC to LB, December 23, 1978.

183 "a bit like pornography": Andrew F. Smith, *The Oxford Companion to American Food and Drink*, 416–17.

183 "The older we get": Beverley Jackson, "Dinner with JC," *Santa Barbara News-Press*, January 9, 1977. In Fitch, *Appetite for Life*, 394.

184 The menu of a 1903 state dinner: "Dining in State," The Old Foodie, May 2, 2006 (http://www.theoldfoodie.com/2006/05/dining-in-state.html).

184 The term "nouvelle cuisine": André Gayot, "Nouvelle Cuisine: The True Story of This Culinary French Revolution" (http://www.gayot.com/restaurants /features/nouvellecuisine.html).

      While the phrase "nouvelle cuisine" was used in eighteenth- and nineteenth-century France, and there has been confusion over who popularized the modern usage, and when, André Gayot wrote that his colleague Henri Gault "forged the name Nouvelle Cuisine" in 1972.

184 "protect the integrity": Steven Englund, "The Simple Lion," *Time*, April 9, 1973.

184 learned to butcher: Francke, Sullivan, and Goldschlager, "Food: The New Wave."

184 "a little mean": Ibid.

185 "A chef, even a bad one": Englund, "The Simple Lion."

185 "If Point was God". Ibid.

185 *la Bande à Bocuse*: Francke, Sullivan, and Goldschlager, "Food: The New Wave."

185 "It is a cuisine of friendship": Ibid.

185 "an evolution seemed necessary": André Gayot, "Nouvelle Cuisine: The True Story of this Culinary French Revolution." Gayot.com.

186 "Down with the old-fashioned picture": Ibid.

186 "*les copains*": Ibid.

187 "a tool of Gallic": "Pass Notes," *The Guardian*, January 23, 1997.

187 Bernard Loiseau, of La Côte d'Or: Lloyd Vries, "French Furor Over Chef's Apparent Suicide," Associated Press, February 25, 2003. Also, William Echikson, "Death of a Chef," *The New Yorker*, May 12, 2003.

187 "it is clearly too old-fashioned": JC, " 'La Nouvelle Cuisine': A Skeptic's View," *New York*, July 4, 1977.

187 "none of [them] seems the glorious temple": Ibid.

188 "Manifesto of Nouvelle Cuisine": "Manifesto of Nouvelle Cuisine," *Nouveau Guide*, October 1973. Gayot, "Nouvelle Cuisine: The True Story of This Culinary French Revolution." Gayot.com. Also, Smith, *The Oxford Companion to American Food and Drink*, 416.

188 "The French Revolution": Gayot, "Nouvelle Cuisine: The True Story of This Culinary French Revolution." Gayot.com.

188 "an accordion-pleated affair": Craig Claiborne, "Food View: Nouvelle Cuisine: Here to Stay," *The New York Times*, December 18, 1983.

188 "Nouvelle cuisine is the greatest": Ibid.

189 "When people go to a French restaurant": Francke, Sullivan, and Goldschlager, "Food: The New Wave."

189 "Without butter, cream": Ibid.

189   "does not develop the essential taste": JC, "'La Nouvelle Cuisine': A Skeptic's View."

189   "Humph!": John Kifner, "The New French Food Revolution? Julia Child Says, 'Humph,'" *The New York Times*, September 5, 1975.

189   "Nouvelle Cuisine was debased": Beck, *Food & Friends*, 90, 273.

189   "just doing the same thing": Kifner, "The New French Food Revolution? Julia Child Says, 'Humph.'"

189   "that Paris PR game": Ibid.

189   "Well, if they can get away with it": Ibid.

190   "One thing to remember": JC to Philip W. Nash, November 13, 1973.

190   "It began with sausage": Englund, "The Simple Lion."

190   In September 1971: John L. Hess, "7 Chefs Cook 'Dinner of Century'—Were There 6 Too Many?," *The New York Times*, September 8, 1971.

191   "quite simply": John L. Hess, "The Life of a Food Critic Has Its Indigestible Moments," *The New York Times*, December 11, 1973.

191   "like putting seven artists": Hess, "7 Chefs Cook 'Dinner of Century'—Were There 6 Too Many?"

191   "The dinner is *énormément trop*": Gael Greene, "Paul Bocuse: Trial by Pig's Bladder," *New York*, February 5, 1973.

192   "Never was there a more elegant hustle": Gael Greene, "Nobody Knows the Truffles I've Seen," *New York*, November 12, 1973.

192   "the very clever French publicity": JC to Philip W. Nash, November 13, 1973.

192   causing her "feminist spirit": Gael Greene, "More Confessions of a Sensualist: The Dinner for Women," *New York*, January 28, 1974.

192   Lillian Hellman: JC to SB, January 13, 1974.

192   *no sacquépage!*: In her letters Julia often used the made-up word "*sacquépage*" to describe the cosmetological work done on her face in France. (She was not vain, but she understood the importance of looking youthful on TV.) Though I can't be sure, I suspect *sacquépage* was an in-joke between Julia and Paul, a conjoining of the name of the doctor she frequented in Cannes—Dr. Sacquépée—and the French word *décapage*, meaning "chemical peel."

193   The *loup* was overcooked: Greene, "More Confessions of a Sensualist: The Dinner for Women."

193   "Dinner with 12 women": JC to SB, January 13, 1974.

194   "'Down with Escoffier'": JC, "'La Nouvelle Cuisine': A Skeptic's View."

194   "Dieu! How can one refuse": Ibid.

194   "Where would any of us be": Ibid.

195   Guérard sank into despair: Francke, Sullivan, and Goldschlager, "Food: The New Wave."

195   "I don't want to make dieting": Ibid.

195   "He is the only one who really did invent": Beck, *Food & Friends*, 273.

195   "I don't think people are really going to want to go out": Kifner, "The New French Food Revolution? Julia Child Says, 'Humph.'"

196   "a really original style of cookery": JC, "'La Nouvelle Cuisine': A Skeptic's View."

197 "for all the world like liquefied bouillon": Ibid.

197 "It's not that I don't appreciate": Ibid.

197 In a 1984 interview: Hudgins, "A Conversation with Julia Child, Spring 1984."

198 "a refreshment of traditional": Ibid.

198 When Michel Guérard helped: Gael Greene, "Full House for the Queen of Clubs?," *New York*, May 10, 1976.

199 culinary puns: Smith, *The Oxford Companion to American Food and Drink*, 416–17.

199 "with a twist": Ibid.

199 "What that movement": Ibid.

200 "the culinary shift to": Christopher Kimball, "Book Review: 'Provence, 1970' by Luke Barr," *The Wall Street Journal*, October 18, 2013.

IO. A GO-TO CULTURAL FIGURE

201 "It's not very *tender*," Julia says reprovingly: From *Julia & Jacques Cooking at Home—Series Highlights*, A La Carte TV (https://www.youtube.com/watch?v=H7mtEoMFJ6o).

202 "It always felt completely natural": JP to the author in a series of interviews, 2013–2015.

202 Johnson had started the business: Anthony Mitchell Sammarco, *A History of Howard Johnson's: How a Massachusetts Soda Fountain Became an American Icon* (Charleston, S.C.: The History Press, 2013), 15.

203 Howard Johnson's included: Howard Johnson International, Inc., company profile (http://www.referenceforbusiness.com/history/He-Ja/Howard-Johnson-International-Inc.html).

204 "We were foot soldiers": JP, *The Apprentice*, 164.

205 "For me, Howard Johnson's reliable": Jacques Pépin, "Howard Johnson's, Adieu," *The New York Times*, April 28, 2005.

206 "Jean-Claude and I": JP, *The Apprentice*, 182.

207 fourteen fractures: Joe Yonan, "Hip Pain Forces Jacques Pépin to Cancel Book Tour," *The Washington Post*, November 1, 2011.

211 "I am in the mood": JP to the author.

212 "speak out on any subject": Hartman and Raichlen, "Julia Child."

212 "nuts and berries": JC to the author.

212 "that dreadful woman": Adelle Davis: Shapiro, *Julia Child*, 160.

212 "never met a healthy, normal nutritionist": Ibid.

212 "the dinner table is becoming a trap": Carol Lawson, "Julia Child Boiling, Answers Her Critics," *The New York Times*, June 20, 1990.

212 "The only time to eat diet food": Nancy Verde Barr, *Backstage with Julia: My Years with Julia Child* (Hoboken, N.J.: John Wiley & Sons, 2007), 64.

212 "Personally, I don't think pure": Karen Grigsby Bates, "Slice of History," *People*, June 7, 1999.

213 "*You*, of all my favorite": Shapiro, *Julia Child*, 165.

213   the organic movement: Hartman and Raichlen, "Julia Child."

213   "There is no room for the cult": Shapiro, *Julia Child*, 161.

213   "I just do not want to be allied": Ibid., 162.

214   Julia spoke out in favor: Ibid. Also, JC to SB, January 15, 1970.

214   she dismissed the Food and Drug Administration: Hartman and Raichlen, "Julia Child."

214   "Rotten apples": JC to ADeV, May 14, 1972.

214   "All this romance about French products": JC to ADeV, May 14, 1972.

215   "We don't believe good food": Shapiro, *Julia Child*, 153.

215   "The Big Mac I like least": "The Hamburger Empire," *Time*, September 17, 1973.

215   "Would you rather have an airline lunch": Hartman and Raichlen, "Julia Child."

215   The first French McDonald's: Rob Wile, "The True Story of How McDonald's Conquered France," *Business Insider*, August 22, 2014. After a dispute with its original franchisee, Raymond Dayan, the Chicago-based chain changed the way its stores in France operated. After shuttering its outlets there for a year, McDonald's worked with a new franchisee; the company dates its first store opening in France to 1979.

216   the sheep farmer José Bové: Suzanne Daley, "Montredon Journal; French See a Hero in War on 'McDomination,'" *The New York Times*, October 12, 1999.

216   there were more than twelve hundred: Wile, "The True Story of How McDonald's Conquered France."

216   a refined recipe for tuna casserole: Shapiro, *Julia Child*, 167.

216   "We've been terribly spoiled": Hartman and Raichlen, "Julia Child."

217   "What do you think of women's lib?" she asked a reporter: Efron, "Dinner with Julia Child."

217   "We who are pro women's rights": Polly Frost, "Julia Child," *Interview*, August 1989.

217   "Women should stop squawking": "Julia Will Cook a 'Series of Spectaculars,'" *The Bridgeport Post*, October 4, 1973.

217   "What are your plans": "Dear Abby," "Julia Child Stirs Up Issues for Planned Parenthood," *The Miami News*, July 15, 1982.

217   "You run into so many situations": Hartman and Raichlen, "Julia Child."

218   "neither French, nor a chef": Amanda Cohen, "Madeleine Kamman, The French Chef Who Battled Julia Child (And Survived)," The Braiser, n.d. http://www.thebraiser.com/lady-chef-stampede-madeleine-kamman/.

218   "not a cook, but she plays one on TV": Regina Schrambling, "A Tribute to Karen Hess," *edibleManhattan*, July 4, 2013.

218   "Why Julia?": Molly O'Neill, "For Madeleine Kamman, a Gentler Simmer," *The New York Times*, January 14, 1998.

218   "very controversial": Marian Burros, "Flinty, Revered Teacher of Chefs," *The New York Times*, August 4, 1993.

218   "I shall grab her": From the Harvard Institute for Learning in Retirement, 1985; quoted in Fitch, *Appetite for Life*, 352.

218 "I was a good fighter": O'Neill, "For Madeleine Kamman, a Gentler Simmer."

218 "How shall we tell our fellow": John L. Hess and Karen Hess, *The Taste of America* (New York: Penguin Books, 1977).

219 "What are these people": Shapiro, *Julia Child*, 156.

219 They deemed Pierre Franey: Betty Fussell, "Food Edenist," *The New York Times Magazine*, December 30, 2007.

219 "Those of us who were new": Ibid.

219 "Julia will be more responsible": Fussell, *Masters of American Cookery*, 48.

220 "Cooking While Gassed": Fitch, *Appetite for Life*, 301.

220 Grilled Dill Pickles: Judy Graubart as Julia Grownup, on "Here's Cooking at You," The Electric Company, PBS, show no. 73 (https://www.youtube.com/watch?v=5-wxb2TEWUs).

221 "I adored Julia": Judy Graubart to the author, June 23, 2014.

221 "Julia Child was directly responsible": Dan Aykroyd to the author, May 1, 2014.

221 "How many times": From NBC video, *Saturday Night Live*, April 17, 1976 (http://www.nbc.com/saturday-night-live/video/bassomatic/n8631).

223 Julia borrowed: JP to the author.

224 "Julia Child" was dressed: Dan Aykroyd as Julia Child in *Saturday Night Live*, Season 4, Episode 8, December 9, 1978.

226 "just so that it would make a noise": Stephen Wadsworth, "Julia Sums Up," *Dial*, April 1981.

226 "We thought it was *terribly* funny": Ibid. Also, JC to the author.

226 Dorie Greenspan: Dorie Greenspan to the author, April 18, 2015.

11. BURSTING OUT OF THE STRAITJACKET

228 "I'm not tired": JC interviewed by John Callaway.

228 "We felt it was time": Child, *Julia Child & Company*, vii.

229 "It didn't take too much": Ibid.

229 "Americans don't want": *MLiF*, 209.

230 "calculator": Bourdain, "Julia Child Is Stirring Up More Treats."

231 "'Diet food'": Child, *Julia Child & Company*, 37.

233 "We wouldn't do the new series": Bourdain, "Julia Child Is Stirring Up More Treats."

235 "shrimp's intestine": Child, *Julia Child & Company*, x.

236 "Whether we were devising": Child, *Julia Child & More Company*, viii.

237 "No question, it was great TV": Sara Moulton to the author, October 10, 2013.

237 Mimi Sheraton praised: Mimi Sheraton, "Cookbooks," *The New York Times*, December 3, 1978.

238 "selling as if it were free": Bourdain, "Julia Child Is Stirring Up More Treats."

238 the *Company* programs: Ibid.

238　"We just KILLED ourselves": Wadsworth, "Julia Sums Up."

239　"It's the Balkanization": RM to the author, May 28, 2015.

240　"After a while, the whole how-to genre": Henry Becton to the author, May 27, 2015.

241　"As soon as you're off the television": Hartman and Raichlen, "Julia Child."

241　"I love working": Russ Parsons, "A Day in the Life, at 90," *Los Angeles Times*, August 7, 2002.

12. PRIME TIME

246　"Actually, now we are into it": JC to SB, October 29, 1980.

246　In a typical week: JC date book, 1980.

246　In a show about rice pilaf: Nancy Verde Barr, *Backstage with Julia*, 31.

247　"Years later, my mother decided": Sara Moulton to the author, October 10, 2013.

252　"How time indeed flies": JC to SB, July 4, 1984.

252　She taped five segments: Episodes available online: "Julia Child Introduces Snack Foods of Nice" (http://www.mefeedia.com/watch/21027823).

254　Kathie Alex: Kathie Alex to author. At the time of writing, Kathie Alex has retired and sold La Pitchoune.

13. THE CELEBRITY CHEF

256　"Julia was a real *authority*": Henry Becton to the author, May 27, 2015.

258　"If I can do it": JC to the author.

258　"The more you do": Hartman and Raichlen, "Julia Child."

258　"I went back into the kitchen": Emeril Lagasse to the author, April 15, 2014.

259　"cool and sexy": Dorie Greenspan, at the Santa Barbara Food & Wine Festival, April 18, 2015.

259　"Plating food": Russ Parsons, at the Santa Barbara Food & Wine Festival, April 18, 2015.

260　Jean-Georges Vongerichten and Daniel Boulud: Greenspan, Santa Barbara Food & Wine Festival, April 18, 2015.

260　"If you don't eat": JP quoting JC, "How 'Reality' TV Cooking Shows Get It Wrong," *The Daily Meal*, July 14, 2014. Also, "Learn to Cook with 'Gusto' Advises Kitchen's Grand Dame," Associated Press, September 27, 1978.

261　"I'm really getting tired": JC to SB, July 28, 1977.

14. "BON APPÉTIT, AMERICA!"

262　"I'll never, never": Hartman and Raichlen, "Julia Child."

262　"a sacred trust": *MLiF*, 302.

262　"You have to show people": Hartman and Raichlen, "Julia Child."

262　"If you want to be a chef": Ibid.

263 "to advance the understanding": www.AIWF.org.

263 *Parade* had a circulation: Philip H. Dougherty, "Advertising; Parade's $1 million Campaign," *The New York Times*, January 28, 1983.

263 "It was meant to be upscale": RM to the author, May 28, 2015.

264 Julia's knees: JC to SB, July 4, 1983.

264 *Dinner*'s elegant mise-en-scène: John J. O'Connor, "TV: Julia Child Series on Dinners," *The New York Times*, November 17, 1983.

264 Food, transportation: Phyllis C. Richman, "Making Dinner at Julia's," *The Washington Post*, April 13, 1983.

265 "I suffer": PC date book, February 8, 1983.

265 Paul had a series: JC to SB, April 18, 1976; July 28, 1979; January 28, 1981; February 26, 1981; May 28, 1986.

265 "Mon pauvre Paul": JC to SB, February 20, 1987.

266 ABC received letters: The Julia Child Foundation for Gastronomy and the Culinary Arts, Timeline: 1980.

267 wandered out of 103 Irving Street: Spitz, *Dearie*, 463.

267 "Let the living live!": JC to the author.

267 "You must be patient": JC to SB, February 20, 1987.

268 "Both Simca and Louisette": JC, Introduction to Beck, *Food & Friends*, xv.

268 double pneumonia: Suzanne Patterson to JC, June 6, 1991, and June 9, 1991.

268 "We were like sisters": Trish Hall, "Simone Beck, a Cook, Dies at 87: Co-Wrote Book with Julia Child," *The New York Times*, December 21, 1991.

268 Provence was becoming: JC to William Truslow, July 5, 1992.

268 She cooked a final: *MLiF*, 301.

268 "I left France": JC to William Truslow, July 5, 1992.

268 The "Merci, Julia" party: Marian Burros, "For Julia Child, an Intimate Dinner for 500," *The New York Times*, February 10, 1993.

271 "Julia's Kitchen": National Museum of American History, Smithsonian Institution, Washington, D.C. (http://amhistory.si.edu/juliachild/jck/html /textonly/visiting.asp).

EPILOGUE: A CIVILIZED ART

272 "I have no fear": Martha Smilgis, "Live! Eat! Enjoy!," *Ms. Magazine*, summer 2003.

272 "eat in moderation": JC to the author.

272 "I think I will go on": Smilgis, "Live! Eat! Enjoy!"

274 "My point is to make cooking": JC interviewed by John Callaway.

274 "Practically every article on Julie": Shapiro, *Julia Child*, 120.

275 "Some children like to make": Child, *Julia Child & Company*, "VIP Lunch," 91.

BIBLIOGRAPHY

BOOKS BY JULIA CHILD

Mastering the Art of French Cooking, with Simone Beck and Louisette Bertholle. New York: Knopf, 1961.

The French Chef Cookbook. New York: Knopf, 1968.

Mastering the Art of French Cooking, Volume II, with Simone Beck. New York: Knopf, 1970.

From Julia Child's Kitchen. New York: Knopf, 1975.

Julia Child & Company, in collaboration with E. S. Yntema. New York: Knopf, 1978.

Julia Child & More Company, in collaboration with E. S. Yntema. New York: Knopf, 1979.

The Way to Cook. New York: Knopf, 1989.

Julia Child's Menu Cookbook. New York: Wings (Random House), 1991.

Cooking with Master Chefs. New York: Knopf, 1993.

In Julia Child's Kitchen with Master Chefs, with Nancy Verde Barr. New York: Knopf, 1995.

Baking with Julia, with Dorie Greenspan. New York: William Morrow, 1996.

Julia and Jacques Cooking at Home. New York: Knopf, 1999.

Julia's Kitchen Wisdom, with David Nussbaum. New York: Knopf, 2000.

My Life in France, with Alex Prud'homme. New York: Knopf, 2006.

TELEVISION SERIES AND VIDEOS BY JULIA CHILD

The French Chef. WGBH, Boston. PBS, 1962–1973.

Julia Child & Company. WGBH, Boston. PBS, 1978–1979.

Julia Child & More Company. WGBH, Boston. PBS, 1979–1980.

Good Morning America. ABC, 1980–1995.

Dinner at Julia's. WGBH, Boston. PBS, 1983–1984.

Cooking in Concert. PBS, 1993.

Cooking with Master Chefs. PBS, 1993–1994.

In Julia's Kitchen with Master Chefs. PBS, 1994–1996.

Julia Child & Jacques Pépin: More Cooking in Concert. PBS, 1995.

Baking with Julia. PBS, 1996–1998.

Julia & Jacques: Cooking at Home. A La Carte Communications, KQED. PBS, 1999–2000.

Julia's Kitchen Wisdom. A La Carte Communications. PBS, 2000.

BOOKS ABOUT JULIA CHILD

Barr, Nancy Verde. *Backstage with Julia: My Years with Julia Child.* Hoboken, N.J.: John Wiley & Sons, 2007.

Fitch, Noël Riley. *Appetite for Life: The Biography of Julia Child.* New York: Doubleday, 1997; Anchor Books, 2012.

Polan, Dana. *Julia Child's The French Chef.* Durham, N.C., and London: Duke University Press, 2011.

Shapiro, Laura. *Julia Child: A Life.* New York: Viking, 2007.

Spitz, Bob. *Dearie: The Remarkable Life of Julia Child.* New York: Knopf, 2012.

BOOKS BY SIMONE BECK

Simca's Cuisine, in collaboration with Patricia Simon. New York: Knopf, 1972.

New Menus from Simca's Cuisine, in collaboration with Michael James. New York: Harcourt Brace Jovanovich, 1979.

Food & Friends: Recipes and Memories from Simca's Cuisine, with Suzanne Patterson. New York: Viking, 1991.

SECONDARY SOURCES

Ford, Betty. *The Times of My Life.* New York: Harper & Row, 1978. Excerpted at http://www.fordlibrarymuseum.gov.

Fussell, Betty. *Masters of American Cookery: M.F.K. Fisher, James Beard, Craig Claiborne, Julia Child.* New York: Times Books, 1983.

Jones, Judith. *The Tenth Muse: My Life in Food.* New York: Knopf, 2007.

Kamp, David. *The United States of Arugula: The Sun-Dried, Cold-Pressed, Dark-Roasted, Extra Virgin Story of the American Food Revolution.* New York: Broadway Books, 2007.

Pépin, Jacques. *The Apprentice: My Life in the Kitchen.* Boston: Houghton Mifflin, 2003.

Smith, Andrew F., ed. *The Oxford Companion to American Food and Drink.* New York: Oxford University Press, 2007.

INDEX

Page numbers in *italic* refer to illustrations.

A NOTE ON THE TYPE

This book was set in Janson, a typeface long thought to have been made by the Dutchman Anton Janson, who was a practicing typefounder in Leipzig during the years 1668–1687. However, it has been conclusively demonstrated that these types are actually the work of Nicholas Kis (1650–1702), a Hungarian, who most probably learned his trade from the master Dutch typefounder Dirk Voskens. The type is an excellent example of the influential and sturdy Dutch types that prevailed in England up to the time William Caslon (1692–1766) developed his own incomparable designs from them.

Composed by North Market Street Graphics,
Lancaster, Pennsylvania

Printed and bound by Berryville Graphics,
Berryville, Virginia

Designed by Cassandra J. Pappas